THE INSTITUTE OF PACIFIC RELATIONS

The Institute of Pacific Relations is an unofficial and nonpartisan organization founded in 1925 to facilitate the scientific study of the peoples of the Pacific area. It is composed of autonomous National Councils in the principal countries having important interests in the Pacific area, together with an International Secretariat. It is privately financed by contributions from National Councils, corporations, and foundations. It is governed by a Pacific Council composed of members appointed by each of the National Councils.

The Institute as such and the National Councils of which it is composed do not advocate policies or express opinions on national or international affairs. Responsibility for statements of fact or opinion in Institute publications rests solely with the authors.

INTERNATIONAL SECRETARIAT AND PUBLICATIONS OFFICE

1 East 54th Street, New York.

NATIONALISM AND REVOLUTION IN MONGOLIA

BY

OWEN LATTIMORE

WITH A TRANSLATION FROM THE MONGOL OF
SH. NACHUKDORJI'S *LIFE OF SUKEBATUR*

BY

OWEN LATTIMORE AND URGUNGGE ONON

ISSUED UNDER THE AUSPICES OF THE
INTERNATIONAL SECRETARIAT
INSTITUTE OF PACIFIC RELATIONS

LEIDEN
E. J. BRILL
1955

PRINTED BY E. J. BRILL, LEIDEN, NETHERLANDS

CONTENTS

Preface VII
A note on sources IX

PART I. NATIONALISM AND REVOLUTION IN MONGOLIA

Introductory 3
The Mongols under Manchu rule 6
Chinese Warlords and Inner Mongolia 22
The Kuomintang and Inner Mongolian nationalism 27
Outer Mongolia: the capacity for independence 30
Satellite dependency contrasted with feudal dependency . . . 36
Anatomy of satellitism 41
The Russian mode of expansion 43
The problem of personality: sketches of two careers 48
Sukebatur and "united front" politics 62
Sukebatur and Choibalsang: personal reputation in a satellite
  society 67
Political heroes: the process of enhancement 78
The track of the orbit in satellite politics 82

PART II. THE LIFE OF SUKEBATUR

Introduction 94
  I. Youth and young manhood 98
  II. Sukebatur the soldier 111
  III. Sukebatur's first revolutionary work 117
  IV. The beginning of the building of the party 129
  V. The journey north 136
  VI. The direction and organization of the armed rising of the
  workers and people against the external and internal
  enslavers 144
  VII. The struggle for the consolidation of the gains of the
  revolution 167
  VIII. His death by poisoning at the hands of his enemies . . . 174
  IX. Under the leadership of Choibalsang on the road of Suke-
  batur 179
Bibliography 182
Indexes 183

PREFACE

This translation of a contemporary Mongol book — the only one, I believe, that has been translated into a Western language — and the accompanying introductory essay on nationalism and revolution in Mongolia are the outcome of two programs. The first is the program of Inner Asian studies at the Johns Hopkins University which I directed from 1947 to 1953 (after which year the Walter Hines Page School of International Relations, under which the program was conducted, was discontinued). Acknowledgments are due not only to the University, which gave me such complete academic independence in conducting the studies, but to the two foundations which made grants enabling the studies to be carried on — the Carnegie Corporation of New York and the American Council of Learned Societies. Acknowledgment is also due to the Department of State's contribution in helping my Mongol colleagues to come to this country and later making grants-in-aid to them under one of its programs of assistance to foreign scholars.

The second program is that of the Institute of Pacific Relations, which for some years has been promoting studies of nationalism in various parts of Asia, and made a grant to me, some years ago, for a study of Mongol nationalism. Nothing in my long and happy association with the Institute has given me greater respect and admiration for the international value of free scholarship than the way in which Mr. William L. Holland, Secretary-General of the Institute, has devotedly supported this program and the other work of the Institute, at times under very difficult conditions.

My most personal acknowledgment of indebtedness is to my Mongol colleagues: the Dilowa Hutukhtu, my mentor and friend for a quarter of a century, only a fraction of whose unique contributions to the Johns Hopkins program of Mongol studies have yet been published [1]; Mr Urgungge Onon, who collaborated with me on the translation of the *Life of Sukebatur* and on much other translation

---

[1] His *Autobiography* and *Political Memoirs* are in preparation for publication. In the translation of the *Life of Sukebatur*, information contributed by him is either acknowledged specifically or identified by the initial "D."

work, and Mr. John Gombojab Hangin, who together with Mr. Onon assembled a great quantity of source material in Mongol, Chinese, and Japanese [2]. Further publications are planned, based partly on these materials.

When the student is working on problems of a nationality that is not his own, and is heavily indebted for information and source material to colleagues of that nationality, whose views are the outcome of their national cultural heritage as a whole, their regional upbringing within that culture, and their personal experiences, it is especially necessary to proceed most rigorously in defining responsibility for selecting, out of the mass of the raw material, what is to be printed as the final product, and in forming the opinions that are presented together with the material. Both for the selection of all material and for all expressions of opinion (except, of course, the opinions of the Mongol author of the *Life of Sukebatur*) I am alone responsible.

This study has had to be completed in odds and ends of time when I have been much preoccupied with legal and political matters. For this reason the commentary is neither as well rounded nor as fully supported by further citations from the literature as I should have liked it to be; but conscious as I am of these defects, what is foremost in my mind is the fact that the work could not have been completed at all had it not been for the many friends who have so generously sacrificed their own time to make it possible for me to keep up some degree of continuity in my research. I owe much to many; to my wife, most of all.

OWEN LATTIMORE

Ruxton, Maryland
April 1955

---

[2] For a publication that stands alone in the literature dealing with Mongol society, based on two years of seminar interviews with the Dilowa Hutukhtu, Mr. Onon, and Mr. Hangin, see Herbert Harold Vreeland 3rd., *Mongol Community and Kinship Structure*, Yale University, New Haven, Human Relations Area Files, 1954.

A NOTE ON SOURCES

In the Mongol sources that have been available to me the main emphasis is "political" in a rather narrow sense — who did what, when; who was "good" and who "bad." There is not enough of the kind of realistic discussion of social cleavages and alliances (and the shifts among them) or of actual economic factors and processes (as distinguished from clichés about "exploitation") to enable an investigator to carry the analysis of the transition from nationalism to revolution as far as it should be carried.

In the Russian sources two periods can be discerned. In 1926, for example, Kallinikov's study of *The national-revolutionary movement in Mongolia,* though a short book of only 118 pages, makes an interesting effort to discuss just those economic and social factors and stages of development that one would expect a revolutionary to discuss. This was a period of great controversy about theory and practice among Russian Communists. It takes a special kind of training that I do not have to be able to express an opinion whether a particular author, writing about Mongolia in a particular year, is likely to have continued to be accepted later as orthodox, or purged for deviation. I have therefore not even attempted to make analyses of this kind when citing Russian sources.

In the contemporary period there are a number of Russian books and booklets about the Mongolian People's Republic. These tend to treat the past in clichés. For recent years they give figures about education, the multiplication of doctors and veterinarians, improvements in the livestock economy, the beginnings of industrial enterprise, and so forth; but as these have little bearing on the period discussed in this book, I have not cited them.

In neither Mongol nor Russian sources (nor Chinese for that matter) have I found an adequate discussion of religion as a factor in politics. I do not mean so much revolutionary campaigns against belief (which appear not to have been so severe in Mongolia as they have intermittently been in Russia) as an analysis of the organizational strength and economic resources of Lama Buddhism. Undoubtedly many great monasteries, with administrative territories and revenues of their own and jurisdiction over a lay population, were better managed than many of the princely Banners. In fact the general indications are that the part of the old order represented by the Church was much more vigorous, even in the period of decay, than the part represented by the princes, so that for the revolutionaries the problem of winning an ascendancy over the position held in society by the Church was a more serious problem than depriving the nobility of its privileges.

I am still accumulating material on this and other problems, and hope in time to be able to do something to fill in the gaps that I have pointed out.

At the moment of going to press I learn from p. 116 of the Chinese translation of a book originally published in Russian or Mongol that Nachukdorji's *Life of Sukebatur* received a "Choibalsang Prize." The Chinese title is *Meng-ku jen-min ko-ming san-shih nien, 1921–1951,* (*Thirty years of the Mongol people's revolution, 1921–1951*), Peking, 1953. The Chinese edition reads as if it had been translated from a Russian rather than a Mongol original. The original text was published at Ulan Batur in 1951. The authorship is ascribed in the Chinese transliteration to "Pu. Hsi-lin-ti-pu" (*i.e.,* Bu. Shirendib) and others. On the reverse of the title page the authorship is ascribed, in Russian transliteration, to "B. Shirendyb and others." Here the Russian "B.", Chinese "Pu." or "Bu." is the abbreviation of a Mongol clan name, while Shirendib or Shirendyb is the personal name.

O. L.

PART ONE

NATIONALISM AND REVOLUTION IN MONGOLIA

Revolutions serve to emphasize very vague ideas and make them appear to have a specific content. . . . This is important to remember because of the generally accepted notion that revolutions advance new ideas. What they actually do is to give morale and organization to radical individuals. This may or may not advance the new idea.

THURMAN W. ARNOLD

The Folklore of Capitalism

(New Haven, 1937, 13th ed. 1950, p. 13)

INTRODUCTORY

Sukebatur, the Sun Yat-sen of revolution in Outer Mongolia, died in 1923. Several years ago, in contributing an introduction to the book by Gerard M. Friters, *Outer Mongolia and its international position* (cited frequently below), I made the comparison between Sukebatur and Sun Yat-sen and also some comparisons between nationalism in Mongolia, China, and Turkey in the 1920's. What I am now trying to do is to carry that line of research a stage farther, by translating the "official" life of Sukebatur — which shows, as no analysis by an outsider possibly could, the way in which, toward the end of the second World War, the régime in the Mongolian People's Republic wanted Mongols to think about their country and its recent past — and by prefacing to this translation an essay which gives the historical background, touches on the differences between Outer and Inner Mongolia, tries to bring into focus the impact of both China and Russia on Mongol affairs, and attempts an analysis of the modes of politics in a satellite state [1].

There was a time when Soviet writers referred to Outer Mongolia as if it were a broad avenue leading into China and the rest of Asia, and as if they expected its government, the Mongolian People's Republic, set up in the turbulent 1920's with Russian aid, to serve as a model for other countries in Asia [2]. Yet looking back from the 1950's

---

[1] In "The historical setting of Inner Mongolian nationalism", *Pacific Affairs*, New York, 9, 3, 1936, p. 404 I wrote: "Since, however, the trend of policy in Outer Mongolia assumes the full development of both economic and social revolution in the future, and since both depend on the ability to draw on the economic resources of the Soviet Union as well as on the ideas of the Communist Party, Outer Mongolia may well be called a satellite of the Soviet Union." Possibly this may be the earliest use of the term "satellite" in what has now come to be its contemporary connotation, and the earliest or one of the earliest descriptions of the satellite relationship.

[2] See, for example S. [= Siren] Shoizhelov (very probably, from his name, a Buryat Mongol), "*Zapadnaya Mongoliya*", ("Western Mongolia") in *Novyi Vostok* (*New Orient*), Moscow, 1923, No. 4, pp. 151–161, who speaks of the Mongols becoming "a cadre of truly conscious warriors for the liberation of the peoples of the East and the ideals of world revolution." The same author, in an article called "*Natsional'no-osvoboditel'noe dvizhenie Mongolii*", ("The national-liberation movement of Mongolia"), in the same publication, 1924, No. 6, pp. 245–254, counts on the Mongols as "one of the most active detachments in the struggle for liberation of the peoples of the East, especially the 400 millions of China."

it is plain that Outer Mongolia never did become of primary importance either in military strategy or as a pilot model of revolutionary methods. In the brief but crushing Russian participation in
the war against Japan Outer Mongolia was used for flank maneuvers,
but the main attack was from Siberia directly into Manchuria. There
is no indication that the Russians even developed a supply line across
Mongolia to aid the Chinese Communists; and it certainly can be
stated definitely that the Chinese Communists never modelled themselves either in structure or in procedure on Outer Mongolia. Even
in Inner Mongolia the present structure of government and organization of the Communist Party are entirely the work of the Chinese
Communists, not of Mongols from Outer Mongolia.

On the other hand there is another aspect of recent political history
in Mongolia which, though it has been almost totally neglected by
Western scholarship, is capable of yielding valuable information to
the student who is interested in comparing different kinds of society
and forms of government with each other. This important aspect of
recent Mongol history involves the problem of "satellite politics,"
which will be analyzed later in this discussion but can be stated in
outline here. "Satellite politics" is in the main a new development in
relations between states. Analysis of it must be preceded by comparing the satellite relationship with other relationships, such as the
alliance, the protectorate, the sphere of influence, and the colony. In
any such study Outer Mongolia is of peculiar interest because from
1911 to the end of the first World War it was a satellite of Tsarist
Russia, and then became the first of the satellites in the orbit of Soviet
Russia. Yet the peculiarity (let alone the importance) of this relationship is generally overlooked. The misleading description of Outer
Mongolia as "in all essentials, a copy of the Soviet Republics proper,
without being formally annexed," is not exceptional but typical [3].

A survey of nationalism and revolution among the Mongols must
cover the whole range between the relative unimportance of Mongolia
as a channel for the dissemination of revolution in Asia, and its
relative importance as the pilot model of the contemporary Soviet
satellite state. In order to set out the data in an orderly manner, a
historical approach is advisable.

Nationalism is a post-medieval development. In social history it is
linked with the growth of the middle classes and their encroachment

---

[3] The quotation is from Walter Kolarz, *The peoples of the Soviet Far East*,
London and New York, 1954, p. 128.

on feudal and royal privileges. In political history it is linked with the concept that the loyalty of a citizen to his nation should take precedence over his loyalty to his class. Because of the weakness of the middle classes in Asia, nationalism in this sense appeared later in Asia than it did in the West; and since it appeared at a time when Western nationalism already existed, when Western nations ruled or dominated most of Asia, and when Western economic activities were helping to create a new kind of middle class in Asia but at the same time were trying to hold it in political subordination, Asian nationalism was inevitably shaped both by imitation of the West and reaction against the West.

As soon as a modern nationalism comes into being, its exponents appeal to the past history of their people for moral and emotional sanctions. Among the ancient deeds and sentiments thus recalled some indeed may be recognized as ancestral to nationalism — after all, in even the most primitive history, whenever men united either to defend themselves or to pillage someone else, the concept of "we" and "they" at once went into operation, and this concept is one of the elements of nationalism — but foreshadowings of nationalism are not the same thing as nationalism itself [4]. In the case of the Mongols it cannot be claimed that what we now call nationalism existed either in the creation of the great Mongol empire of the thirteenth century, the overthrow of the Chinese part of that empire in the fourteenth century and the retreat of the Mongols into Mongolia, or the conquest of both Mongolia and China by the Manchus in the seventeenth century.

---

[4] For a discussion of this point, including mention of the medieval Orkhon Turks of Outer Mongolia, see Owen Lattimore, Introduction to Louis M. J. Schram, C.I.C.M., *The Monguors of the Kansu-Tibetan frontier: their origin, history, and social organization*, Philadelphia, American Philosophical Society, *Transactions*, 1954, N.S. 44, 1, pp. 16—17.

THE MONGOLS UNDER MANCHU RULE ·

The Mongols whom Chingis Khan led to conquest were a collection of tribes rather than a people. They were at chronic war with each other until he united them by force, and he used them to found not a nation but an empire [1]. When the Chinese part of that empire fell, the Mongols who were left in Mongolia, or who withdrew from China into Mongolia, did not unite "nationalistically" either to restore Mongol rule over China or to defend themselves against the Chinese; they fought each other more than they fought the Chinese [2]. When they came under Manchu rule, the Mongols neither adhered to the Manchus as a united people nor resisted the imposition of Manchu

---

[1] Nationalist glorification of the past confronts Communist and Soviet-satellite writers with special problems, inasmuch as patriotism is "good", but the rule of one people by another is "bad". Thus in an Outer Mongolian publication entitled *Monggol-un arat tumen, erke chiluge, tosagar toktanil-un tukhai temecheksen* (*How the Mongol common people struggled for freedom and the establishment of independence*), a long passage on pp. 3—8 praises Chingis for uniting his people and giving them a land and culture of their own, but is immediately followed by a passage condemning imperialism and the enslavement of other peoples as "dirty business." My copy of this book is a photostat which unfortunately does not show the author's name or date and place of publication; but the date is established approximately by the final passage, which cites a 1945 radio address by Choibalsang.

[2] For Mongol troops in Chinese service, after the fall of the Mongol dynasty, fighting against "barbarian" tribes south of the Yangtze, see Erich Haenisch, *Sino-mongolische Dokumente vom Ende des 14. Jahrhunderts, Abhandlungen der deutschen Akademie der Wissenschaften zu Berlin, Klasse für Sprachen, Literatur und Kunst,* Jahrg. 1950, No. 4. Berlin: Akademie Verlag. 1952. pp. 60; cited, with comment, in Owen Lattimore, "Inner Asia, from inside and out," *Pacific Affairs,* 27, 2, New York, June 1954, p. 170. We may now expect much new light on this whole subject from a doctoral dissertation at Columbia University, as yet unpublished, by Father Henry Serruys, C.I.C.M. According to a personal letter of 15 July, 1954 from Professor C. Martin Wilbur, Father Serruys has assembled "hundreds of references" from Ming history "and put all of the little pieces together to reconstruct the situation. He shows in great detail that Mongol troops were on all sides of the fighting that brought about the downfall of the Mongol Dynasty and the eventual triumph of the Ming; that large numbers of Mongols stayed in China, some continuing in the Ming bureaucracy; that there was a general movement of Mongols both outwards to the frontiers and inwards towards China during these 20 years. His study rather explodes the idea that the establisment of the Ming was a nationalistic movement."

authority in the manner of a nation defending itself against foreigners. It is the piecemeal inclusion of the Mongols in the Manchu empire that accounts for the "Outer," "Inner" and other divisions of Mongolia and the Mongols.

For decades before they occupied Peking in 1644 and set up their empire over China, the Manchus, while they were still in Manchuria, fought against a number of Eastern and Southern Mongol tribes. Not "the Mongol people" as such, but a number of Mongol princes or chiefs adhered voluntarily to the Manchus, bringing their followers with them. Others were conquered, but after conquest were raised to the status of auxiliaries to assist the Manchus in their campaigns against China.

A second phase began in the second half of the seventeenth century, when the Manchus were already firmly seated in China and in control of what is now Inner Mongolia. After prolonged tribal wars it began to look as though the Northern Mongols (the Khalkhas) would be conquered by the Western Mongols, known under various tribal names such as Oirat and Ölöt (Eleuth). Many Khalkhas fled southward into Inner Mongolia. Their princes appealed to the Manchu emperor for support, and with Manchu intervention the Western Mongols were defeated and driven back. Outer Mongolia thus came within the Manchu empire as a special kind of protectorate, somewhat different in status from the administrative subdivisions of Inner Mongolia, and more loosely and indirectly ruled. One reason for this was that some of the Northern Mongols were looking to the Russians rather than to the Manchus for support against the Western Mongols, and the Manchus were cautious not to assert themselves so strongly as to encourage a drift of the Mongols into the Russian orbit.

The Western Mongols had been badly mauled. A portion of their territory was annexed to the northwestern part of Outer Mongolia. They had also been at war among themselves, in a manner typical of tribal politics, and one group broke away and migrated to the lower Volga, in Russia. They became the Kalmuks. The main body of the Western Mongols, however, still remained in the northern part of what is now the province of Sinkiang. They were still a formidable power. For a time, some of them dominated Tibet. They were the kind of people among whom in the past barbarian invasions and conquests of China had repeatedly originated, the process regularly taking the form of decades of tribal warfare leading to the emergence of a talented leader, the "snowballing" of tribes under his banner and then, if the defenses of China were weak, invasion of China. The Manchus, being of this kind of origin themselves, were well aware of the traditional pattern. At the beginning of the eighteenth century, taking advantage of internal dissensions in Tibet, they turned the flank of the Western Mongols by extending Manchu authority into Tibet. They were then ready to crush the Western Mongols completely, and this they did in the second half of the eighteenth century, with a great slaughter not only of armed men but of the whole population. As a partial replacement of the population, the Western Mongols who had migrated to the Volga were invited to return. Some of them came back to Sinkiang, where their descendants still live; others remained on the Volga, and these are the Kalmuks [3].

Thus the three phases of extension of Manchu rule over the Mongols, and their consequences for the Mongols of today, may be recapitulated as follows:

1.   Southern and Eastern Mongols. Closely associated not only with the Manchus, but with the Manchu conquest of China. Princes favored by the Manchu court, and often given Manchu princesses in marriage. Since the connection of each tribe with the Manchus was separate, there was little cohesion among the common people of the tribes, and when the Manchu dynasty fell in 1911 there was no widely agreed idea among the Mongols of Inner Mongolia about what to do about their future.

2.   Outer Mongolia: Khalkhas, with an annex of Western Mongols in the Northwest. Not really conquered by the Manchus; their chiefs preferred accepting Manchu overlordship to being conquered by the Western Mongols. Association of princes with the Manchu court less frequent than that of Inner Mongolian princes. Manchu rule more indirect. Contact with Chinese, and effect of Chinese agricultural colonization, much less than in Inner Mongolia. Strong historical

---

[3] There is a popular etymology, often repeated — most recently in Olaf Caroe, *Soviet empire*, (London, 1953, p. 71) — which traces the name Kalmuk to a Turkish word meaning "to remain." According to this explanation the Kalmuks were those who "remained" on the Volga when their kinsmen returned to Sinkiang. (The descendants of those who returned to Sinkiang are *not* known as Kalmuks.) On the other hand, another popular etymology is that given me by the Dilowa Hutukhtu, himself a Khalkha but having a considerable knowledge also of Western Mongol dialects, both those of the Altai and those of the Kalmuks. According to him, the proper form is Kalimak, from a root *kalima-* "to overflow." It will be noticed that this involves a directly opposite sense; instead of being Kalmuks because they "remained" on the Volga, they are Kalimaks because they "overflowed" to the Volga from their ancient homeland.

tradition of being the main body of the Mongol stock, living in the true ancient Mongol homeland. An unmistakeable sense of being a nation, as well as a group of tribes, predisposed them to seek a common, national answer to the problem of their future when the Manchu dynasty fell.

3. The Western Mongols. Widely scattered, from Outer Mongolia (the Altai) through Sinkiang into Alashan (an annex of Inner Mongolia) and into the Tibetan plateau (Mongols of Kokonor) and South Russia (the Kalmuks). Little cohesion. On the other hand, a "recalcitrant" tradition of being the only Mongols who really fought hard and long to resist Manchu rule. Hence a certain predisposition toward chauvinistic, "anti-everybody else" nationalism, breaking out in occasional individuals like Dambijantsan, who will be mentioned again later, a Kalmuk from the Volga who was prominent in Western Outer Mongolia for a number of years and was fanatically anti-Tsarist Russian, anti-Soviet Russian, and anti-Chinese.

At this point, however, some other characteristics of the Manchu period (1644–1911) must be discussed because of their bearing on the origins of nationalism.

The Manchu conquest was the last great traditional conquest of China — traditional in the sense of belonging to a well-known type. It originated on the landward side of China, north of the Great Wall. It was initiated by a tribal chieftain who first disciplined the warriors of his own tribe and then agglomerated to them the chiefs and warriors of other tribes. Even before they had entered China the Manchus had also begun to enlist Chinese troops (from whom were created the hereditary "Chinese Bannermen") and Chinese administrators capable of collecting revenue for their new masters and carrying on all the other complex business of managing an empire. These procedures were not new discoveries of the Manchus. They were part of a well-known tradition.

The alternate phase of this tradition came when a dynasty of barbarian origin was overthrown and replaced by a genuinely Chinese tradition. A hitherto neglected aspect [4] of this alternate phase is that, just as barbarians habitually or traditionally conquered and ruled China with the aid of Chinese, so Chinese enlisted and employed barbarians in overthrowing and expelling barbarians. The history of China and the history of the barbarians were in fact symbiotic. In one

---

[4] In the work of Father Serruys (see above, p. 6, n. 2) we may look forward to interesting material for filling this gap.

phase of the cycle more power was in barbarian hands and less in
Chinese hands. In the alternating phase, more power was in Chinese
hands and less in barbarian hands; but in both phases, although the
Great Wall divided the Chinese farmer from the barbarian herdsman
and hunter, it divided them only within an inclusive symbiosis. It was
for reasons of this kind that Chinese history was so largely repetitive
and cyclic, and so slow in evolving through recognisably different
successive periods. Power passed from one group of hands to another,
but essentially dynastic power remained the same kind of power.

The Manchu conquest was the last of the series because it was
accompanied (in fact slightly preceded) by a revolution in military
technology and an economic revolution, especially in the economics of
transportation.

It would take too long to refer here in more than the briefest outline
to the history of firearms in China. The main points are as follows:
gunpowder weapons were used in China as early as the twelfth and
thirteenth centuries [5] but though the Chinese were advanced enough

---

[5] According to L. Carrington Goodrich, A short history of the Chinese people,
New York, 1943, pp. 148—149, gunpowder was used in firecrackers in China in
the sixth century A.D., and in warfare in the 12th and 13th centuries. But note
that it was used virtually simultaneously by their "barbarian" opponents, first the
Jurchen and then the Mongols; and the Mongols used gunpowder in Europe in
1241. See also the mentions in O. Franke, Geschichte des chinesischen Reiches,
Berlin-Leipzig, 5 vols., 1930—52; vol. 4, p. 287 (with footnote in vol. 5, p. 155),
vol. 4, p. 467 (footnote in vol. 5, p. 234). For gunpowder weapons the Chinese
used the word p'ao as early as the 13th century. The Mongol word is boo, and
the two seem obviously related. The Russian word is pushka. The suggestion has
been made that the Russian word is a borrowing from the German; the German
word (büchse in its modern form, the "barrel" of a gun) goes back to Greek
πυξίς , "a box made from the wood of the box tree." (A primitive way of making
a cannon is to drill a hole through a section of log and wrap this "barrel" with
rawhide, which shrinks as it dries.) A. G. Preobrazhensky, Etymological dictionary
of the Russian language, Columbia University Press reprint, New York, 1951,
questions the derivation of pushka from German büchse (older form buhsa),
because the Slavs, unlike the Germans, did not confuse p and b in borrowed
words. He traces an alternative line back to Bulgarian, Serbian, and Albanian
forms beginning with p. A non-German origin for the Russian word seems to
coincide with the theory that firearms were introduced into Russia by two routes,
one from Germany and one from the East or Middle East, with the eastern route
somewhat earlier, as argued by V. Mavrodin, "O poyavlenii ognestrel'nogo
oruzhiya na Rusi," ("On the appearance of firearms in Russia,") Voprosy istorii
(Questions of history), Moscow, 8—9, 1946, pp. 98—101. While this article is
weakened by claiming fantastically early dates for firearms or gunpowder in Asia,
it makes a good case for Russian technological borrowing from the Middle East,
with at least in part a Turkish nomenclature. If there should be a word of 12th
century currency from one of the Iranian or Indian Indo-European languages,

to be pioneers in the use of such weapons, though perhaps not the originators of them, some factor to encourage further development, and especially quantity production, must have been lacking in the Chinese technological, economic, and social complex. By the seventeenth century the necessary techniques had progressed much farther in Europe than in China. Toward the close of the Ming dynasty the Chinese were glad to have cannon cast for them by the Jesuit Adam Schall; and the use of these cannon delayed the final Manchu conquest. The same Adam Schall stayed on in China after the fall of the Ming and served under the Manchus [6].

It is also important to note that the use of firearms was at the same time developing rapidly in Russia, and that the use of firearms had much to do with the swift Cossack penetration and conquest of Siberia which brought the Russians to the northern edges of Mongolia and Manchuria at the very time that the Manchus were establishing their empire. Thus in the main the Manchus effected an "old-fashioned" conquest, using the traditional arms and tactics; but even as they were doing so new and improved firearms were appearing in quantities that were destined to change the character of war and the relationship of firepower to mass numbers. They were also to change the social character of war, both within China and on the tribal frontiers of China, because the traditional superiority of the mounted archer was conditioned socially by the fact that the pastoral and hunting tribes, though small in numbers compared with the huge population of China, produced this élite kind of warrior in numbers that over and over again in a long history had proved decisive [7]. The

---

related to Greek $\pi \upsilon \xi \acute{\iota} \varsigma$ and serving to link Russian *pushka*, Mongol *boo*, and Chinese *p'ao*, we should have interesting evidence of the technological combination of the Chinese invention of gunpowder, and devices for using gunpowder to propel missiles, invented west of China. On the other hand Joseph Needham, *Science and civilization in China*, Vol. I, Cambridge, 1954, pp. 134–135 and 206, is convinced (personal letter of 20 Nov. 1954), that "when we come to piece all our information together, we shall be able to trace a continuous thread to the metal-barrel projectile-launcher within the Chinese culture-area." Professor Needham's authority is eminent, but pending the outcome he anticipates, I remain impressed by the general indications of great activity in the development of explosives in a wider area that included China, Iran, and the Arab fringe of the Iranian world.

[6] René Grousset, *Histoire de la Chine*, Paris, 1942, p. 324.

[7] Because archery, especially mounted archery, required constant practice, those who used the horse and the bow in their ordinary life had an advantage over levies of peasants. Early firearms were inferior in range and accuracy; but as soon as they could be produced in sufficient numbers, peasants and townsmen could be turned into musketeers more quickly than they could be made into good

new age definitely supplanted the old age when the Manchus used firearms in their intervention on behalf of the Khalkha Mongols against the Western Mongols [8].

This new factor not only meant that China could never again be conquered in the old way. It also meant that when the Manchu dynasty fell, it could not fall in the old way. For although China was penetrated by firearms, it was not penetrated and transformed by the industrialism which in the West was to continue the improvement and enormously increase the production of firearms. In a country which does not produce its own armaments, civil war as well as international war is at the mercy of the sources of supply.

The revolution in economic values was parallel to that in military values, and linked with it. For two centuries the Manchus were able to rule their empire in the old manner, but they were unable to check the growth of the power of the Western nations whose ships had appeared over the ocean horizon in Ming times. Up to this time, such pirates as the Japanese had been able to harass the coasts of China; but the new foreigners were armed, organized, and backed in such a manner that they could take up permanent positions on the coast, force their trade into the interior, and dictate what commodities were to be exchanged. In due course this control was extended and tightened by the construction of railways — also at the insistence of the foreigners.

Up to this time it can scarcely be said that there was such a thing as a national market in China. The country lived in geographical regions, marked off by mountains and rivers, and most trade was within the regions. Only relatively small surpluses and a few special commodities like silk, tea, iron, and salt were traded between regions, and foreign trade was negligible. Now a national market was being created and at the same time China was being made a part of the world market, but neither the national market nor China's participation in the world market was under the control of the Manchu govern-

---

archers, and replaced more quickly if they became casualties. The Manchus were in a dilemna. They wanted to maintain their own Bannermen as an élite of archers assuring rule over the unarmed Chinese, and this was probably one reason why they did not enthusiastically push the early development of firearms; but inevitably, as firearms became more plentiful, there were more Chinese than Manchus to use them. See the brief citation of Manchu edicts on the subject in Owen Lattimore, *Inner Asian Frontiers of China*, 2nd. ed., New York, 1951, p. 138, n. 58.

[8] Grousset, *op. cit.* p. 343.

ment or the Chinese Republic that succeeded it. The railway network was not designed to integrate a national economy but to tie a power-less China into the world market; factories to take advantage of the cheapness of Chinese labor were not placed at the points that might have been indicated by the location in China of raw materials, transport facilities, and consuming markets, but where they served the needs of foreign investors, foreign naval and military protection of the investment, and the convenience of foreigners both in import-ing commodities into China and in exporting commodities from China.

These changes affected not only China but China's relations with the Mongols, and prepared the way for a future Mongol nationalism as well as Chinese nationalism. When the Manchu empire disinte-grated and fell, power could no longer pass into the kind of hands that would have set up a new Chinese dynasty of the old style, replacing a barbarian dynasty of the old style. It had to pass into new hands, and of the claimant hands the most important were those of the warlords, the merchants, industrialists and bankers who drew their wealth from China's new economic superstructure, and the in-tellectuals who represented the penetration into China of Western education and technology. The most important conservative force was that of the landlords representing the traditional wealth and social status based on land-rent; but many landlords were linked with war-lords, merchants, and intellectuals.

A warlord was a man who dominated a region within China by command of an army equipped with rifles and a small amount of artillery. The warlords were the most irresponsible of the nationalists. They did not sell out their country to foreigners just for the fun of it, as some of the radical literature in Chinese and other languages would suggest; a man like Chang Tso-lin, for instance, the famous warlord of Manchuria, could only survive on the sufferance of Japan's regional domination over Manchuria, but nevertheless, while tied to Japan's interest, he maneuvered to the best of his ability to limit Japan's control over him. But China's munitions industry was weak, and a warlord, competing with other warlords, was partly dependent on foreign supplies, and the wars of warlords divided China into regions, in a competition for the control of railways leading to ports at which the arms could be obtained. We still lack an adequate analysis of this period, and of the significance, in this context, of a hinterland warlord like Feng Yü-hsiang, who with no direct access to the sea was more nationalistic than other warlords partly because, having to be more economical in the expenditure of force, he had to cultivate popular support [9].

Merchants, industrialists, and bankers were inevitably nationalistic because their position would obviously be stronger in a fully independent China than in a country where foreign merchants were more secure than Chinese merchants, foreign industrialists than Chinese industrialists, and foreign bankers than Chinese bankers.

Intellectuals had before them the obvious prospect that, in a future in which China was inevitably going to be transformed by new kinds of knowledge of Western origin, they would have better careers in developing a country that was really their own, not hampered by the vested political and economic interests of foreigners.

Landlords were the most conservative nationalists because they represented the least changed economic activity in the life of China. The more exclusively a man was a landlord, the less ardent he was as a nationalist; the more he was linked also with trade, manufacture, or banking, the more willing he was to accept economic and social change, for these middle class interests, though not radical in themselves, were willing at times to make quite radical concessions, including concessions that would rouse the political enthusiasm of peasants, if they needed popular support to further their major interests in trade, manufacture, and banking, which imperatively needed national independence.

These changes in China affected the Mongols in the following ways:

In the early period of the Manchu empire the position of the Mongols as a people and especially of their princes as a class, was a favorable one. They had a sound economy, based on the herding of livestock, almost entirely free of drought and flood, the two great plagues of agricultural China. The major factor of instability was animal disease; but diminished herds recuperate much more quickly than devastated fields — especially since the pastoral nomad, unlike the landfast peasant, can move away from an endangered area with all his remaining possessions. Moreover the Mongol economy was exceptionally well-rounded as a self-sufficient economy, providing the basic requirements of food (meat and milk), housing (felt tents), fuel (dry animal dung) and transportation. Under the old conditions of

---

[9] See Owen Lattimore, "China and the barbarians," in Joseph Barnes (ed.), *Empire in the east*, New York, 1934, p. 31.

overland trade, there was only a limited demand for the surplus products of this economy, and therefore almost all Mongols lived well, and dressed well. Both Mongol and Russian accounts in the revolutionary years repetitively denounce "Manchu oppression", "Chinese exploitation," and the "despotic behavior" of Mongol nobles; but the fact is that, until rather late in the nineteenth century in some cases, and early in the twentieth century in other cases, even the poor Mongol suffered much less from such elemental privations as cold and hunger than the poor peasant in agricultural Asia.

The Manchus favored the Mongols because, in the tradition of a conquering dynasty of barbarian origin, they began their rule by trying to maintain, at the edge of the conquered territory, a "reservoir" of tribal auxiliaries who were, by definition, to be well treated in order to keep them loyal to the house ruling over China but, equally by definition, were to be exhorted to keep up the ancient barbarian military virtues and prevented, by positive laws and regulations, from becoming assimilated to the Chinese [10]. Mongols were to enter Chinese-inhabited regions only for specified purposes of trade, pilgrimage, or when princes and their retinues came to the Manchu court. Each Mongol prince collected his own revenue and dispensed justice among his subjects. The Manchu court took a ceremonial tribute from each prince, but China as a nation did not collect taxes from the Mongols. The relationship of Mongol prince to Manchu emperor was feudal, and as is typical of a feudal system, various devices were used to keep the feudal princes territorially divided and to weaken any sense of unity among the Mongols as a people.

Conversely, Chinese were in theory prevented from entering Mongol-inhabited country except as traders or appointed officials; and traders were not allowed to bring their wives with them from China or (in theory again) to cohabit with Mongol women. Chinese were forbidden to settle on Mongol land either as purchasers or as tenants of Mongols. In some areas, like Manchuria, and some of the adjacent Mongol Banners in Jehol province, where farming seems always to have been practised, there was a special need for seasonal farm labor. For this purpose Chinese migrant laborers were granted permits, but were supposed to return within the Great Wall after the harvest season.

It may seem odd at the first glance, but was in fact quite logical, that it was the Mongols themselves who first evaded these regulations.

---

[10] For a discussion of the inner and outer tribal "reservoirs," see Owen Lattimore, *Manchuria, Cradle of conflict*, New York, 1932, pp. 38—41.

It was all very well for the Manchus to want to keep the Mongols as contented, unsophisticated barbarians and happy warriors; but Mongol princes who went periodically to the Manchu court in Peking saw there the luxury enjoyed by Manchus attached to the court or settled in Peking as part of the garrison. They saw no reason why they should not enjoy their own provincial versions of the same luxury. Accordingly it was Mongol princes who encouraged Chinese merchants and paid well for Chinese artisans to come to Mongolia to build for them palaces modelled on those of the Manchu nobility in Peking. In order to increase their revenues to cover this growing expenditure, those princes whose territories were favorably situated began to arrange for Chinese tenants to cultivate part of their tribal lands, which they set aside for the purpose. In the early stages of this expansion of agriculture the grain that was produced was not sent "back" into China but "out" — that is, deeper into Mongol territory, where Mongols who had no grain were willing to exchange livestock, wool, and hides for it. The economics of this kind of exchange were simple. Under the conditions of overland trade, using animal transport, the profits of transporting grain through settled country diminished very rapidly at any distance over 100 miles in settled country, requiring expenditure at inns; but grain loaded on camels, grazed daily on open pasture, could be carried many hundred miles into Mongol country at a good profit. Thus Chinese agricultural colonization did not, in the early stages, represent an accretion to the farming economy of China so much as a springboard for the projection of Chinese trade deeper into Mongolia.

This kind of relationship lost its balance in proportion as the traditional Chinese economy became unbalanced by Western trade and economic domination. The old, self-sufficient Chinese economy offered only a limited market for Mongol products. The Chinese, for example, had little taste for woolen textiles. While on the one hand this limited the market for the Mongols, on the other hand it meant that the value of wool in Mongolia itself was so low that even the poorest families could afford to use all the wool they needed to make felt to cover the wooden frames of their round tents; that all could wear warm sheepskin clothes in the bitter winter; and that, the demand of the market in China for beef and mutton being limited, and the demand for milk and cheese non-existent, there were ample supplies for the basic Mongol diet.

These conditions could not survive the influence of the seaports on

Chinese trade and colonization, especially when this influence was extended by the construction of railways, which at the turn from the nineteenth to the twentieth century began to affect the northern Mongols and the Mongols of western Manchuria (Peking-Mukden Railway, Trans-Siberian and Chinese Eastern Railways) and in the second decade of the twentieth century the Mongols of central Inner Mongolia (Peking-Suiyuan Railway). Channels were thus provided through which Mongol raw materials, still in limited demand in the Chinese consuming market, could pass right through China and enter the world market. Chinese traders profited as middlemen, and the impact of money values, replacing old barter values, was sharply increased. The effect, as always in the case of underdeveloped economies, was that the price of consumer goods needed by the Mongols increased much more rapidly than the prices they received for their raw materials. Princes, moreover, increased their demands on their subjects in order to have more to sell to the Chinese traders, in order to indulge themselves in more luxuries.

Economic change was preceded and accompanied by military change. Mongol feudal levies were called up, in the old traditional manner, to serve their overlord the Manchu emperor in the T'aip'ing Rebellion (1851–65), against the Nienfei peasant rebels in the northern provinces of China in the 1850's and 1860's, against the British and French in 1860, against Moslem rebels in the 1860's and 1870's, against the Japanese in 1894–95, and in the Boxer Rebellion of 1900. Mongol irregulars, moreover, served with both the Russians and the Japanese, but especially the Japanese, in Manchuria in the Russo-Japanese War of 1904–05. In these campaigns the Mongols (most of them from Inner Mongolia) showed that they were the most superior of the old-style troops in the service of the Manchu dynasty — but at the same time nothing could hide the fact that the day of the old-style troops was done. The best troops available to the Manchus were increasingly, from decade to decade, not Manchu Bannerman and Mongol levies, but new-style armies of Chinese, with relatively modern equipment, under Chinese commanders — a change that confirmed the transformation of the dynasty itself from being a Manchu dynasty ruling over China to being an essentially (though archaically) Chinese dynasty of "Emperors of China."

A few details from this half-century illustrate the conservatism of Mongol society, the disintegration of that society, and the first stirrings of a Mongol nationalism. A manuscript of a ballad in the old grand manner recites the glories of Senggerinchin, a prince of the Khorchin Mongols in western Manchuria, who fought the T'aip'ings, the Nienfei, the French and British, and then, campaigning once more against the Nienfei, was killed by them in battle. This ballad, of a kind sung by minstrels at the courts of princes, rings with the old feudal loyalty and the contempt of the Mongols, as soldiers of a dynasty of conquest, for the rebellious subject Chinese [11].

On the other hand, as early as the 1870's there was a mutiny in one of the Banners of the Ordos, among levies who had been summoned to serve against the Moslem rebels in Northwest China. The cause of the mutiny was that remittances from Peking to pay the troops had been pocketed by the prince of the Banner. The soldiers seized the prince, made him wear the kind of tattered gown they did, and try for several days the attractions of the kind of life they led. These troops were eventually allowed to go home — an indication that their mutiny was too strong to suppress [12].

Again, a Mongol soldier's ballad of the Chinese-Japanese war of 1894—95 stresses not loyalty but the resentment of the conscript against the fact that the rich were able to buy their way out of service, while the poor, abandoning father and mother and all they had, must be to horse and away for Mukden.

Outer Mongolia was less affected at this time, but in 1900 there was a mutiny of some 2,000 men who had been mobilized at Uliasutai to be sent down to China in connection with the Boxer Rebellion. The men were kept idle for several months; the pasture was poor, the Banners from which they had been levied refused to send any more money, maintaining that they had fulfilled their obligations. The men mutinied and broke into the market gardens tended by Chinese around the town of Uliasutai, where they pastured their hungry horses. The mutineers were abetted by their senior officer, himself a prince; he refused to name ringleaders to the higher authorities. Finally the mutineers were allowed to go home. It is noteworthy that some of these men are said to have been influenced by Dam-

---

[11] For biographical notice, see under Sêng-ko-lin-ch'in (the Chinese rendering of his name), in Arthur W. Hummel, ed., *Eminent Chinese of the Ch'ing period.* Washington, 1944. The notice is by Teng Ssu-yü. The Chinese rendering of his name was further transformed, by the British troops against whom he fought, into "Sam Collinson."

[12] An[atolii] Kallinikov, *"Aratskoe revolyutsionnoe dvizheniya v doavtonomnoi Mongolii"* ("The popular revolutionary movement in pre-autonomous Mongolia"), *Revolyutsionnyi Vostok (Revolutionary East)*, 5, 1934, p. 146.

bijantsan (of whom more later), a Kalmuk from the Volga, who as early as 1890 had agitated against both the Manchus and the Chinese in this region [13].

There can be no doubt, however, that in the complex of disruptive factors that was gathering momentum against the old order in Mongolia, by far the heaviest impact was that of Chinese colonization. The checks against colonization, based on an original assumption that it was worth the while of the Manchus to preserve a special Mongol order loyal to the Imperial House, had become futile. Manchu administration, though hortatory in the tone of its pronunciamentos, had in any case become lax in execution by the end of the eighteenth century, though subject to fits of savage repression. By the opening of the nineteenth century considerable communities of Chinese settlers had been established in originally Mongol areas, especially in Manchuria, under the patronage of Mongol princes but in evasion of Manchu regulations. As the decades went by, it was increasingly obvious that the loyalty of the Mongols no longer meant, for the Manchus, the kind of balance of military power that enabled them to impose their will as sovereigns of China, suzerains of Inner Mongolia, and overlords of Outer Mongolia and Tibet. The only compensatory move open to them was to act increasingly as emperors of a China of which Mongolia and Tibet were external possessions; and this meant that increasingly the important favors were those that were granted to Chinese officials who were loyal to the régime. The change of course took place not only more gradually, but more unevenly, in different regions, than can be described in a few words, and seems always to have been implicit in a gradually changing mode of action rather than in any explicitly formulated declaration of policy.

Some important changes of policy can however be noted, of course, such as the relaxing, in 1803, of the rules forbidding Chinese settlement in Manchuria (though seasonal laborers, as mentioned above, had been permitted to come in and were supposed, at the end of the season, to go home). A century later, in 1908 [14], the old administration of the Manchurian provinces as a special domain of the Manchu imperial house was abandoned, and a provincial system was set up which followed the norms of provinces inside the Great Wall. The

---

[13] An[atolii] Kallinikov, as cited (continuation) *Revolyutsionnyi Vostok*, 6, 1934, p. 54.

[14] An intermediate step was taken in 1876. See Owen Lattimore, *The Mongols of Manchuria*, New York, 1934, p. 97.

date of this change, following on Japan's victory over China in 1894—
45 and over Russia in 1904—05, followed again in 1907 by the first of
several treaties between Japan and Russia defining their spheres of
interest in Manchuria and Mongolia [15], is enough to show its significance: Manchuria could no longer be held as an outer domain. It had
to be integrated with China.

When an administrative decree is not in fact a new departure, but
significant because it gives authority to processes that are already
under way and gathering momentum, the result is likely to be a great
acceleration of pace. In Manchuria, for example, before 1900 (arbitra-
rily including Jehol as a Manchurian province, according to later
usage), Chinese settlements large enough to be organized as *hsien* or
counties were established in 1729, 1738 (two), 1778, 1802, 1806, 1875,
1877, and 1882, or nine in all. The reason for their organization was
that the administrative framework of a Mongol Banner could contain
only a few hundred Chinese — at most a thousand or two — whose
agricultural and handicraft production was ancillary to the Mongol
economy. In numbers of this order of magnitude, heads of households
could handle all minor problems of the Chinese according to recognized and accepted custom, and more important problems arising
between Chinese and Mongols could be settled by the Mongol
authorities. Beyond this order of magnitude the problems became so
many and so serious that they burst the relatively crude Mongol administrative framework, and it was necessary to appoint Chinese
officials to deal with the Chinese community and, on behalf of the
community, with the Mongol authorities.

The rate of acceleration is shown by the fact that in the same region
more than 25 counties were organized between 1900 and 1911 (end
of the Manchu empire), and more than 20 between 1912 and 1931
(invasion of Manchuria by the Japanese). The later-founded counties,
moreover, have as a rule, though not always, larger populations,
which accentuates the acceleration [16].

---

[15] For these treaties, see Ernest B. Price, *The Russo-Japanese treaties of 1907—
1916 concerning Manchuria and Mongolia*, Baltimore, 1933. It is from these
treaties, setting a dividing line between Russian and Japanese spheres of influence,
that the term "Eastern Inner Mongolia" (*i.e.* east of that line) derives.

[16] See the table of "Chinese counties and county towns established in Mongol
territory in Manchuria," in Lattimore, *The Mongols of Manchuria*, as cited, pp.
288—291. See also, in the same book, the discussions of "Early colonization: the
Mongols as the privileged people," beginning at p. 63, and "Modern colonization:
the Chinese become the privileged people," beginning at p. 89.

Even Outer Mongolia was affected. From very early times there was a certain amount of "market garden" cultivation by Chinese around towns like Urga, Kobdo, and Uliasutai. In the 1880's and 1890's Chinese colonists began to grow grain in northern Outer Mongolia, near the Siberian frontier, where water was available for irrigation. This colonization was speeded up at the turn of the century to implement a policy of building up a screen of Chinese population all along the Russian borders of Outer Mongolia and Manchuria [17]. Chinese colonization in Outer Mongolia had one notable peculiarity: it was "islanded," with vast stretches of Mongol-inhabited territory separating the Chinese settlers from other Chinese-inhabited territory — in contrast to Inner Mongolia, where each new Chinese settlement represented an expansion from land already colonized. Because of this isolation, Chinese colonization was never able to dominate Outer Mongolia as it did Inner Mongolia.

---

[17] See the article "Mongolia," by G. C. Binsteed, in *The China Year Book*, ed. H. T. M. Bell and H. G. W. Woodhead, London, 1919–20. Also Gerard M. Friters, *Outer Mongolia and its international position*, Baltimore, 1949, p. 157. Anatolii Kallinikov, *Natsional'no-revolyutsionnoe dvizhenie v Mongolii*, (*The national-revolutionary movement in Mongolia*), Moscow, 1926, p. 24, gives the area of Chinese farmland in Outer Mongolia in 1911 as 70,000 *desyatiny*, or approximately 175,000 acres, but gives no figure of Chinese farming population.

CHINESE WARLORDS AND INNER MONGOLIA

In the accelerated sweep of the Chinese into eastern (Manchurian) and southern Inner Mongolia the chief significance of the Chinese Revolution in 1911 was that it delivered the Mongols into the hands of Chinese warlords with limited local interests. From 1911 to the establishment of Chiang Kai-shek's regime in 1926—27 there was no central government strong enough to impose a continuous national policy on the warlords who had at their mercy the various sectors of Inner Mongolia. (Outer Mongolia, of course, immediately slipped out of China's control.)

It is in the light of these conditions that modern Mongol nationalism must be studied, and the differences between Outer and Inner Mongolian nationalism analyzed.

Colonization was immensely profitable to the warlord who controlled a Chinese province or group of provinces adjoining Mongol land. The land could be taken away from the Mongols very cheaply, sometimes by violence and sometimes by chicanery. The colonists were in the main very poor people — often famine refugees. The land was taken up in large blocks by the warlords themselves or their agents and associates, and the colonists were placed on these holdings as share-croppers. There was no landlordism in China more oppressive than that of the colonized regions.

While in China the Revolution of 1911 meant the passage of power into new hands, there was in Inner Mongolia very little power to change hands, and there were no new hands to reach out for power. Such power as there was lay in the hands of hereditary princes and monastic foundations. There was no middle class. Trade was in the hands of Chinese. There was not even enough manpower to make possible the rise of Mongol warlords to compete with Chinese warlords. Inevitably, therefore, Inner Mongolian nationalism was sporadic in its manifestations and inevitably, when it did manifest itself, it had more the character of the rebellion of a minority than that of the revolution of a people; although (equally inevitably) it had from the beginning one revolutionary characteristic, that of class conflict.

Each warlord pressed his encroachment on the Mongols at his own pace. The result was that when the Mongols rose in rebellion they rose in different places at different times. There was no general Inner Mongolian nationalist movement, with a unified leadership, until the 1930's.

As so often happens in history, the pattern that comes later to be associated with a well-defined period appears first in an anticipatory form well before the period for which it is considered typical.

Actually the first important risings of the Mongols of Inner Mongolia were against their own princes rather than against Chinese colonists or the Manchu government — and this undoubtedly was a symptom of the decay of the Mongol society and economy. In areas near to the Chinese, where the decay was most rapid because of Chinese trade, the princes held on to their luxuries as long as they could. Thus the fall in the standard of living bore most heavily on poor people, and they turned their resentment against their princes. Kallinikov lists a rising as early as 1858 in one of the Banners of the Ordos, in protest against increased levies demanded by the prince. About 300 families refused for three months to carry out their feudal corvée services. In this case the Manchu government authorities at Kueihua (Suiyuan) intervened. The people were considered to be justified and the prince was made to reduce his demands [1].

This rising was notable for the first appearance of the *duguilang*, a form of organization that flourished from then on in the Ordos, spread widely through Inner Mongolia, and made one notable appearance in Outer Mongolia. *Duguilang* means "in a circle." It means a ring without a ringleader, as explained to me by the spirited Inner Mongolian nationalist leader Merse (Kuo Tao-fu), who was killed in 1932 (supposedly on the orders of Chang Hsueh-liang, the ruler of Manchuria) after the Japanese had invaded Manchuria and it was feared, with reason, that the Mongols would go over to the Japanese because of the way they had been treated by the Chinese. The members of a *duguilang* are all supposed to be equal. Their names, if they are written down, are written in a circle or "round robin," so that no one can be singled out as the leader [2]. If there are several *duguilang*

---

[1] Kallinikov, as cited above (first instalment) *Revolyutsionnyi Vostok*, 5, 1934, p. 145.

[2] This is an old and perhaps the original meaning of the English term "round robin," now often used of a message that is sent to a number of people in turn: " ... a peticion ... signed by most of them, in the manner of a circle, because itt should not bee knowne whoe was the principall of the mutiny." Citation from the year 1612 in Ernest Weekley, *An etymological dictionary of modern English*, London, 1921, *s.v.* "robin."

in a movement, the number of those in one who know members of another is limited, so as to decrease the danger of betrayal. Today when all revolutionary activity is apt to be attributed to Russian instigation, it is well to note that this "cell" method of organization seems to be instinctive among people who organize against oppression and who, because of their weakness, find secrecy imperative. Sun Yat-sen invoked the same principle in China — also at a period before there could be any question of imitating a Russian model.

Kallinikov, as a Marxist writer, suggests that the *duguilang* may be a "clan survival," and cites Engels on clan survivals as weapons against oppressing classes [3]. This suggestion, which sounds rather doctrinaire, may in fact be slightly beside the mark but not altogether off the target. It is certainly beyond dispute that the Mongols, in spite of their long division into separate feudal principalities under Manchu rule, retained in their social tradition and social psychology ideas of "the good of the tribe" — such as the idea that, "for the good of the tribe," it could on occasion be demanded that a bad prince be replaced by a better one (of the same family, of course). On the other hand the specific *duguilang* form of organization may have been borrowed from Chinese secret societies. This is suggested by the first recorded appearance of a *duguilang*, near the Chinese province of Shensi, where secret societies flourished from of old. It is also suggested by the fact that the Chinese, when describing a *duguilang*, call it a *kung hui* — a term used for many kinds of public associations, guilds, and in modern times clubs [4].

It is certainly significant that the *duguilang* form of organization seems always or almost always to have combined resistance to Chinese colonization with resentment of the Mongols against the incapacity or corruption or oppression of their own princes. The reasons are not far to seek. Often the prince, seeing that he was not strong enough to resist Chinese demands for cession of land, would try to do at least the best he could for himself, working in with the Chinese authorities,

---

[3] Kallinikov, as cited (first instalment), *Revolyutsionnyi vostok*, 5, 1934, p. 145.

[4] This is probably why Antoine Mostaert, in his *Dictionnaire ordos*, 3 vols., Peking, 1941—44, renders *duguilang* as *Nom donné aux clubs révolutionnaires qui vers la fin des Ts'ing furent érigés en Üchin et Otok pour s'opposer aux impots excessifs, à la vente des terres mongoles, etc.* So also J. van Hecken, *Les missions chez les mongols aux temps modernes*, Peiping, 1949, p. 174, n. 22: *La bannière d'Otok est divisée non officiellement en huit régions, dont les habitations forment un club ou cercle et qui se réunissent à des endroits fixes, qui donnent leur nom au club.*

taking up land, and investing in Chinese trading companies. It was not unknown for a prince to become in this manner more of a Chinese landlord than a Mongol prince.

There were, of course, also converse developments. As time went on Mongol nobles occasionally became nationalist leaders. These were not usually ruling princes, but cadet members of a princely line. Such men had the habit of authority and decision, but seeing no future in trying to follow the decaying pattern of the old order, would set themselves up as popular leaders. These changes of attitude even affected the lama priesthood. Kallinikov (rather surprisingly for a Soviet writer) notes this. Large monasteries that had secular territories under their jurisdiction were often less exacting in their demands on their subjects than ruling princes, and commoners would therefore try to transfer from princely jurisdiction to monastery jurisdiction [5].

There were even demands for reform by high members of the clergy. About the last decade of the Manchu dynasty the man who was recognized as the incarnation of the Gungjo Gegen or Living Buddha, in the Ordos, wrote a short book called *The teaching of the Gungjo Gegen* that was considered quite daringly radical for its time and was widely popular. In sententious alliterative Mongol verse it denounces the conventional sins of pride, luxury, greed, display, "riding in sedan chairs" and "acting like Chinese" among the great, both clerical and secular. It reads vapidly enough now, but what was radical about it at the time was that the doings of the great were not supposed to be commented on at all [6].

Before passing on to the period of the Chinese Republic, one notable rising among the Tumet Mongols near the Yellow River deserves a special comment. These Mongols had long been more agricultural than pastoral. They had no hereditary princes of their own, but among them there lived a noble of Khalkha descent, from Outer Mongolia, to whom the Manchus had granted land and retainers near the town of Kueihua [7]. Heavy assessments following

---

[5] Kallinikov, as cited (first instalment), p. 141.

[6] *Gung-un joo-in gegen-u surgal*, Hsinking, 1943, issued in Manchuria in the period of Japanese domination. During this period Japanese imperialism occasionally permitted the dissemination of quite radical ideas among the Mongols, especially anti-clerical ideas.

[7] In Mongol, *khamjilagh*, often rendered by Russian writers as "serfs." They were families which were the hereditary retainers of noble families. The root meaning is "to be joined to, to belong to." In the administration of a Mongol Banner, it could be a cause of dispute whether a member of one of these retainer

a famine season made these retainers rebel. They attacked the noble's "palace" in the town and killed his wife and several nobles who were related to her. The rising spread and a large punitive force was sent in. Chinese peasants also began to rise against their own landlords and a "united front" of Chinese and Mongols was formed which, from 1892 to 1894, kept up a partisan war against both rich Mongols and Chinese landlords. At the end of this bloody struggle there was more confiscation of Mongol land for colonization [8]. It is probably significant that the leading Mongol Communist in Inner Mongolia under the present regime, Ulanfu or Ulanhu (whose Chinese name is Yün Tze) comes from this region which for more than half a century has had a tradition of joint Chinese-Mongol peasant radicalism.

It should also be noted that violence did not always begin with Mongol risings against the Chinese. In exactly the same period there was widespread Chinese terrorism against the Mongols in Jehol province. Members of Chinese secret societies were united and led by a Chinese landlord named Liu to kill or drive out all Mongols, and thousands of agricultural Mongols fled at this time into the Banners of the Jerim League Mongols of western Manchuria. The Chinese organization was also nationalistic and anti-Manchu, but when the imperial government had suppressed the disturbances, it increased the confiscation of land for colonization instead of treating the Mongols as allies of the Manchu régime [9].

These two kinds of violence, Mongols against Chinese and Chinese against Mongols, created a tradition of banditry all along the Inner Mongolian frontier — a tradition in which recurrent phases of anti-landlord, anti-rich-man, anti-provincial-government radicalism alternated with the organization of private bandit armies by the landlords themselves. There were border landlords who lived in fortified manors and after the harvest was in would lead or send bands of their retainers on freebooting forays that ranged for hundreds of miles in a great curve sweeping from the Ordos bend of the Yellow River up into northwestern Manchuria [10].

---

families could be commandeered for Banner service, or whether he should be considered immune because his noble needed him. Mostaert, *Dictionnaire,* as cited, gives: *"aide; serf attaché spécialement au service d'un noble."*

[8] Kallinikov, as cited (first instalment) p. 147. Note that the beginning of the rising was at about the time of the first appearance of Dambijantsan in Western Outer Mongolia, proclaiming the coming end of the Manchu empire (see below).

[9] Kallinikov, as cited (first instalment) p. 148.

[10] Owen Lattimore, *Mongols Journeys,* New York, 1941, pp. 14—17.

dealt with the Mongols almost exclusively through their princes and the more important Living Buddhas, but upheld their power against any demands made on them by the Mongols as a people. When Chinese policy operated by intimidation, it was the prince who was ordered to make his people move out of land wanted for colonization. His authority to do so was backed by Chinese troops when necessary. When a deal was made, princes and important lamas were let in on the deal. In this way the powers of princes and lamas were enhanced within the structure of the old society at the same time that the power of the Mongols as a people was being steadily endroached on. The result was to make Inner Mongolian nationalism more radical, because it was clear that Mongol interests could not be defended as long as the old social order was both preserved and exploited by the Chinese, and because the Mongols could not resist colonization unless they resisted the orders transmitted to them through their own authorities.

This new tendency led to the emergence of a new nationalism of which the most important leader and symbol was Prince Demchuk-donggrub of West Sunid (Te Wang or Prince Te). Coming to the fore on the eve of the Japanese invasion of Manchuria in 1931, Prince Te succeeded for the first time in organizing a general movement of the whole of Inner Mongolia, from Manchuria to the Ordos. His most important demand on Chiang Kai-shek was that Inner Mongolia should no longer be divided into sectors, each attached and subordinated to a Chinese province, which prevented unity of Mongol action. He maintained that Inner Mongolia was a flank position on which China was highly vulnerable in face of the menace of Japan, because the Mongols could not be expected to resist Japan solely in the interests of China. They must have interests of their own to defend. He therefore demanded autonomy for Inner Mongolia, under a government chosen by the Mongols, not appointed by the Chinese.

Te Wang's movement was doomed, for three main reasons.

First, Chiang was not powerful enough to force the warlords of the border provinces to agree to the loss of their sectors of expansion into Mongolia, which were extremely valuable to them. When forced to compromise between Mongol demands and the obstinacy of the warlords, his compromises were always in favor of the warlords.

Second, Te Wang's movement was a coalition. He succeeded in giving a certain amount of initiative and opportunity to young, idealistic, energetic Mongols some of whom were radical enough to be quite outspoken about being anti-clerical and hostile to hereditary nobles whose demands for high positions were often not justified by their ability. At the same time, in order to hold his coalition together, he prevented any general assault on the old society. Princes and high lamas were received with the old pomp and ceremony at his headquarters and no attempts were made to take their privileges and revenues away from them. One of the consequences of this coalition policy was that the influence of defeatists and of both princes and lamas who had notorious records of collaborating with the most outrageous Chinese policies for personal profit reached right into his headquarters. The provincial warlords who hated him most bitterly knew everything that was going on and were able to begin lobbying within the national government against each move he made even before he started to make it.

Third, Japanese aggression overwhelmed almost all of Inner Mongolia. From Manchuria in 1931 the Japanese moved into Jehol in 1934 and into western Inner Mongolia in 1936–37. They made enough moves favorable to the Mongols to prevent unity of action between anti-Japanese Mongols and Chinese, and at the same time prevented unity among the Mongols by sudividing Inner Mongolia, dealing with Te Wang in only one of these subdivisions. By the end of the war Te Wang was disliked by the Chinese as a "Japanese puppet," but deeply respected by most Mongols. In their eyes he was no puppet of the Japanese. Not being strong enough to resist them, he had resorted to evasion. Even under the difficult conditions of Japanese occupation, he succeeded in greatly increasing national consciousness among the Mongols of Inner Mongolia. Perhaps his greatest service to his people was his energetic encouragement of education. By the end of the war there was a greater increase in the number of young people who could read and write, and had some idea of Mongol problems, and of the world in which the Mongols lived, than there had been in the whole history of Manchu and Chinese rule of the Mongols. The Chinese Communists, when they came to power, proclaimed Prince Te a "war criminal" — understandably, since he was the only Mongol leader who attempted armed resistance to them. They defeated him and drove him westward, but do not seem to have hunted him down. For some years there has been no news of him. He may have been captured and imprisoned or put to death without public announcement; but it is also possible that he is living in obscurity somewhere in the western part of Inner Mongolia, or even that he has crossed the border into Outer Mongolia.

OUTER MONGOLIA: THE CAPACITY FOR INDEPENDENCE

At this point the broad distinctions between Inner and Outer Mongolian nationalism can be defined.

Manchu rule was more indirect in Outer Mongolia than in Inner Mongolia. During the incursion of the Western Mongols in the seventeenth century some of the Mongols near Siberia began to go over into what is now Buryat Mongolia and to ask for Russian protection. The Manchus took note, and made their policy in Outer Mongolia one of minimum interference, so that the princes themselves would prefer to adhere to the Manchu empire rather than that of the Russians. In addition, both trade and colonization affected Outer Mongolia much less than Inner Mongolia. In this connection, it should be pointed out that the Russians who, even in Tsarist times, described the way in which Outer Mongolia was being drained of wealth by Chinese trade and usury, and the excessive exactions of some of the Mongol princes and monasteries, were describing those Mongols whom they first met when they crossed over the frontier from Siberia into Mongolia. These things are relative, and most of the Russians had no way of knowing that all the abuses, decay, and signs of breakdown they described were much worse in Inner Mongolia.

Not only did the old order still have, by 1911, much more vigor and capacity to survive in Outer Mongolia than in Inner Mongolia, but it had the great advantage of not being contiguous to Chinese provinces and therefore not weakened by being divided up into sections administratively attached to Chinese provinces. Outer Mongolia could still talk to China through whatever national government existed in China. It did not have to approach the national government through the hampering local interests of one or more provincial governments. In this there lay also another advantage for the Northern Mongols. The increase in the power of China as a state did not come until the rise to power of the Kuomintang in the 1920's. The first consequence of the Revolution of 1911 was the weakening of China as a state — both as a state dealing with other states and as a government capable of asserting authority over its own turbulent provincial warlords. The border provinces that held control over portions of Inner Mongolia were immeasurably more powerful than the small, divided Mongol tribes whom now, in the absence of a national policy, they began to plunder and oppress with complete recklessness; but at the same time it was obvious in Outer Mongolia that if the Republic was too weak to subdue its own provinces it was too weak to reach out over the dividing barrier of Inner Mongolia to undertake the conquest of so large a territory as Outer Mongolia — and if China as a nation could not do this, then neither could even the most powerful of the provincial warlords hope to do what the nation could not do. For the Mongols of Outer Mongolia, therefore, the sufferings of the component regions of Inner Mongolia were not so much a warning of imminent danger to themselves from China, as an indication that it was in the best interests of Outer Mongolia to have as little to do with China as possible. It was for this reason that various Inner Mongolian leaders urged at one time or another that there should be a concerted Inner Mongolian movement to break away from China and join Outer Mongolia; while in Outer Mongolia, though a few individuals did now and then try to excite an ambition to annex Inner Mongolia, the generally prevailing opinion among leaders of both the Left and Right was that it was best not to move into a region that would involve Outer Mongolia in both the domestic and the international politics of China.

In view of Outer Mongolia's relative capacity to take advantage of the Chinese Revolution against the Manchus to declare independence, the first question that arises is: Why did those who then spoke for the Mongols ask to be taken under the protection of Tsarist Russia? The official answer of the present régime in Outer Mongolia, which can be matched by many quotations from Soviet writers, was succinctly stated by the late Premier, Marshal Choibalsang:

> "After the extinction of the Manchu Daiching [= Ta Ch'ing] dynasty in China, our own Mongol clerical and secular feudal interests, taking advantage of the popular movement which was agitating for independence and freedom throughout the country, began to strive to create a separate country, in the hope of promoting their own feudal power.

> "The Mongol nobles who hoped to create a separate national state made some of their own more important feudal personages their representatives and sent them to Tsarist Russia, to request aid in freeing Mongolia from Chinese rule, which exactly coincided with the Tsarist Russian government's colonial policy, and ac-

cordingly the Tsarist government of Russia willingly received their request with approval." [1]

Here we have twined together two of the cardinal themes of the Left — the unlimited greedy selfishness of the "feudal" interests of a backward Asian country, and the unlimited greed for expansion of an imperialist power — since "colonial policy" must in this context be taken to mean "ambition to take over." It is fairly obvious that this explanation does not go deep enough. The truth is that Tsarist Russia's ambition to expand was not unlimited. There was a forward school that wanted to extend Russian influence in Mongolia and to make Russian control more direct and forthright; but in the drafting and execution of policy this school repeatedly lost to the more conservative view that Russia's interests would be best served if Russian influence were just sufficient to prevent Mongolia from falling again under the control of China, or passing to the control of Japan. Beyond this, it was held, it was best not to go. The old order in Mongolia should survive intact as far as it was able to, and Mongolia should remain not only a buffer but as inert a buffer as possible between Russia and the actual power of Japan and the potential power of China.

Nor is it true that all feudal nobles and high ecclesiastical personages in Outer Mongolia were greedy, selfish, and nothing else. There were many honest men who did the best they could according to their lights; and if their lights were dim it was not because of personal wickedness, but the dimness partly of their historical conditioning and partly of the time into which they were born. Revolutionaries tend to make history too simple. They burn with a fire in which they try to sear away the infinite complexities of individual character and the infinite multiplicities of social variation, so that they can confront the absolutely bad with the absolutely good. But revolution is not in fact a melodrama of the "good" against the "bad." It is the most tragic form of history, in which good men often make bad decisions not for evil reasons but for reasons of human weakness that may range from ignorance, or partial knowledge (which is often more treacherous than ignorance) to such things as a mere hesitancy in making up their minds which, in less urgent times, would not matter much either to them or to their fellows. By the same token, revolution is also a phase

---

[1] Kho. Choibalsang, *Concise history of the Mongol revolution.* (For bibliographical identification, see below, p. 63, n. 2.)

of history in which the irony is often supplied by the "good" decisions made by "bad" men.

Let us turn, for a comparison, to the very words of those "more important feudal personages" who, as Choibalsang wrote, went to Russia. They carried with them an appeal one passage of which read:

> "Formerly the Mongol Khans, Wangs, and Jassaks were rulers of their own subjects and, enjoying revenues from their lands, lived in tranquillity. In recent times Chinese officials, taking power into their hands, and in every way interfering in Mongol affairs, and especially under pretext of reform colonizing Mongolia and changing its ancient customs, are diminishing local authority. This is truly sad." [2]

In a previous comment on this passage I wrote:

> "It would be hard to draft a better expression of a conservative, static nationalism which sought to prevent the extension of Chinese power into Mongolia, but not to transfer power from the Chinese state to the Mongol people." [3]

True, as far as that goes; but it seems to me now that a more extended and rounded comment is needed. For one thing, I had at the time of my previous comment read very little of the Mongol chancellery documents of that time and so did not note a very important point: the language here used follows a traditional, "elevated" style; it was the only language that the chancellery clerks of the time knew how to write. It could be fairly paraphrased:

> "Mongolia has a stable social order of its own. The Mongols are not aggressive against anybody. Recently, however, the Chinese have been encroaching on us. Chinese colonization especially upsets the old conditions and alarms us. We would like to be left alone."

These men had a "static" nationalism because they were born into a new time which neither they nor anyone else in Outer Mongolia yet understood, and inherited their ideas from an older time which they did understand. They canot be accused of "selling out their country," because that moral judgment would apply only if they or others in

---

[2] Cited in Doksom, "*Istoricheskie uroki 15 let revolyutsii. Doklad predsedatelya Malogo Khurala Doksoma na yubileinoi 21-i sessii Malogo Khurala i kratkoe soderzhanie doklada Amora*," (Historical lessons of 15 years of revolution. Report of Doksom, chairman of the Little Khural, at the jubilee 21st session of the Little Khural and short résumé of the report of Amor), *Tikhii Okean*, (*Pacific Ocean*), 3(9), Moscow, 1936, p. 82.

[3] Owen Lattimore, Introduction to Gerard M. Friters, *Outer Mongolia and its international position*, as cited, p. xx.

their country had been capable of seeing how a true independence could be established, without leaning on the support of another country, and of organizing and carrying out in detail the sweeping reforms that would have been necessary to generate the popular enthusiasm to support such an independence.

Something of this seems to have been sensed by Doksom, the revolutionary Mongol who originally cited this passage, and from whom I quoted it [4]. He prefaces his citation by saying:

> "The letter which this delegation took to Petersburg shows that the Mongol feudal [interests], in turning to the Russian Tsar for help against the Chinese, were concerned above all with their own interests and not with the interests of the Mongol people." [5]

He follows the citation, however, by "hedging" his position and the manner in which he does so is, I believe, a significant revelation of the link of continuity between Tsarist and Soviet Russian policy toward Outer Mongolia:

> "Thus there can be no doubt that the Mongol feudal [interests] were concerned above all with their own interests. Nevertheless their coming out against the Manchu-Chinese oppression corresponded also to the interests of the whole Mongol people and was a step forward on the path of struggle for the national emancipation of Mongolia, however inconsistent that step may have been." [6]

These words are tantamount, it seems to me, to an admission that it was not in fact possible for Outer Mongolia at that time to achieve autonomy, that is, a partial independence of China, except at the price of becoming partially dependent on some other country.

If this definition be accepted, the way is open to a further analysis that I believe has never been attempted before. The old feudal order in Outer Mongolia had been weakened, but not nearly as badly weakened as in Inner Mongolia. There had been rebellions, but no attempted revolutions [7]. The characteristic rebellion was against the

---

[4] Doksom was at that time chairman of the Little Khural, the Continuing or Executive Committee in which the authority of the Outer Mongolian People's Republic was vested in the three-year intervals between sessions of the Great Khural.

[5] Doksom, as cited, p. 82.

[6] *Ibid.*

[7] A possible exception is the series of *duguilang* rebellions, beginning in 1905 in Darkhan Beile Banner of Jasaktu Khan Aimak, organized by a petty official named Ayusha or Ayushi, later honored as a forerunner of the Mongol Revolution. Though he does not appear to have advocated the deposition of princes (deposition, that is, without replacement by "better men," also of noble line), it has

bad rule of a prince, but without demands that all princes be de-
posed and some other form of rule created. The outlook not only of
nobles and high lamas but of the common people and the leaders
who were beginning to emerge among them was still confined within
the framework of a feudal society, and the feudal society was still
so much the only known form of society that even "independence"
could only be thought of in feudal terms.

In Tibet as well as in Outer Mongolia the feudal structure was a
pyramid. The Manchu emperor in Peking did not concern himself
with the lower strata of the pyramid. He was the patron of an
authority that was vested in the apex of the pyramid, and it was because they were fortified by the sanction of this patronage, which
included the assurance that they would be interefered with as little as
possible locally, that the top feudal personages of Tibet and Mongolia moved with assurance in the ordering of their domestic affairs [8].

It is the habit of thinking in dual terms of authority over those
below and the backing of a patron which explains why it was in the
outlying territories of Tibet and Mongolia, where the most autonomy
had survived, that the Dalai Lama for Tibet and the Jebtsundamba
Hutukhtu or Living Buddha of Urga for Outer Mongolia, backed by
the great princes, reacted instinctively or automatically to the fall of
the Manchus not by striking out boldly for a full independence but by
searching for a new patron. The Dalai Lama turned to England, or
rather to the British government in India, and the Mongols to the Tsar
because the need of a patron was a habit of their political thinking [9].

---

been argued that the reforms and limitations in feudal privileges, levies, and
corvée services that he demanded constituted a true political "platform," including
a degree of self-government for the common people of the Banner which "in fact
decreed the end of feudal service." It is also claimed that for a while his
duguilang maintained a dual system of power in the Banner, that of the *duguilang*
and that of the prince. See Kallinikov, as cited (second instalment) pp. 47–50.

[8] In Inner Mongolia, by allowing Mongol affairs to be increasingly interfered
with by the adjacent Chinese provinces, the Manchu emperors had in effect
abdicated from this position of patronage.

[9] Discussions with my friend and former student Dr. Parshotam Lal Mehra first
led me to believe that in order to depict a feudal structure clearly, there must
be an emphasis on the patron at the top of the structure to balance the usual
emphasis on authority over the lower ranks of the structure. Dr. Mehra has included some remarks on the politics of the Dalai Lamas, drawn from these discussions, in his Johns Hopkins doctoral thesis (unpublished) *The Younghusband
expedition: an interpretation*, 1954. The importance of Mongol patronage in
creating the institution of the Dalai Lama in its early form, and of Manchu
patronage in revising it in its later form, can be documented from L. Petech,
China and Tibet in the early 18th century, Leiden, 1950.

SATELLITE DEPENDENCY CONTRASTED WITH FEUDAL DEPENDENCY

This analysis leads up to the new suggestion that I should now like to make: that the habit of thinking I have just described permeated the whole society of Mongolia, and not just the hereditary class of nobles and the self-perpetuating class of high lamas. It also affected the new leaders who were beginning to emerge among the common people. They were at a loss how to move from mere rebellion to real revolution involving great economic changes and a sweeping redistribution of power socially until they, too, were able to move with the assurance — and moral assurance was as important as assurance in the form of arms and other aid — of being backed by a patron of their own. This patron was the new revolutionary order in Russia [1].

Naturally, one would search the revolutionary literature in vain for a frankly stated analysis of this kind. For the Russians, it would not be politic to make such claims in such plain words. For the Mongols, it would be injurious to national pride. I am convinced that it is the right analysis, however, for the following reasons:

1. It goes a long way toward explaining why the historical record shows practically nothing in the way of intermediate, evolutionary stages in Outer Mongolia between rebellion and true revolution. They jumped suddenly from rebellion to revolution when the Russian Revolution provided them not only with inspiration, and not only with a

---

[1] Because the terms "patron" and "client" are complementary, I hesitate to use the expressions "patron" and "patronage" without making it clear that I believe there is an essential difference between a satellite government and a client government. Joseph R. Levenson, in an extremely perceptive article, "Western powers and Chinese revolutions: the pattern of intervention," *Pacific Affairs*, 26, 3, New York, September 1953, describes the "client" relationships of governments in China to foreign powers that partly coerced them and partly supported them against their own anti-foreign nationalists. It seems to me that the essential difference between the two forms is that in the patron-client relationship juridical equality is lacking (because of treaties granting extra-territorial privileges to the patron or patrons), and both patron and client accept the subordination of the client as permanent or at least indefinite; while in the relationship between a satellite and the state in whose orbit it revolves there is at least in theory not only juridical equality but harmony of aims in creating an eventually homogeneous economic system and social and political structure.

model for action and a standard for creating new institutions, but with a political patron.

2.   While it cannot be supported by direct statements in the revolutionary literature, it is indirectly supported by the fact that Russian writers about the Mongol Revolution are so often smug, complacent, and — to use the appropriate word — patronizing.

3.   It is also supported by a use of words in the Mongol literature that occasionally sounds mechanical or sycophantic but more often glows with genuine warmth. Unwavering personal loyalty is one of the good and admirable characteristics of the feudal cast of mind; the Mongol heritage is feudal; and the words of a Choibalsang, for instance, have always the ring of a frank loyalty to his Russian backers, not the tinny sound of sycophancy. Choibalsang was no sycophant [2].

4.   It helps to explain the fact that the satellite relationship of Outer Mongolia to Russia has been less troubled by conflicting nationalisms than that of any other Russian satellite. This point needs further elaboration.

In the nationalism of a Western democracy, as I have suggested above, it is an essential concept that the loyalty of an individual to the

---

[2] The following example of Choibalsang's attitude and manner of expression is taken from the closing passage of his *History of the Mongol revolution*, as cited, p. 119 of Mongol text:

"The Mongol people, when they raised the banner of the struggle for freedom and independence, the banner of the people's revolution, triumphed through the brotherly aid of Soviet Russia.

"In 1921 the Russian proletariat and fighting men of the Red Army fought and struggled beside the Mongol People's Revolutionary Army for the cause of their self-determination of national independence.

"In 1939 the fighting men of the Mongol People's Revolutionary Army stood shoulder to shoulder with the fighting men of the Red Army at the Khalkha River to defend successfully the sacred frontiers of our land from the attack of the Japanese aggressor. [This was when the Japanese, with consequences disastrous to them, undertook an exploratory campaign to find out if there were soft spots on the Outer Mongolian frontier, or any hesitation on the part of the Russians to back up the Mongols.

"All through the period of 20 years the Mongol people have been creating conditions of freedom, independence and happiness with the brotherly aid of the great Soviet Union...."

In this passage and indeed throughout the book one could easily assume that Mongols and Russians were something like equal in strength, and thus, though Russian help is generously acknowledged, the Russians are by inference somewhat played down and the Mongols played up, because in fact the Mongols could never have overcome the Chinese invasion of 1919—21, or Baron Ungern-Sternberg's incursion, or attempted Japanese aggression in the 1930's, without Russian aid the scale of which is never revealed in details of numbers of men or tonnage of arms and supplies.

nation must override loyalty to class interests. Reduced to a hypothetical formula for Mongolian nationalism, this could be worded as
follows:

> Positive aspect: All Mongols have in common a fund of interests
> that they do not share with any other people, e.g. the Chinese.

> Negative aspect: No Mongol individual, social group, or geo-
> graphical subdivision can be loyally nationalistic if he (it) has ties
> with another nation, or with an individual, social group, or geo-
> graphical subdivision of another nation stronger than his (its) ties
> with the Mongol nation as a whole.

This hypothetical formula appears to fit very well the Inner Mongolian movement led by Prince Te, but it certainly does not fit Outer
Mongolian nationalism from the moment that the revolutionary
leaders Sukebatur and Choibalsang came under the influence of Russian revolutionaries. From the Communist point of view the relationship between nationalism and class conflict is delicate and of key importance. Russian and other Communist discussion of the problem is
complicated and full of specialized jargon — possibly because discussion in more simple terms could easily result in the Soviet concept of
nationalism being represented, to the peoples affected, as nothing but
a device for subjecting peoples less numerous and strong than the
Russians to a Russian hegemony. I do not propose to go into the
literature of the subject, partly because it would take more space than
is here available and partly because I believe that the problem itself
can be analyzed in much simpler terms from a point of view that is
entirely independent of Marxist terms.

For Outer Mongolian nationalism, a hypothetical formula could be
written down as follows:

> Question: Do not all of us Mongols have in common a fund of
> interests that we do not share with any other people, even the Rus-
> sians who have helped us?

> Answer: No, because we know from experience and the open
> record that among us Mongols the people who know how to con-
> duct an administration, how to apportion taxes, how to organize and
> command troops, or even such a simple thing as how to read and
> write are in the overwhelming majority either members of the
> privileged classes or people who are associated with and dependent
> on them. They are hereditary nobles, the clerks in Banner offices of
> the nobles and in the national government, Living Buddhas and
> other heads of great monasteries, and lamas trained in handling the
> corporate affairs of great monasteries, many of whom, because of
> this training, hold key government positions. Most of them, like us

more revolutionary Mongols, want national independence; but they want it in a form that will preserve as much as possible of their privileges and their ascendancy. We know that individuals among them have, even in the recent past, hoping to preserve their special interests, been willing to deal with Chinese warlords whom we fear, or with the Japanese who are potentially an even greater danger. Our only defense against the kind of outside protectors they will try to call in is to find outside protectors of our own. There is only one answer: the revolutionary Russians. We must rely on them while we gain time to train up a new generation of Mongols to run things in a new way. These new men we must, for our own safety, find to the maximum possible extent in families that have no ties with the old privileged classes, and that will increase the antagonism between us and the right-wing nationalists. In order to get the Russian help — which is the only thing that will pull us through — the Russians, too, must feel they are getting something out of it. That is going to mean not only that they will take the lead and we shall have to go along as subordinates in international policy, in which they are much more experienced than we are. It is also going to mean that we have to accept their schedule of priorities when it comes to planning their economic development, our economic development, and the relationship between the two.

I believe that this way of putting it throws light not only on the Mongol satellite relationship but on relations between Russia and other satellites, and provides the beginning of a method for analyzing the range of differences among satellites, instead of discussing them, as is usually done, as if they had been uniformly subjugated under a new colonialism as posessions of a new Soviet imperialism. Why, to touch on only one comparison, should there never have been a really dangerous revolt in Outer Mongolia, even when Japan in the 1930's provided a hope of intervention, while Yugoslavia revolted after only a few years and found the internal cohesion to do so successfully?

The answer, or part of the answer, may lie in the fact that the Mongols are an unusually homogenous people, with only small national minorities; the principal question was the very strong survival of the vested interests of the aristocracy and the monasteries. Over this question, both right wing and left wing were prepared to call in foreign intervention, and to pay a price for it. In Yugoslavia the old vested interests had been shattered in the devastating and prolonged partisan fighting against a ruthless German occupation, complicated by bitter civil war, and without effective foreign aid until a late stage. When it was all over, there were several alternatives for Yugoslavia; but successful restoration of the old order was not one of them. On

ANATOMY OF SATELLITISM

Turning now to a comparison of the satellite relationship with other relationships of alliance and subordination, the first point to be noted is that while all sovereign countries are juridically equal, it is rare to find two countries that are exactly equal in power. There are only two very great powers, the United States and the Soviet Union, which in making agreements with other states need to consent to almost no abatement of their own sovereignty. Great, but not very great, powers must make concessions; medium powers must make more concessions; small powers must make such wide concessions that it is sometimes difficult to decide whether the resultant shrinkage in practice of a sovereign independence that is juridically equal and unimpaired should lead us to classify the small power in question as a protected ally or a true satellite.

The unmistakable satellite may be defined as the country whose domestic policies, as well as its international relations, simply cannot be discussed with candor and realism without reference to the domestic policies, social and economic character, or "way of life" of the protecting or controlling country in whose orbit it moves. There are also, however, countries that have much less effective sovereignty than the satellite, such as the protectorate and finally the colony, whose sovereignty is institutionally vested in the possessing country. An essential difference between these classes of countries with abated sovereignty or no sovereignty at all is that the satellite is under strong pressure, sometimes amounting to coercion, to remodel its internal life, social structure, political institutions, and economic methods on those of the country in whose orbit it moves, while normally the protectorate and the colony are prevented, by the policies of the protecting or owning country, from doing these very things.

It seems clear that a satellite is not a colony and stands somewhere between the protectorate and the "subordinate ally" — the ally which, in negotiating its alliance with a much stronger country, has had to waive, or at least to cease to exercise, some degree of effective sovereignty, though retaining juridical equality. In listing the satellites of Russia, Finland should be excepted and described as a sphere of influence. Mongolia and North Korea in Asia and Poland, Czechoslovakia, Hungary, Rumania, and Bulgaria in Europe differ unmistakably from Finland in one most important respect: in each of these countries the satellite relationship with Russia is maintained with the energetic and willing cooperation of a political party within the satellite state. China, because it commands resources of power of an altogether different order of magnitude, is undoubtedly to be classed as an ally, not a satellite.

Carrying the descriptive analysis a step further, the following may be listed as the specific characteristics of a satellite:

1. The régime in the satellite country came to power with the aid of the régime in the country in whose orbit it moves.

2. The régime in the satellite country does not merely accept, but actively wants the satellite relationship.

3. It could not survive without the support and protection of the dominating power.

4. The individuals, social classes, or groups within classes who are the core of the régime identify their interests with those of the dominating country (and those of the régime in the dominating country) more unequivocally and more consciously than does the population at large.

5. Outside of the régime there exists in the satellite country either an actual or a potential, latent opposition which is as hostile to the protector of the régime as it is to the régime itself.

6. If the opposition were to overthrow the régime, the result would probably not be full independence but gravitation into the orbit of some country other than, and probably hostile to, the country protecting the actual régime.

7. The régime in the satellite state therefore must, and wants to, model itself on the régime in the protecting country; its aim is to develop the satellite state under policies that will eventually make it homogeneous in social composition, economic characteristics, and political institutions with the state in whose orbit it moves. It regards the fulfillment of such policies as a desirable process of catching up.

8. Because of all the foregoing characteristics, any variations within the dominant state are promptly reflected within the satellite state.

THE RUSSIAN MODE OF EXPANSION

With these characteristics in mind it becomes easier to analyze the Russian mode of expansion and to find some of the reasons why Russia in some cases insists on annexation and integration into the Soviet Union, in other cases is satisfied with the satellite form of control, and in still other cases, as in Finland, with even less than satellite subordination. Russian expansionism is different from that of Germany, Japan, and Italy in the 1930's. The governments of these three countries described themselves as "have-not" and in need of "Lebensraum." Their doctrines are easily paraphrased: "We have problems of population, production, distribution, employment, and profits. We have no intention of solving these problems within our own frontiers. To do so would mean lower profits and a lower standard of living for those who are the strongest supporters of our régimes. We therefore claim the right to force other peoples and countries to make good our deficits." By adopting policies of aggression they were able, as long as they were successful, to distribute enough benefits among enough of their own people to make themselves popular enough so that they never had to face a united domestic opposition.

Russian policy is based on theories and practices of self-sufficiency. Eventual expansion of the Soviet system is regarded as desirable — indeed, as the inevitable outcome of history — but Russian policies of expansion are regarded as optional. Delayed expansion does not threaten the kind of internal collapse that Germany, Italy, and Japan feared. The Russians, though they have overreached themselves on occasion, usually delay expansion while waiting for situations to ripen. While waiting, their primary concern is to buffer their frontiers against what they regard as the danger of counter-attack and "imperialist war." Consequently in any territory bordering on the Soviet Union the first priority is to prevent the success of local régimes, or the penetration of foreign influences, hostile to the Soviet Union. This kind of frontier and foreign policy can be implemented, according to varying conditions, by the use of satellites, by the projection of spheres of influence, or by neutralization.

There appears to me to be inherent in the Russian mode of expansion something for which I propose, tentatively, the name of "doctrine of the irreversible minimum." I suggest this only tentatively because I have nowhere found it defined in the expert literature on Russia or in the admittedly limited amount of Russian literature on this kind of problem that I have read. It seems to me that we can detect something that can be called by this name (even if the Russians themselves have never formulated a term for it) in a number of situations where the analyst's problem is to try to determine the degree of partial success, or of disappointment, when a phase of Russian policy did not result in expansion by annexation. My suggestion is that in a number of cases, large enough to be significant, there have been changes in the balance of power which, on a Russian evaluation of aims and achievements, would obviously fall short of complete success, but still represented at least some gain in Russia's favor, and a gain not likely to be reversed by foreseeable changes of fortune.

An example is the relationship between the new kind of state created by the Bolsheviks in Russia and the new kind of state (but not the same new kind of state) created by Kemal Atatürk in Turkey after the first World War. Kemal cancelled the privileges that capitalist countries had enjoyed in Turkey under the "capitulations" (the equivalent in Turkey of the "unequal treaties" in China). He recovered control over the rights of naval passage of the Dardanelles, which had been dominated by Britain and France. These changes were regarded by Russia as satisfactory minimum improvements to Soviet security in the Black Sea and the Balkans and not likely to be reversed to Russia's disadvantage. For the sake of this "irreversible minimum" Soviet policy was content to make loans without interest for the strengthening and industrial development of Turkey, regardless of Kemal's hostility to Turkish Communists.

In the light of this concept, it could be said that the present cool relations between Turkey and Russia and cordial relations between Turkey and the Western coalition mean a disappointment for any more sanguine hopes the Russians may have been nourishing but not a reversal of the minimum. The minimum is still there because it is still Turkey that controls the Dardanelles, and because American economic influence in Turkey, though it is very greatly increased, is not reinforced by the old kind of extraterritorial privilege.

An even more striking example, little appreciated in the literature of the subject, is the history of Soviet policy in China. It is I think invariably assumed that the breakdown of the Kuomintang-Chinese Communist alliance in 1927, the beginning of civil war between

Chiang Kai-shek and the Communists, and the establishment of good relations between Chiang and the capitalist powers added up to a great defeat for Russian hopes of Revolution in Asia. A disappointment it obviously was, even a defeat; but not a total defeat. The new government in China, though hostile to Russia, was hostile also to foreign privilege. It undermined the "unequal treaties." Although its power was still limited, it was much more nearly an independent government than the previous warlord governments. As I wrote several years ago:

> "Russian policy was 'defeated' in the sense of not realizing the full potentials of the situation; but it was not defeated in the sense of not realizing any of the potentials. The government which came into power was not friendly to Russia; but it was better able to defend itself against Russia's enemy, Japan, than any previous government of China. Russian appreciation of the importance of a Chinese government able and willing to defend itself, in spite of its hostility to Russia and to social revolution, is proved by the fact that between 1937 and 1941 the Kuomintang Government, which had always been hostile to Russia and more friendly to America than to any other country, received far more aid against Japan from Russia than it did from America." [1]

The same concept can be usefully applied to a number of other situations. Postwar Finland, for example, has been handled by the Soviet Union with a tolerance that is in many ways surprising. Undoubtedly this is partly accounted for by the desire not to drive Sweden into the Western coalition; but it may well be also accounted for in part by a Soviet conviction that an irreversible minimum has been attained: that Finland cannot again be dominated by an anti-Soviet power, as it was for a while by Germany, and that in view of this strategic gain there is no need for a policy of drastic Sovietization in Finland.

Certainly in the case of Mongolia the concept of an irreversible minimum seems to suggest possible explanations of things that are not self-explanatory, such as the willingness of the Russians to go slowly in pressing internal Sovietization of the country, and to refrain from annexing it. When both Chinese troops and "White" Russians who had Japanese backing had been driven out of Mongolia, a policy of Russian support for Mongol independence promised to create a situation favorable to the protection of the Siberian frontier. In order to

---

[1] Owen Lattimore, Introduction to Friters, *Outer Mongolia and its international position*, as cited, p. xvii.

Comparative Political Chronology

	CHINA	OUTER MONGOLIA	RUSSIA
1911	Revolution	Revolution	Deputation of Mongol princes received
1913	China and Russia recognize Outer Mongolian autonomy		
1915	Tripartite Kyakhta Treaty between China, Russia, Outer Mongolia		
1917	Warlord period, 1916–27		Russian Revolution
1918		Sukebatur, Choibalsang form revolutionary groups	
1919	China cancels Outer Mongolian autonomy		International intervention against revolution
1920	Contact between Sun Yat-sen, Russia	Groups amalgamate as People's Revolutionary Party	1920–22 Far Eastern Republic in Siberia
1921	Chinese Communist Party founded	Ungern-Sternberg defeated. Mongolian Republic founded. Youth League founded	
1922		Premier Bodo purged	End of foreign intervention (except on Sakhalin) New Economic Policy
1923	Borodin advisor to Kuomintang	Death of Sukebatur	Buryat-Mongol Republic founded
1924	Kuomintang-Communist cooperation	Death of Urga Living Buddha. Danzan purged. First Constitution	Russia recognizes Chinese sovereignty in Outer Mongolia. Stalin advocates "Socialism in one country" Death of Lenin
1925	Death of Sun Yat-sen. 1925–27 Nationalist Revolution	1925–28 Right-wing period	
1927	Kuomintang-Communist split		
1929		1929–32 Left-wing period	First Five-Year Plan
1931	Japan invades Manchuria		
1936		Soviet-Mongol Mutual Assistance Pact. Choibalsang ascendancy begins	Soviet purges begin
1937	Japan invades China		

| 1940 | New Constitution | |
| 1941 (Pearl Harbor) | | Russia invaded |
| 1945 Japan defeated. New Period of Russo-Mongol-Chinese relations |
| 1950 Chinese Communists victorious | | |
| 1951 | Death of Choibalsang | |

make this advantage irreversible, it was enough to assure the Mongols that Chinese and Japanese would be kept out. It was not even necessary to insist on the immediate deposition of the Urga Living Buddha as titular theocratic ruler. He remained in fact the nominal head of the state until his death several years later. (There is an interesting parallel between the way in which the Mongols did not depose the ruler who was the symbol of the old order, but did put an end to his real power by requiring that his decrees be countersigned by the new government, controlled by the revolutionaries, and the way in which Kemal, in Turkey, at almost exactly the same time, acknowledged the Sultan as titular monarch, instead of deposing him forthwith, but kept him in custody so that he could not organize a counterrevolution.)

THE PROBLEM OF PERSONALITY:
SKETCHES OF TWO CAREERS

Quick sketches of two personalities will show something of the texture and color of Mongol life under satellite conditions. For this purpose I select two careers that could not possibly be treated in a dispassionate manner by the official *Life of Sukebatur*, to which this essay is an introduction; for that document is designed to present to the best advantage the views of a political party, and by assertion or suggestion to discredit all other views. The careers of the two men I have selected serve well to bring into focus two essential aspects of the time in which they lived: the survival into the twentieth century of medieval conditions and with them a medieval psychology, both in society and in individuals; and the fact that, in spite of these survivals from half a millennium ago, the political life of a country like Mongolia is not only real politics but urgently contemporary politics. If this cannot be understood by modern Western men, it is not only Mongolia but the whole of Asia that cannot be understood.

The Jebtsundamba Hutukhtu or Living Buddha of Urga was the preeminent religious figure of Mongolia in the age of the Manchu empire. The first "incarnation" to appear in Mongolia was born in Khalkha in 1635, son of the Tushetu Khan. [1] He played an important role in the first relations of the Khalkhas with the new Manchu dynasty in China. The second, also the son of a great prince, was born in 1724. He died in 1757; the Manchus then stepped in, decreed that henceforth the sons of great princes could not be recognized as Living Buddhas, and from then on all "Incarnations" of the Jebtsundamba Hutukhtu were "discovered" in Tibet [2].

---

[1] See the admirable chapter "The Hubilgans [Reincarnations] of the Jebtsundamba Hutukhtu," pp. 480–582 of vol. 1 of A. M. Pozdneev, *Mongoliya i mongoly* (Mongolia and the Mongols), St. Petersburg, 2 vols., 1896–88. Unfortunately only vol. 1 has been accessible to me.

[2] Pozdneev was one of the great Mongolists. His strength was his knowledge of Mongol written sources and the spoken language. As a traveller he was a sympathetic but unsentimental, accurate, and extremely realistic observer. He was unable, however, to use Chinese sources to elucidate Manchu policy in dealing with the Mongols. In brief, that policy was to prevent any of the great

The eighth and last of the line was born in Lhasa in 1870, the son of a kind of major domo of the Dalai Lama. From the age of about 17 he began to surround himself with dissipated youngsters and to drink, carouse, smoke, gamble, and frequent the company of women. Even at this age, he was cruel. One of his escapades was to burn the hair and beard off an old retainer with kerosene. Pozdneev, who saw him in 1892, describes his expression of childish willfulness, but also notes that nothing he could do could lessen the people's infatuated religious faith in him [3].

This ability to accept a debauched human being as a religious symbol of unimpaired sanctity was characteristic of the West, too, in the middle ages; its survival as such a strong characteristic of the social psychology of the Mongols well into the twentieth century is part of the strange and fascinating mixture of the middle ages and the twentieth century in Mongol political life for several decades.

In his later years the Jebtsundamba Hutukhtu was a besotted drunkard. For many years he was blind, probably as the result of syphilis. He made no attempt to hide his depraved sexual life. When he became the ruler of Autonomous Mongolia, his most important consort was treated with imperial honors.

The Dilowa Hutukhtu (a man as chaste and even saintly in his life as the Jebtsundamba Hutukhtu was depraved) described him as he was in 1920 in the following words:

"....he was very hard to do business with because he was such a fearful drinker. He would sometimes sit cross-legged for a week drinking steadily night and day. The officials attending him would be changed frequently but he would go on drinking, never lying down to sleep and never moving except to go out to the toilet. At times he would seem to be completely unconscious, with his head lying on his chest; he would not seem to understand anything that was said to him. Then he would raise his head and demand another

princely lines from combining secular and religious power; to control the religious relations with Tibet of the various parts of Mongolia; and (an important point in the 18th century) to prevent the Western Mongols from having independent access to and influence in Lhasa. For information from the Tibetan side see L. Petech, *China and Tibet in the early 18th century*, as cited. For some remarks on Manchu religious policy, see Owen Lattimore, Introduction to Louis M. J. Schram, C.I.C.M. *The Monguors of the Kansu-Tibetan Frontier, Transactions of the American Philosophical Society*, n.s., Vol. 44, pt. 1, Philadelphia, April, 1954, p. 10. New and valuable light on religious institutions and religious policy is to be expected from Father Schram's second volume on the Monguors, not yet published.

[3] Pozdneev, as cited, Vol. 1, pp. 546—550.

drink, and the new drink would seem to sober him up so that he could conduct business. Even after a bout like this he would not sleep except in naps of two or three hours at a time. Yet he was a very able politician and kept control of things within the limits of his rapidly vanishing power." [4]

This description does not mean that the Jebtsundamba Hutukhtu would be repudiated on religious grounds by even a saintly lama. Pozdneev, in the pages from which I have quoted, says that the Mongols treated the strangest eccentricities of the Jebtsundamba Hutukhtu as enigmas, to be explained if possible by looking into the scriptures as if they were omens, and that a way could always be found to turn them to his credit. The Dilowa Hutukhtu has spent nearly a quarter of a century in exile and seen much of the world beyond the old Outer Mongolia in which he was born — Inner Mongolia, China, Japan, India, Tibet, and the United States. It could be said of him, adapting Tennyson's *Ulysses:*

> *Much has he seen and known, cities of men*
> *And manners, climates, councils, governments —*
> *Himself not least, but honored of them all.*

Yet when he sits down to the writing of his memoirs the pull of time takes him back to a Mongolia in which the middle ages were still alive, and he writes, again of the Jebtsundamba Hutukhtu:

"The reason why this Eighth Bogda had become notably more powerful and strong than previous Incarnations was, in addition to the fact that the Mongols universally, generation by generation, had believed in, honored, had faith in and reverenced each [incarnation of the] Bogda as a true divinity, this Eighth Gegen ever since childhood had been especially sharp and intelligent. Throughout Khalkha, whenever in any district there was any such fear or suffering as fire or flood, sickness or disaster, he knew it in advance and let it be known to give warning. His ordinary regulation of religious matters was always known to the public, and in consequence of this being repeatedly demonstrated in detail, he became famous for it and won the confidence of all.

"At the age of 18, as the result of a serious illness, he lay dead for three days and nights, and when he came to life again there was no mark of the sickness apparent on him, and for such marvels as this the Mongols had complete faith in him and followed him." [5]

---

[4] The Dilowa Hutukhtu, *Autobiography* (unpublished).
[5] The Dilowa Hutukhtu, *Political memoirs* (unpublished).

This was the man who, like the Dalai Lama in Tibet, became automatically by virtue of his position a more and more important man in the last decade of the Manchu empire, even before that decline accelerated to the Revolution of 1911. In both countries, the Manchu policy had been to exalt the leading religious figure as a device for preventing the emergence of secular politics. In Mongolia, as the Manchu supervisory system became more and more inadequate and incompetent, there was no way for secular politics to begin except by competition between the major princely houses, and this would have meant regional dissension as well as rivalry between nobles. The only way to avoid this kind of weakening of the nation was to encourage the great religious symbolic figure to act, if he was capable of action at all. Manchu policy had overreached itself in one respect: the Jebtsundamba Hutukhtu, being of Tibetan origin, was at least not related to the great princely houses, and all nobles could work with him.

The Dilowa Hutukhtu's unpublished *Political memoirs* reveal that as early as 1909 — two years before revolution broke out in China — the Jebtsundamba Hutukhtu issued a "decree" in the following terms (the Dilowa Hutukhtu is, of course, quoting not directly but from memory):

"Now is the time to make firm our Mongol faith and church, to protect our territory and homeland, and to devise a policy for dwelling in longlasting peace and happiness. Merely to sit still and let slip this opportunity would, apart from losing the chance to dwell in power and happiness, mean to look upon all kinds of suffering and to become unable to rule over our own land and territory. Since I understand this whole matter, if I were not to let all of you know my mind, then alas the belief and reverence of all the Mongols for my Eight Incarnations would have been of no use. Therefore I cannot bear merely to sit quiet and not to speak of what I know, and so have spoken my mind to all of you. Let all of you lamas, princes and officials consider well your own devices and promptly let me hear in detail what you have thought and considered. For you simply to remain inactive, honoring and respecting your own generations [i.e. giving priority to your individual and family interests] and looking after your own affairs and, alas, impeding the important affairs of the Mongol nation will not do."

In the summer of the next year, 1910, the great princes of the four Aimaks of Khalkha (this excludes the Altai region, which though a part of Outer Mongolia is inhabited chiefly by Western Mongols who are not Khalkhas) asked for an explanation of the previous year's "de-cree." The Jebtsundamba Hutukhtu replied:

"The secrets of Heaven may not be revealed in advance. But if without fail you duly obey whatever I have said, and all confirm what I do, I can make a policy."

The account goes on to say that the princes:

".... presented a document of confirmation stamped with seals of all of them.... [saying] it was necessary to establish an independent Mongol state, and accordingly the five territories, namely the four Aimaks and the Shabi administration were each to appoint four delegates to discuss and determine the affairs of Mongolia. When the names of the princes were selected and reported they were appointed...." [6]

The Amban, the imperial representative at Urga [now Ulan Batur] got wind of this and the Mongols quieted down for the time being, but it was these preliminary debates that led to the final step, the decision in the summer of 1911 to declare the Jebtsundamba Hutukh-tu the spiritual and temporal sovereign of Mongolia, and to send a deputation to Russia to ask for support. One thing that is quite clear about these events is that they not only took place before the out-break of revolution in China in October, 1911, but that there was never the slightest collusion, common action, or even consultation be-tween the Mongols and those who were planning the Chinese Revolu-tion. Moreover the Chinese were planning the overthrow of the em-pire, which meant a new political structure in China; the Mongols were planning separation from China, to be accompanied not by overthrow of the existing system of authority in Mongolia, but the "stepping up" of what had been the domestic system of authority under the Manchus to be a new government separate from China.

From this time on the Jebtsundamba Hutukhtu acted as partly the leader and partly the moderator of a coalition governing a satellite state. There were those who, from time to time, thought that com-plete independence was possible; but it is clear that the weight of the coalition was against them and that the Jebtsundamba Hutukhtu realized that Mongolia could not maintain even a partial and strongly conditioned independence unless the governing régime could obtain the support of a foreign government — which is as much as to say

---

[6] *Ibid.* The Shabi administration was in charge of the lands, herds, and herds-men (*shabi* or "disciples") providing revenues that went directly to the support of the Jebtsundamba Hutukhtu and his religious and household establishment.

that he grasped the essential quality of a satellite state and satellite politics.

At first he was in a strong position because his coalition overwhelmingly preferred Russian support, even at the price of the Russian restraints that made them accept "autonomy" instead of full independence. Later, when the Russian Revolution broke out, he had to mediate between those who wanted to negotiate a fresh attachment, either to China or to Japan — with even, as the documents show, some idea of asking for American protection [7]. The idea of accepting a continuation of the Russian association, with Russia under a new kind of government, was not at first — as it is easy to assume today, looking back — an alternative on a totally different level. Of republics the Mongols had some idea. China was a republic. Of the nature of a republic controlled by Communists they could not be expected to know as much as people in countries where "modern" systems of government had been modern for generations. It was the fact that the new Russian alternative was on a footing something like that of the other alternatives that made it possible for Sukebatur to obtain a document officially sealed by the Jebtsundamba authorizing him to negotiate with the "new" Russians on the Siberian horizon.

It was also as the pivotal figure in a coalition that the Jebtsundamba Hutukhtu had to accept the harsh reimposition of Chinese control in 1919, the year of calamity with its Chinese and "White" Russian incursions; and it is interesting to see how this incident is described in the *Life of Sukebatur* from a revolutionary and nationalistic point of view as a national humiliation, not just as a blow to the prestige of an individual whom the revolutionaries disliked and distrusted. It was as the symbol of a coalition, again, that the Jebtsundamba Hutukhtu dealt even with Baron Ungern-Sternberg. All of this goes to make it understandable that Sukebatur's left-wing revolutionary nationalists, when they came to power with Soviet Russian support, were content to do so by entering the national coalition and careful not to split it dangerously by ejecting the Jebtsundamba Hutukhtu. Instead, they merely shifted the center of gravity to the left for the first few years, maintaining the Jebtsundamba Hutukhtu in a position of honor but without real power until his natural death in 1924.

---

[7] The Dilowa Hutukhtu, in his unpublished *Autobiography* and *Political memoirs*, relates his experiences as a member of a mission sent to Peking by the Jebtsundamba Hutukhtu where they tried (unavailingly) to interest the American Legation in the idea of intervention in Outer Mongolia.

At this point I interpolate excerpts from two documents that show, more vividly than any political analysis can, the mentality of the old Mongol society, represented by the Jebtsundamba Hutukhtu, and that of the revolutionary generation, and the watershed between them. The first document is referred to only briefly in the *Life of Sukebatur,* but cited at length by Choibalsang in his *Concise history* of the Mongol revolution (for bibliographical reference, see below, p. 63, n. 2). It is the "decree" issued by the Jebtsundamba Hutukhtu, after both the Chinese and the "White" Russians had been driven out, in an attempt to mollify the Red Russians on the one hand and at the same time to win the initiative away from Sukebatur and his revolutionary Mongols:

"A decree of the Sun Effulgent, Myriad Yeared, Holy Emperor Khagan. Perfect in faith, having maintained Our Incarnation for Eight generations by the pronouncement of Fate from of old, this is to enlighten all Our disciples, clerical and lay .... [under our rule] .... determining treaty agreements, honoring religious customs, compassionately loving Our people, every household had abundance and every man sufficiency, the rain was opportune and the wind favorable 8 .... [after Chinese intervention] .... Our children 9 and disciples, the great and the small, elders and infants, men and women were prey to an insupportable resentment. In their prayers they appealed to the spirits in heaven above and called the dragons of the earth to witness .... the Soviet government drew near to protect us and these reactionary [Chinese], having again and again entertained secret hostile intentions, left .... It was only out of fear of the might and power of the army of this Red party, from which they could find no place to escape, that they returned to their own country. Was this not an infallible fulfillment of true faith in the infinite power of the Savior Buddha?
"Now, having already recovered our own government, we must restore our sovereignty as it was before, bring our internal government into conformity with the times and reform it, strive for good foreign relations, and give priority to the strengthening and defense of our frontiers. Opposition to one teaching 10 or following another teaching is in no way involved. In this connection, according to what We hear, those who went north to find help [meaning Suke-

---

8 A translation of the Chinese *yü shün feng tiao* but (as Mongols frequently do) reversing the usual Chinese order, which is *feng tiao yü shün.*

9 The Mongol word means literally "seed," used here as a pair with "disciples," thus corresponding to the expression "my son" as used by a priest.

10 Were it not inappropriate for the Mongol language in a decree drafted by an old-style chancellery clerk in the year 1921, the obvious translation here would be "ideology."

batur and his group] can hardly be expected to understand fully as yet such matters as that the central government has stabilized itself, and the General and Army of the White party [Ungern-Sternberg] have gone back to their own country. Moreover the fact that, in the first place, people began to fight jointly with the People's Party, because their suffering at the hands of the [Chinese] was so serious, was undoubtedly merely because they were mistaken in not knowing accurately that their national government had thus firmly stabilized itself. In this moreover they were guilty of an error of faith. If they were to ally themselves with Our intent and purpose to promote religion and the well-being of all creatures, all Our disciples, near and far, would unanimously be reassured and understand the efforts We have made on behalf of Church and State and all the people, and now and for the future would be able to make the distinction between the inaccurate and the accurate, the obscure and the obvious. That which should be first and foremost in the acquisition of virtue is to take the opportunity to join in Our supreme desire to regard all creatures with compassion. Pacifying their thoughts, laying down their arms and returning to their allegiance [11] they should strive to aid in supporting their State and Church. If there should be those who do not accept this teaching of Ours, they may declare and submit their own proposals and ideas.

Given under Our seal and proclaimed. Obey!"

The second document, also cited at length by Choibalsang, is a proclamation to the people by Sukebatur and his revolutionaries. It is of the same year as the one just cited, but a little earlier, before the defeat of the Chinese and "White" Russians:

"....We must purge our territory by driving out troops and bands of looting and plundering bandits, the treacherous and wicked robbers of all kinds who have been going about telling all sorts of lies and with arms in their hands.

"We must establish peace and security in our Mongol homeland.

"To summon representatives of the whole of our Mongol people, to open a great national conference at which all may discuss and express their approval, to organize a decent government of our nation, to ensure respect for the power and rule of the people, to study and determine a code of laws, we have in accordance with the trend of the times chosen and appointed seven men ....who have organized a temporary ruling body to decide all matters relating to the government of the Mongol people....

---

[11]) Although the text reads simply "coming back," it undoubtedly echoes the traditional Chinese formula *kuei-fu*, meaning the "submission" that takes place when a subject returns to his allegiance.

"All matters of our Mongol People's Government will be determined by the temporary authorities who with all the power at their command will be guided solely by the sovereign interests of the freedom of the people. To believe in and have faith in this is to trust the decree of Heaven and to have faith in the grandeur and magnificent destiny of our Mongol people. Therefore be you great or small, far or near, in equal honesty and sincerity when you look on the present unlimited sorrow and suffering of your own Mongol nation, all who are wise and intelligent, all who are defenders of a firm loyalty, and all who are fearless and patriotic should rally to the making of a peaceful future that will truly fit the conditions of our times.

"Reflecting on the ancient heroic prestige, fame, and glory of the Mongol nation,

"Each and all, every man according to the degree of his ability should join and take part in the great task of reviving our Mongol nation and causing it to flourish...."

On one side of the watershed between these two documents we have traditional authority trying to recover the initiative and stop action, calm the people down, and cause them to reflect that probably those who ruled them in the past can best rule them in the future. On the other side is an appeal to action and an invitation to new talent — to all who consider themselves patriotic and intelligent to come forward and take a part in managing the affairs of their country. The difference in language is of great interest from the point of view of political psychology. The Living Buddha's decree is in an elevated style, encrusted with literary phrases showing Chinese influence and unintelligible to most Mongols, together with religious exhortations that express the passive, submissive traditions of Buddhism. The revolutionary manifesto is in a much more direct language and besides its fervent nationalist appeal shows considerable skill in adapting plain, familiar words to the introduction of new ideas — and always ideas that suggest action.

It is not that the Jebtsundamba Hutukhtu's decree is a stupid document. Far from it. Within the traditional manner it shows a considerable skill in diplomacy — but a skill for which events were already moving too fast. Nor can the revolutionary manifesto be called particularly subtle: its one inspiration is to ride the tide of action and to range action behind the revolutionary leadership.

My second example is Dambijantsan, the Ja Lama [12], whose

---

[12] This name, which like so many Mongol names is of Tibetan origin, appears

death is mentioned in the *Life of Sukebatur*. The first record of him that I have found is in Pozdneev's account of his journey of 1892 [13]. Pozdneev, accepted as a man of consequence by the Mongols among whom he travelled, was asked if armed forces were gathering in Siberia to invade Mongolia and liberate it from Chinese (*i.e.* Manchu imperial) rule. They had been told to expect this by a certain Dambijantsan who had told them that he was the son of Temursana, son of Amursana, who after leading the last stand of the Western Mongols had died in 1755. They said that he appeared to be a man of between 30 and 40, that he was going to liberate the Mongols, and that he would soon be back from the north with his army.

Pozdneev was able to identify him as a man of the Little Derbet *ulus* of the Astrakhan region, *i.e.* a Russian Kalmuk from the lower Volga. The Russian Consul in Urga, using the extraterritorial authority then enjoyed under treaty, had arrested him and deported him to Russia. In a short but striking passage Pozdneev shows the temper of the time in the last decade of the nineteenth century in Outer Mongolia. Credulity and ignorance were such that any man of forceful personality could easily win acceptance on his own terms. When Pozdneev asked how Amursana, who died in 1755, could in 1892 have a living grandson of 30 or so, he was answered with the "irrefutable argument" that this man wore a gold ornament of a particular kind on the peak of his conical hat. (Such matters were regulated by protocol under the imperial-feudal system. The penalties for wearing a badge of high rank illegally were, at least nominally, severe. Therefore a man could not possibly be audacious enough to go under false pretensions. Therefore he must be what he said he was.)

Inquiring further, Pozdneev was astonished to find how deep was

---

in various spellings. Many Mongols — particularly, I believe, those who speak the Western dialects — pronounce it Dambijaltsan. It is common practice to abbreviate the names of important persons, and thus he also appears as Ja Lama and Jal Lama, from the abbreviation of the second half of his name. In 1926, hearing stories about him from Chinese caravan men, I wrote the name down as *Chialama* and translated it "False Lama" because the caravan men took *ja* to be a Mongol pronunciation of Chinese *chia* (false). (Owen Lattimore, *The desert road to Turkestan*, London, 1928, pp. 212—219, and Boston, 1929, pp. 235—242, with photographs of the fortress where the Ja Lama was finally killed). There is a considerable literature on the Ja Lama from which I shall cite here only a few sources, as my object is merely to show what kind of figure he cut. I hope later to publish a study of his life.

[13] Pozdneev, as cited, vol. 1, pp. 45—46. Pozdneev's spelling is Donbichzhantsan, *i.e.* Donbijantsan. The name is not listed in his index.

the prevailing resentment against "Chinese" rule and still more astonished at the bitterness of the people against their princes. He noted
that the feeling was against the princes, not the Church; one of the
complaints was that they "insulted" the Church [14].

This passage is extremely important. In the last decades of the old
order the kind of foreigners travelling in Mongolia who were likely
later to write about their experiences were normally important enough
to have special arrangements made for them. They were entertained
by the more wealthy and important people, often by princes. Accordingly, although they might mention poverty now and then, they
had a strong impression of a serene and confident upper class. Only
rarely and accidentally do we discover, as in this passage, that the
slow breakdown of the old order had in fact prepared, long in advance, a seedbed of rebellion and even revolution that when the time

----

[14] Other sources confirm that the rule of the Church was often less harsh than
that of princes, with the result that men tried to get out of their Banners to be
accepted as *shabi* of a monastery. See Kallinikov, as cited (first instalment), p. 141.
Kallinikov's explanation is that by acquiring more dependents in this way the
Church improved its position relative to that of the princes. The most important
shabi, of course, were those of the Jebtsundamba Hutukhtu (see above, p. 52, n.
6), and on this we have the following from Choibalsang, *Concise History* of the
Mongol revolution, p. 5 (for bibliographical identification see below, p. 63,
note 2):

"At that time our Mongol nation consisted of seven parts, the four Aimaks of
Khalkha, the Shabi divison, and the two Aimaks of Durbet [the Altai-Kobdo
region in the northwest]. The people of the Shabi division were by origin men
from all the Aimaks of Khalkha who in those times were offered as presents of
honor [by their princes] to the Jebtsundamba Hutukhtu to become his "disciples," and collectively were known as the Bogda's Shabi. Apart from taking
part in the various services of the Jebtsundamba Hutukhtu they did not engage,
like the other Aimaks of Khalkha, in the joint national burden of feudal services, such as posts and relays and civilian and military services, but were
exempted and went about at their own free will.

"In the period of the autonomous government the power and advantages of
the clerical feudal interests attained an additional development. In order to
increase the profit and income of the monasteries and great lamas people from
all the Aimaks were transferred to the Shabi feudal jurisdiction.

"On these grounds there was a sharpening of conflict between Aimak and
Shabi over the conditions of internal administration in Mongolia. The resulting
destructive struggle was not confined to the people of the Aimaks and Shabi;
it also became sharp between the clerical and secular feudal groups. Consequently this internal struggle in the country ended in cancelling Mongolia's
autonomy and making it ready to become a colony of China."

On the subject of monastic administration and relations between monasteries
and Banners there is much new and basic information in the Dilowa Hutukhtu's
contribution (a description of his own monastery) to H. H. Vreeland 3rd., *Mongol
community and kinship structure*, cited above.

came would burst suddenly and unexpectedly into terrible harvest.

The next important notice of Ja Lama in Russian sources appears to be that of Maiskii [15], who puts his first arrival in Western Mongolia at 1890 rather than 1892. Maiskii's informants were local Russian traders and settlers who had known Ja Lama for years. After the Russians had sent him out of Mongolia, Ja Lama disappeared for ten years. He is next heard of, according to Maiskii, as in the employ of an expedition led to Tibet in 1900 by the famous explorer P.K. Kozlov. Unable to go to Lhasa himself, Kozlov sent Ja Lama there; but Ja Lama never rejoined him and disappeared for another ten years. It is presumably in this second ten-year gap that we should place the Dilowa Hutukhtu's picaresque account of Ja Lama as a successful "gold-brick" confidence man; he made much ado about certain heavy packages that he had with him on his journey to Lhasa, insisting that every night they must be placed in his own tent. By the time he got to Lhasa everybody knew about this mysterious pack-load. It was a custom that travellers could put their valuables in one of the religious treasuries in Lhasa and receive a sort of letter of credit, on which they drew for local expenses while travelling to various places of pilgrimage. The Ja Lama did this, acting like such an important man that nobody insisted on actually inspecting his "treasure." After interesting and profitable travels — for pilgrimages are often also trading ventures — he disappeared. When the authorities finally decided to open his "treasure," they found nothing but stones [16].

Resuming Maiskii's account, Ja Lama is next heard of in 1910 at Karashahr, in Sinkiang, among the Torgut Mongols of that province. Then in 1912 he reappeared in Mongolia at Kobdo. He now claimed to be not only the grandson but the reincarnation of the great Amursana. The Durbets and other Western Mongols were wavering. There was traditional dislike between them and the Khalkhas, and they did not know whether to adhere to an independent Outer Mongolia or to attach themselves to the Chinese province of Sinkiang, where one of the important Mongols, Prince Palta [17], had declared for loyalty to China. Ja Lama decided the day in favor of Outer Mongolia with his

[15] I. Maiskii, *Sovremennaya Mongoliya* (*Contemporary Mongolia*), Irkutsk, 1921, pp. 255—256. This is the Maiskii who later became much better known under the English spelling of his name, Ivan Maisky, as Ambassador to the Court of St. James.

[16] The Dilowa Hutukhtu, *Autobiography* (unpublished).

[17] See brief listing in Friters, *Outer Mongolia and its international position*, p. 346.

propaganda for a renascence of the Mongols — and especially the Western Mongols. He acquired great influence not only over the people but over the Durbet princes.

In May 1912 he had made such headway that he laid siege to the town of Kobdo, with its large Chinese trading community and Manchu-Chinese garrison. It fell in August. Ja Lama was now one of the important men of autonomous Mongolia. He was military governor of the Kobdo region, and the Jebtsundamba Hutukhtu conferred on him (or recognized his assumption of) both the religious title of Nom-un Hutukhtu and the secular position of a Banner prince. (This double status is not to be understood as simply a sign of the breaking up of the old order; such things occurred intermittently throughout the history of Lamaism in both Tibet and Mongolia.)

In this period he was one of the radical reformers in the new Outer Mongolia. He built a monastery to which he drew lamas from other monasteries. He enforced a strict religious discipline, saying that in these new times there should be "few lamas, but good ones" — and that the rest should be sent back to the herdsman's life. He wanted to develop agriculture and to found schools. His long-range aims, however, were still his personal aims. It was said that he wanted to conquer Sinkiang and part of Tibet, and joining these to the Western Mongols of Outer Mongolia to found a new Western Mongol state.

In February 1914, however, there was a crisis of some sort, of the reasons for which Maiskii is not quite sure. At any rate, there was a detachment of Russian Cossacks in Kobdo (sent there when the Russians had begun to take a hand in the affairs of Outer Mongolia), and they arrested Ja Lama (who was still a Russian subject), and sent him to Siberia. He was imprisoned first in Tomsk, then near Irkutsk, then sent into exile in the far north, in Yakutia. Here he met some of the revolutionary intelligentsia among the Russian exiles, and is said to have improved his education, learned some political ideas, and even to have played a part in the revolutionary events of 1917–18. Eventually he managed to get sent back to his native region of Astrakhan.

In 1918 he returned to Mongolia, where he received a tremendous popular welcome but was cold-shouldered by the authorities at Urga. Maiskii does not say so, but it may be that in these disturbed times, with the clear possibility that relations with China would again become important, the record of his savage treatment of the Chinese in Kobdo might have become an embarrassment; or it may simply have been feared that he would start a separatist movement in the Kobdo

region [18]. Not feeling certain of his position, he gathered some followers and went down to an oasis in low desert mountains called the
Ma-tsung Shan, in a sort of no-man's land between Outer Mongolia
and the Chinese provinces of Sinkiang and Ninghsia, with their Mongol fringes. Here he built a fort, in and around which he gathered
about 300 troopers and some 500 tents of people.

This is as far as Maiskii's account takes us, but we know from the
Life of Sukebatur how the new government eventually felt it necessary to send a detachment down to his stronghold, which negotiated
its way in to see him and then shot him down. (There are many sup-
plementary details in the unpublished *Autobiography* and *Political
memoirs* of the Dilowa Hutukhtu, whose monastery and administrative district lay on the edge of the western territory in which the Ja
Lama was most active, and who knew him personally.) The official
reason for killing him was that he was in dangerous contact with
Chinese border provinces from which Outer Mongolia might be
attacked. There is probably some truth in this. The account of the
Chinese caravan men who told me tales about him in 1926 was that,
on an understanding with the governor of Sinkiang, he had begun
developing a new, protected caravan route to replace those that had
been closed by Outer Mongolian independence [19], and there is support also in the fictionalized but very true-to-life account of this last
phase of the Ja Lama in a Russian adventure-book [20].

What stands out as characteristic of the political life of Mongolia
in the 1920's however is the fear that one bold adventurer with 300
troopers at his back and a proved ability to excite old tribal passions
and loyalties might be able to change the whole fate of a vast country
of some 600,000 square miles, with a population of the order of one
million. The Mongols had just lived through about fifteen years in
which again and again great events had been decided by small numbers. The importance of the critical decision and the deciding event
comes to the fore again and again in the *Life of Sukebatur*.

---

[18] Many sources testify to his extreme cruelty. Maiskii relates that after a clash
with some "Kirghiz" (*i.e.* Kazaks of the Altai) Ja Lama ordered the breast of a
Kazak leader to be cut open and the heart torn out, and then the skin flayed
from the body to be used for some "religious" (*i.e.* shamanistic) purpose. For
equally lurid details (and some striking photographs) see Hermann Consten,
Weideplätze der Mongolen, Berlin, 2 vols. 1919 and 1920, vol. 2, pp. 214 *et seq.*
Consten was in Mongolia in 1912.

[19] Lattimore, as cited.

[20] This story is one of the episodes in V. A. Obruchev, *V debryakh tsentral'noi
Azii* (In the ruins of central Asia) Moscow, 1951. See review by Owen Lattimore
in *Pacific Affairs*, 27, 2, June 1954, pp. 166—168.

SUKEBATUR AND "UNITED FRONT" POLITICS

Within this framework and against this background the *Life of Sukebatur* can be studied as a document that gives us considerable insight into the way in which "modern" political issues penetrate into countries in Asia where until recently political life was either static or archaic or limited by foreign rule.

The first point of interest is the date of publication, because values change with time in satellite politics. In the Mongol introduction, to which is attached the name of the Propaganda and Enlightenment Bureau of the Central Committee of the Party, and which is decidedly more official and formal in tone than the text of the *Life* itself, the remarkable statement is made that this *Life,* published in 1943, the twentieth anniversary year of the death of Sukebatur, is the first full biography ever published of the man who is regarded as the "father" of the Outer Mongolian People's Republic. The statement is remarkable because it shows that there has never been in Outer Mongolia a political cult of Sukebatur comparable to the cult of Sun Yat-sen in China under the Kuomintang, or that of Kemal Atatürk in Turkey.

The most probable inference is that people in Mongolia had been encouraged to think of Sukebatur as a prominent figure in revolutionary history, especially in military revolutionary history (he is typically referred to in the biography of Choibalsang as "the fearless Sukebatur") [1] but by no means as the unique creator of the modern Republic. There is support for the inference in the desultory char-

---

[1] *Nukur Choibalsang-un uiles ba amidural,* by Yu. Chidenbal (pronounced Tsedenbal, and usually so rendered in Russian and Western mention of him). The only edition accessible to me has been a copy of the Chinese translation in the Hoover Institute and Library at Stanford University, *Ch'iao-pa-shan t'ung-chih-ti shih-yeh yü sheng-huo,* by Ts'e-teng-pa-la, translated by Hsieh Tsai-shan, Shanghai, 1951, described as being from an "original" edition by the Inner Mongolian Newspaper Association, 1945. The underlying Outer Mongolian edition must also have been issued in 1945, as the book opens with accounts of two 1945 speeches by Tsedenbal — 1945 being the year of Choibalsang's fiftieth birthday. There is no statement whether this edition is an abridgement, adaptation, or full translation. Both Mongol and Chinese titles may be translated *The deeds and life of comrade Choibalsang.* (Tsedenbal is a personal name. The "Yu." is an abbreviation of his clan or family name, which may be the old tribal name usually written, after its Chinese form, "Yunghsiehpu.")

acter of the bibliography attached to the *Life* of Sukebatur. The first two references (as is to be expected in a satellite state at that date), are to Stalin. The next is to the official two-volume *History of the Mongol revolution* by Choibalsang, Sukebatur's early political collaborator, comrade-in-arms, and eventual successor [2]; but the only Choibalsang titles listed that deal specifically with Sukebatur are a lecture of 1942 and a contribution (the contents of which may not be limited to discussion of Sukebatur) to a volume celebrating the twentieth anniversary of the Mongolian People's Republic. It is probably significant that these dates are so close to the publication of the *Life of Sukebatur* in 1943. They seem to indicate a period, and a surprisingly late period, in which after something rather like neglect there was a concerted interest in Sukebatur. There follows in the bibliography a reference to what appears to be a general ideological work by Tsedenbal, author of the official biography of Choibalsang noted above, Vice-Premier under Choibalsang, and after Choibalsang's death in 1952 his successor as Premier.

Only at this point does there come a reference to what obviously must be a most important source, the *Favorite sayings of Sukebatur* by his widow, Yangjima [3], who seems to hold in Outer Mongolia a position analagous to that of Madame Sun Yat-sen in China as an honored survivor of a revolutionary generation that was great in its

---

[2] Kho. Choibalsang, *Monggol arat-un undusun-u khubiskhal-un anggha eguschu baigolokdaksan tobchi teuge (Concise history of the original organizing of the Mongol people's national revolution)*, 2 vols., Ulan Batur, 1934. This has been available to me only in a one-volume edition which may or may not be a revision or abridgement of the two-volume edition, entitled *Monggol-un khubiskhal-un teuge, (History of the Mongol revolution)*. It carries no indication of place or date of publication, but must have been printed in Inner Mongolia, as evidenced by the use of Chinese characters for the headings of the pages of *errata*. (The Kho. standing before Choibalsang's name is an abbreviation of his clan or family name, Khorluin (? Khurluin).

[3] This name means "pretty," "beautiful." It is a borrowing from the Chinese, *yang-tze* (shape, form) with some change of meaning. In Russian transcription it is written "Yanjima". The Russians do not have a terminal" "-ng" in their own language, and must adopt a convention when transliterating Chinese and Mongol. In Tsarist times -ng was transliterated by writing -n with a "hard sign" following it. Since the "hard sign" was dropped as a Soviet reform, -ng is written as -n; and if a word ends in -n, with no -ng sound, this can be shown by writing -n followed by a "soft sign," (which has not been discarded from the Soviet alphabet). The new Kyrillic alphabet in Mongol is modelled on the Russian. This explains why in both Russian and Kyrillic transcription Choibalsang, for instance, is written Choibalsan, though pronounced Choibalsang and so written in the old script.

time but is now not only past but to some extent outlived. Then comes a reference to a speech about him by Maksurjab, one of the great Mongol warriors from 1911 to his death in the 1920's [4]. The remaining references are of a general and archival nature.

A clear clue to the significance of this *Life* at the time it was published is provided by another statement in the Introduction:

> "....especially at this time when the fascist bandits confront all decent humanity with fear and terror, it is more than ever imperatively desirable to study and understand the history of our own motherland and the place in it of the life of Sukebatur...."

---

[4] There is a biography of Maksurjab by Choibalsang, under the title *Arat-un Khatan Bagatur Maksurjab-un khuriyanggui teuge (The People's Mighty Hero Maksurjab, an abridged history)*, Ulan Batur, 1942. One of his ancestors was ennobled under the Manchus for military prowess and thus he is of interest as representing one of the few noble families not claiming aristocratic descent from the age of Chingis Khan. He grew up poor, however, led the life of an ordinary working commoner, and took up agriculture. He rose rapidly to fame in 1911 as one of the nationalist leaders from the west; most of the leaders, especially the more radical ones, were from the east of the country which was more open to the political consequences of economic penetration stimulated by railways on three sides — in Siberia, Manchuria, and North China.

Maksurjab was a ruthless warrior who like Ja Lama revived the ancient shamanistic "magical" practice of tearing out the hearts of enemies killed in battle (but it does not appear that he sacrificed prisoners for this purpose, as did Ja Lama). An interesting study could be made of the revival of these barbaric practices, such as draping the skin of a slain enemy over one's saddle, cutting off his head and tying it to the tail of one's horse, and so on, in the period from about the last decade of the nineteenth century to the early 1920's. Along the borders of Inner Mongolia and in the Ordos these practices were taken up by Chinese bandits. It is probable that they were revived among the Mongols for a paradoxical reason. In purely Mongol areas, with no contacts with Chinese, there was no banditry. Most Mongols had seen no fighting for a long time until banditry began to ravage the southern and eastern Mongols and war and revolution swept into Outer Mongolia. Many travellers have commented on how peaceful and docile "the descendants of the warriors of Chingis Khan" had become. Then, when suddenly pitched into a new warlike age, old legends of battle and "war-magic" were revived, and men who had no military training and had been taught all their lives to be meek in the face of authority worked themselves up to a pitch of desperate courage by carrying out these savage rites.

I believe that Maksurjab's "title of honor" of "Mighty Hero" was awarded by the Jebtsundamba Hutukhtu for his part in the fighting at Kobdo in 1912; this became "People's Mighty Hero" under the new government. He was more a military than a political leader. After holding important commands under the Jebtsundamba Hutukhtu he served under Ungern-Sternberg; but when Sukebatur and Choibalsang's Partisan Army began to raise the country against both Ungern-Sternberg and the Chinese he joined them and took a leading part in fighting and disarming the "White" Russian detachments in his home country in the Northwest. Choibalsang's book about him contains little political ideology; it is written with the zest of one warrior writing about another.

In political tone, this is a pure "united front" statement. In January, 1943, the German tide had begun to ebb at Stalingrad. Victory over Germany would carry with it the assurance of victory over Japan, whether Russia, and Mongolia as an ally of Russia, took part in the fighting or not; and this in turn made it sure that the most important country in Asia, after the war, was going to be China. For the Mongols, therefore, the question of the character and policy of the postwar government of China was of primary importance. There is no indication anywhere, so far as I know, of what their own forecast on the future of China may have been [5]; but we are certainly entitled to assume, from the many and strong assertions of Mongol faith in Russian protection and guidance, in this book and elsewhere, that they would accept the Russian analysis of the probable future of China.

In this connection there are two significant questions of Russian policy to be assessed.

In the first place, there is evidence that the Russian leadership, like most of the leadership of Russia's democratic allies, hoped toward the end of the war and for a while after it ended that there was going to be "peaceful coexistence." Certainly there was a good deal published in Russia in these years that can be regarded as an attempt to prepare people's minds for this possibility.

In the second place, part of the Russian calculation (and part of almost everybody else's calculation) was the assumption that the Chinese Communists were strong enough to remain a permanent part of China's political life, but not strong enough to overthrow Chiang Kai-shek's government and seize power completely [6]. This assump-

---

[5] In July 1944, in Ulan Bator, I had a very brief conversation with Marshal Choibalsang on the subject of Chinese politics, in which he expressed himself in very downright terms on the inability of the Chinese to get together and fight a national war of liberation to rid their country of the Japanese, without the acute distrust that was then evident between the Kuomintang and the Chinese Communists. He was diplomatic enough to speak of "the Chinese," without laying the blame exclusively on the Kuomintang. The tenor of what he said was that the Chinese had always claimed to be more civilized and sophisticated than the Mongols; but in the midst of a war against invaders they were quarrelling among themselves, while the Mongols, whom the Chinese considered barbarous and backward, were ready to defend themselves and united to a man. Nothing that he said indicated any special or "inside" knowledge of Chinese politics.

[6] The most recent confirmation that the Russians underestimated the Chinese Communists is to be found in Vladimir Dedijer, *Tito*, New York, 1953, p. 322, where it is asserted that in 1948 Stalin admitted to Eduard Kardelj, the Yugoslav Foreign minister, that in negotiating with the Chinese Communists at the end of the war the Russians ".... told them bluntly that we considered the development

tion carried with it the further assumption that the Chinese Communists would have no more than a regional power entitling them to minority representation in a coalition government [7].

Because of these two elements in the Russian policy of the time, I interpret the "united front" tone of the words quoted above, and indeed the whole movement to reemphasize Sukebatur (and such nationalist heroes as Maksurjab) as indicating a Mongol "contingent policy" of getting into a position in which Mongolia could, if it were advisable, turn a friendly face toward a postwar government in China containing Communists but not controlled by Communists. For a policy of this kind it would be useful to emphasize the "united front" origins of Mongolia's own government.

It is, however, a formidable characteristic of all Russian and Communist conduct of policy that a short-term, "contingent" policy is never pursued so single-mindedly as to make it awkward to drop it and swiftly substitute another. All short-term policies are in fact alternative to each other and subject to a long-term, overall concept of policy based on the doctrine of "historical inevitability" which assumes that eventually the whole world will be included in a Soviet order of economic production and political administration.

---

of the uprising had no prospect, and that the Chinese comrades should seek a *modus vivendi* with Chiang Kai-shek, that they should join Chiang Kai-shek's government and dissolve their army. The Chinese comrades agreed here with the views of the Soviet comrades, but went back to China and acted quite otherwise . . . . and now, as we see, they are beating the Chiang Kai-shek army. Now, in the case of China, we admit we were wrong."

[7] My own view of this hotly debated question is that at the end of the war the Chinese Communists had such a strong regional position that they were confident that they could not be overwhelmed in a civil war and could, if they negotiated toughly enough, retain that position and their own armed forces and, on this basis, win representation in a national government. They were not, in my opinion, over-confident enough to think they could win control over all China through a civil war. It was only after negotiations failed and fighting had gone on for some time that they realized, before the Russians or anyone else did, that Chiang Kai-shek's generals, political organizers, and administrators were being so inept that they were driving people in such increasing numbers into the arms of the Communists that the Communists were going to win the civil war outright. It was the fact that the Chinese Communists were based on a strong regional position that set them apart from the strong Communist parties of such countries as Italy and France, where the Communists were scattered all over the country and did not have at the end of the war a region of their own with a government in it that was a "going concern."

SUKEBATUR AND CHOIBALSANG:
PERSONAL REPUTATION IN A SATELLITE SOCIETY

That this kind of thinking, intended to keep various contingencies in focus with each other, is characteristic also of the ideologists of recent and contemporary Mongolia is indicated by the way in which Sukebatur and Choibalsang are treated in relation to each other. An understanding of this treatment enables us to identify the political phase in which the *Life of Sukebatur* was published and is therefore important in the evaluation of the book as a political document.

Even with the small amount of corollary material available to us it is clear that Sukebatur and Choibalsang are written about, for the purpose of shaping the political thought of their countrymen, not as it were abreast but in echelon. At first Sukebatur appears in the lead, with Choibalsang parallel to him but somewhat in the rear. Sukebatur is emphasized because it is quite clear from the beginning that he is more nationalist and, though radical, less Communist than Choibalsang. As the situation changes Choibalsang is moved up, still parallel with Sukebatur but first abreast of him and then ahead of him; and at the same time there is an increasing emphasis on the difference between "bourgeois" nationalism and the kind of nationalism, infused with the spirit of Communism, that Choibalsang represents more strongly than Sukebatur did.

Thus Sukebatur, without being obliterated, drops back to a position of less importance. The next stage may be a similar advance in echelon of the reputation of Tsedenbal, the present Premier, to a position eventually ahead of that now held ideologically by Choibalsang. Such enhancement of Tsedenbal will probably await a new phase — which has not yet begun — in the transformation of the present "people's democracy" structure of the Outer Mongolian People's Republic into a fully socialist structure.

The echelon treatment of Sukebatur and Choibalsang can be illustrated by comparing the "canonical" biographies of the two men.

From the *Life of Sukebatur* we know that he was the founder of a revolutionary group that was anti-Chinese and radical to the extent that Sukebatur and some of the group believed in drastic reforms of the privileges of the clergy and hereditary nobility, but knew nothing of Marxism. This instantly suggests a comparison with Sun Yat-sen in China, who was against the privileges enjoyed in China by foreigners, against the regional warlords, and had rather vague ideas of a future socialism. At an early stage, Sukebatur came in touch with Choibalsang, who had a group of his own, in close contact with two Russian Communists [1]. After the two groups were in contact, Sukebatur also met a Russian representative of the Comintern.

Sukebatur welcomed the views of the Russians and the "activist" attitude of Choibalsang with an enthusiasm comparable to that of Sun Yat-sen when, in somewhat similar circumstances, he accepted Russian advisors and an alliance with the Chinese Communists. As for Choibalsang and his Communist, partly Communist, or Communist-influenced Mongols, they were content to act as a vanguard group under Sukebatur's leadership, without for the time being trying to take over control, like the Chinese Communists in the ways in which, without fusing with the Kuomintang, they joined the Kuomintang as individual members [2].

For additional details on the early life of Choibalsang and for the stages by which his reputation was advanced we must turn to the biography of him by Tsedenbal which has already been cited. Here we find that the emphasis on the indispensability of Russian help in establishing the independence of Mongolia and the constantly

---

[1] Their names were Kucherenko and Gembarzhevskii. The spelling of their names, not clear from the Mongol transcription, is to be found on p. 38 of N.V. Tsapkin, *Mongol'skaya narodnaya respublika* (*Mongolian people's republic*), Moscow, 1948. They were killed by Baron Ungern-Sternberg when he was occupying Urga. Choibalsang writes of them in his *Concise History*, as cited, p. 22:

> "The Russian proletarian Kucherenko, while working at the Russo-Mongol printing office, talked about and explained to the members of [Choibalsang's] group the events of the Great October Revolution, and how the Soviet Government had won full freedom for the minorities who had been oppressed within Tsarist Russia, and the Russian proletarians had taken their own place in the government and, together with the minorities, had abrogated the enslaving treaties drafted by the Tsarist government and explained their willingness to aid such peoples [*i.e.* China and Mongolia, bound by "unequal treaties"] in the struggle for independence. The members of the group, through Kucherenko and Gembarzhevskii as intermediaries, were well acquainted with the situation in Russia.

> "Thus starting from its very beginnings the Mongol People's Revolutionary Party was closely linked with the Russian revolutionary proletarians who struggled to help it day by day in its work and devoted themselves unto death to the cause of the Mongol Revolution."

[2] Compare Owen Lattimore, Introduction to Friters, *Outer Mongolia*, as cited, p. xxxi.

reiterated idea that Mongolia must continue to rely on Russia for the future, already so noticeable in the *Life*, are extended to a suggestion that Russia is the true source of the ideas of the Mongol Revolution. Early in the book (for example, on p. 8) the statement is made that "the revolutionary movement of 1905 in Russia influenced the bourgeois revolution in a number of countries, and in China, in the same way, a bourgeois revolution also began." This statement is made presumably because it is pertinent to Mongolia also, as then being a part of the Manchu empire [3]. In Tsedenbal's book, moreover, there is much more detail about the early Russian and Communist contacts of Choibalsang than there is in the *Life of Sukebatur*.

From Tsedenbal we learn (p. 11) that Choibalsang, born on February 8, 1895 in a very poor family in the northeastern corner of Outer Mongolia near the Mongol-inhabited region of Barga in northwestern Manchuria, was placed in a monastery at the age of thirteen because of his mother's faith in Lamaism. At the age of seventeen (p. 12), in 1912, when the Jebtsundamba Hutukhtu was being set up as Khagan of Outer Mongolia, he ran away to Urga, travelling nearly 2,000 kilometers on foot, and after Dickensian experiences as a waif he was, through the aid of "one of the sages of the pre-revolutionary generation, Danchinov" (presumably, from the Russian termination of this name, a Buryat) able to enter a school for interpreters. This must have been a school for interpreters in Mongol and Russian, under the auspices of the Russian consulate.

Because of his good record at this school Choibalsang was sent on to a middle school in Irkutsk, in Siberia, in 1914. Here (p. 13) he "frequently heard news of the Russian proletarian revolutionary movement and the worker's fight for freedom," was a witness of the Bolshevik summons to the workers in the October Revolution, and

---

[3] The attribution of exceptional ideological importance to the Russian 1905 Revolution may be of particular interest to those who specialize in studying the appearance, disappearance, and reappearance of certain themes in Communist exegesis. In the second of his two 1934 articles which have been so frequently cited above, Kallinikov opens with the assertion that the increasing number of insurrections in Outer Mongolia after 1905 is hard to explain otherwise than by the influence of the Russian Revolution of 1905, when "Soviets of workers' deputies" were formed in Krasnoyarsk and Verkhneudinsk (the latter right on the Outer Mongolian frontier), and he cites the Buryats, under Russian rule, as links between Siberia and Outer Mongolia. At this point an editorial note is inserted, warning that the author has insufficiently worked out the motive forces of the national liberation movement in Mongolia. In 1945, we have Tsedenbal reviving this Russian theme.

first heard of Lenin. In 1918 he and all other Mongol students were recalled from Irkutsk and it was as early as this year (p. 14) that he founded his secret revolutionary group, which apparently from the very beginning was in contact with Gembarzhevskii, "leader of the Russian workers' group active in Urga," and Kucherenko, "a printer in the Russo-Mongol printing establishment."

Another statement by Tsedenbal is that the Mongol Revolutionary Youth League was founded in August 1921 with Choibalsang as the secretary of its Central Executive Committee (p. 38). The date is important. A few months before, on March 1, the first Great Khural had been called into session, and on March 13 it had passed a resolution founding the Mongol People's Temporary Revolutionary Government. By the end of June Ungern-Sternberg had been defeated, and on July 8 the revolutionary Mongols entered Urga. They were not able, however, to take over complete power. There were still at Urga

"influences that were either pro-Chinese or anti-Soviet. It was only natural that the Church dignitaries — whose active participation in political life dated only from 1911 — and some of the princes felt themselves increasingly menaced by the new and revolutionary wing of the Mongol National Party." [4]

Comparing these events and dates it seems a reasonable speculation that Choibalsang, in face of the complicated problems that were looming up, decided to leave the People's Revolutionary Party under Sukebatur as a coalition of all factions except the extreme Right, and to safeguard the interests of the Marxist Left by founding a Revolutionary Youth League that could eventually become the nucleus of a Communist rather than Nationalist Party. This speculation is supported by the Youth League's reputation for being more Communist than the official Party [5]; a reputation not inconsistent with the fact

---

[4] Friters, as cited, p. 125. Friter's statement is supported by the account in the *Life of Sukebatur* of the way in which one wing of Sukebatur's own party had swung over to support of the Living Buddha before Sukebatur could enter Urga. It was with this support, apparently, that the Jebtsundamba Hutukhtu felt encouraged to issue a proclamation condemning any "subversive Red movement" and summoning "Sukebatur and others" to make their submission to him. See text, below, pp. 155—6, also excerpts from the decree, above, pp. 54—5.

[5] Lattimore, Introduction to Friters, as cited, p. xxxv. In 1926—27 a representative of the Right Wing of the Chinese Kuomintang, who was then working for the Left Wing (but never Communist) General Feng Yü-hsiang, who was receiving arms from Russia through Outer Mongolia, made an interesting journey to Outer Mongolia. His book (Ma Ho-t'ien, *Chinese agent in Mongolia,* translated by John De Francis, Baltimore, 1949), contains the following statements: Youth League was founded by "only 13 men, under Russian guidance"; its member-

that in spite of the personal orthodoxy of Choibalsang, there was at one time a tendency toward "Left deviation" within the Youth League [6]. It would be interesting to know whether Sukebatur concurred in the founding of this League, or whether it was an independent move by Choibalsang.

Tsedenbal then gives the following summary of Choibalsang's subsequent career (pp. 38—39):

1921: Deputy to People's Revolutionary Temporary Government; Political Commissar, People's Army; Commander, Western Army [7], in addition to his connection with the Revolutionary Youth League which has already been noted.

1922: Commissioner, Eastern Frontier, and Inspector-General of the Army.

1923: Sent to Russia for study after Sukebatur's death.

---

ship, as of 1926—27, represented "the masses" more than did the membership of the People's Revolutionary Party (p. 107); the Russians instigated the organization of the Youth League to counter the swing to the right in 1921 (p. 109); whereas the Russian Communist Youth League was subordinate to the Russian Communist Party, the Mongol Revolutionary Youth League "had equal rank with the Mongol People's Party and even dominated it ... it was nothing less than a branch of the Communist Party"; the liquidation of Bodo and others in 1922—23 "was entirely due to Soviet Russia's direction of the Revolutionary Youth League", (p. 113); the People's Party made an attempt to purge the League, but "because of Russian intervention the Revolutionary Youth League came out on top"; in 1922 the declaration was made that the Youth League "....is not a Communist organization. From now on, however, it will initiate activities in cooperation with the Comintern...." which leads the Chinese author to state the "disavowal of Communism was merely designed to counter Mongol opposition." (p. 114). On p. 112 the table of organization of the Youth League is given.

It should be noted here that the *Life of Sukabatur* states (see text below, p. 179) that "the Party has produced and trained its own future successor, the Mongol People's League of Revolutionary Youth" — a wording which, in spite of the immediately following conventional reference to training the youth, seems to imply not just training the future membership of the People's Party, but an offshoot of the Party which will eventually succeed the Party.

[6] Lattimore, in Friters, as cited, quoting Anatolii Kallinikov, *National-revolutionary movement*, as cited, pp. 78—80.

[7] It was this army that "mopped up" the last "White" Russian detachments in Western Outer Mongolia. Maksurjab served with Choibalsang on this campaign. For details of these Russian detachments, see I. I. Serebrennikov, *Velikii otkhod* (*The great exodus*), Harbin, 1936, based on the personal memoirs of many of these Russians, some in manuscript, some published obscurely in books, pamphlets, and journals, mostly in China. It provides a much clearer understanding of what happened in the course of the breakup and demoralization of the "White" armies than such popular but confused and lurid accounts as Ferdinand Ossendowski, *Beasts, men and gods*, New York, 1922.

1924: Commander-in-Chief, People's Revolutionary Army. At the
First Great Khural, elected a member of the Little Khural
(continuing committee; see above, p. 34, note 4), of which
he was from then on continuously a member.

As Tsedenbal does not list the years 1925–27 in this summary,
Choibalsang must then have been in relative eclipse — an interval
almost certainly to be explained by the fact that "the years 1925 to
1928 [were] a period of the revival of the feudal-capitalist ('right
wing') forces in Mongolia." [8] We have here in fact an interesting
indication that there was no liaison, or no effective liaison, between
Chinese Communists and Mongol Communists or pro-Communists
and that the main influence of China on Mongolia at that time was
the example of the nationalism of the Kuomintang. In an earlier passage, however, on p. 26, Tsedenbal does make one reference to these
years, crediting Choibalsang with a fight against the "Right deviation." He claims that this fight saved the party, and refers especially
to an "open letter" in which Choibalsang criticized the Party leadership in 1925. With this fight eventually won, we can resume Tsedenbal's summary of Choibalsang's career:

1928: Elected, at the fifth session of the Great Khural, Chairman
of the Praesidium of the Little Khural, (p. 39).

1930: Referring back to pp. 27–28 we find the Right Wing accused
of a Machiavellian plot in this year; losing ground as Right
Wingers, they planted their men in the Party and turned it
on a course of excessive Leftism, advocating fantastic and
utopian theories that caused the people to lose faith in the
Party, with the result that in "certain regions" there were

---

[8] Friters, as cited, p. 134. This statement is supported by Ma Ho-t'ien's obser-
vations, as of 1926–27 in his *Chinese agent,* cited above. He states that Dambadorji, 28 years old, who was then Chairman of the Central Executive Committee
of the People's Party, was anti-European and anti-American, as well as anti-
Russian (p. 162). He could "speak a little Chinese" and "is all for Outer Mongolian independence, but until that is possible he is in favor of forming a self-
governing state joined to China. He is against the Russian seizure of military and
political control of Mongolia and is very thick with the representatives of the
Kuominchün" (pp. 97–98). [The Kuominchün were General Feng Yü-hsiang's
troops. Though more radical than the Kuomintang, they were allied with the
Kuomintang which they supported, shortly after this, in the break with the Communists.] Ma Ho-t'ien also reported that Dambadorji had been educated in
Russia but was "strongly in favor of joining with the Chinese Kuomintang in order
to reduce the power of the Russians." Ma advocated that the Kuomintang find
a way to support him against the Revolutionary Youth League (p. 115). Ma also
makes the flat statement that "most of the leaders in the Mongol People's Party
are Rightists who advocate union with China" (p. 115).

counter-revolutionary risings. [This sounds like an *ex post facto* allocation of blame for the failure of the attempt to collectivize the herding economy of Mongolia in the period from 1929 to 1932, described by Friters as "one of violent socialization."] [9] Tsedenbal credits Choibalsang with having given a warning at the Seventh Party Congress, 1928, against abolishing private property and attempting socialization before the proper economic foundations had been laid.

1931: At the sixth session of the Great Khural, Choibalsang was appointed Minister for Foreign Affairs and also Minister for Agriculture and Livestock (p. 39). [Both appointments were of special importance; the first, because this was the year of Japan's invasion of Manchuria; the second, because it enabled Choibalsang to prepare for the reversal of the policy of collectivization.]

1932: At a joint session of the Party Central Executive Committee and the Control Commission the "Left deviation" was criticized and reversed. It was declared that the correct course for Mongolia was "gradual development toward noncapitalism." Tsedenbal adds that Choibalsang was the one who "faithfully executed" this "new turn" (p. 29).

1934: Tsedenbal says that 1934–39 "was an especially important period in the history of our Party." The ninth Party Congress, 1934, took up the implementation of the "new turn" [away from collectivization]. Choibalsang, who was in Russia for medical treatment, telegraphed saying that mistakes had been made, but also successes won. The stress must now be on unity and strength, in view of the growing menace of Japan [which had invaded Manchuria in 1931, set up the puppet state of Manchukuo in 1932, and added to it the province of Jehol, containing important Inner Mongolian territories, in 1933]. The implication is that Choibalsang was the healing influence after a period of party strife (pp. 29–30).

1935: Choibalsang appointed First Assistant Minister of State. [It is not clear what Mongol term is translated by the Chinese *kuo wu*, lit. "state affairs." This term is used in the Chinese rendering for the United States "Department of State," which is a Ministry of Foreign Affairs, but it is clear from the context that "foreign affairs" is not here intended, since on the

---

[9] Friters, as cited, p. 134. See also Lattimore, Introduction to Friters, p. xxxvi, with reference to the Report of Doksom, then Chairman of the Little Khural, "*Istoricheskie uroki 15 let revolyutsii*," (Historical lessons of 15 years of the revolution), in *Tikhii Okean (Pacific Ocean)*, No. 3(9), Moscow, 1936, p. 86, condemning this extremist policy as "an extremely dangerous, harmful, and incorrect deviation to the left."

same page, as can be seen above from the summary made for the year 1931, "foreign affairs," for which Choibalsang had been made Minister, is rendered by *wai chiao, lit.* "external ralations."] (p. 39).

1936: Choibalsang added to his other duties that of Minister of Interior. In this capacity he "exposed" the "duplicity" of Gendung, leading to the purging of Gendung and Demid (pp. 32, 39) [10].

1937: Choibalsang now held concurrently the offices of First Vice-Premier, Minister of Interior, Minister of War, and Commander-in-Chief of the armed forces (p. 39).

1939: Choibalsang is described as being, from this year, continuously or permanently Prime Minister and Minister of Foreign Affairs (p. 39).

From this point on, Tsedenbal's account reports no new developments in Choibalsang's career and almost nothing new about the affairs of Mongolia. The only dates mentioned subsequent to 1939 are 1940 (the new Mongol Constitution) and 1941 (a congratulatory telegram from Stalin). These dates may indicate that the original Mongol edition was published in the early 1940's and then brought more or less up to date by prefacing to it the 1945 speeches by Tsedenbal in order to make the 1945 edition that apparently underlies the Chinese translation (see above, p. 62, note 1).

By comparing the two "canonical" biographies, that of Sukebatur and that of Choibalsang, we can learn much of the method that is used, in a one-party state, for establishing the official stature of political heroes. In the *Life of Sukebatur* Choibalsang is placed in an unassailable position as one of the founding fathers of the new Mongol state, but he appears throughout as one who never tried to assert an importance greater than that of Sukebatur himself. In Tsedenbal's account of Choibalsang, first published only two years later but with the war already ended or ending and Mongolia standing in a position of new importance, the importance of Choibalsang is greatly enhanced. No claim is made that he was the "real" leader even while

---

[10] Gendung had been Prime Minister and as recently as 1934, when on a visit to Moscow, had concluded financial and economic agreements with the U.S.S.R. favorable to Mongolia. There is a Report by him to the Seventh Great Khural, reproduced in *Tikhii Okean (Pacific Ocean)*, No. 1 (3), Moscow, 1935. Demid was Minister of War. That these two had in fact been in a plot seems to be confirmed by a pamphlet, *Krasnaya ruka nad Vneshnei Mongoliei, (Red hand over Outer Mongolia)*, by Captain Bimba, a Mongol deserter to the Japanese, published (no date) during the war in Japanese-occupied Shanghai as Japanese propaganda.

Sukebatur was alive; but he is moved forward, identified as more of a political originator in his own right, and no longer treated as if he were just a loyal follower and lieutenant of Sukebatur and no more.

An important detail in this enhancing of his stature in the years before the death of Sukebatur is the identification of Choibalsang as the founder of the Revolutionary Youth League in 1921, whereas the founding of the league is not even mentioned in the *Life of Sukebatur*, and the League is referred to only at the very end — where, significantly, it appears as the "future successor" of Sukebatur's own People's Revolutionary Party.

In writing the biography of Choibalsang, however, the main problem was obviously to establish his importance in the troubled and critical years between the death of Sukebatur in 1923 and the recognition of Choibalsang as the sole and undisputed head of Party, Government, and armed forces in 1939. Here the critical statements which establish the whole method, are the statements that he opposed the "Right deviation" of 1925–28; that in 1928 he warned against the attempt to abolish private property which was the main feature of the "Left deviation" of 1928–32; that after 1932 it was he who "faithfully executed" the "new turn" away from collectivization and toward gradual non-capitalist development; and that in 1936, as Minister of Interior, he directed the purge of those previously in power, including the former Premier, Gendung.

These references are not matched by similar references in the samples to which I have had access (and admittedly they are only scattered samples) of the literature that is contemporary, or more nearly contemporary, to the events described. For instance Kallinikov's book on *The national-revolutionary movement in Mongolia,* published in 1926, to which reference has already been made, has no mention at all of Choibalsang although it has a section, important for this early period of revolutionary history, on the Revolutionary Youth League, of whose Central Executive Committee Choibalsang was secretary, and although it mentions a number of men whose careers and reputations have since come to be considered secondary or even tertiary in importance as compared to those of Sukebatur and Choibalsang. Kallinikov does not even mention Choibalsang as one of the founders of the People's Revolutionary Party.

Even more remarkable is the lack of emphasis on Choibalsang in Doksom's "big" Report of 1936, also previously cited. According to Tsedenbal it was Choibalsang who "faithfully executed" the "new turn" in 1932 away from the "Left deviation" against which he had warned in 1928. Tsedenbal adds that the period that began with 1934 was "especially important" and lists Choibalsang as the Minister of Interior who conducted the purge of 1936. Yet Doksom, an important part of whose Report is devoted to the "new turn" and the errors first of the Right and then of the Left in earlier years, does not even mention Choibalsang in connection with all these events. He is in fact mentioned only once, and then just in passing, as an early associate of Sukebatur.

Attention may also be drawn to the passage in the *Life of Sukebatur* describing the last illness of Sukebatur (see below, pp. 175—6 of text). Here it is said of Choibalsang that he "had gone to the eastern frontier on special business" (p. 104). The funeral oration was pronounced by Maksurjab, and in it Choibalsang was not mentioned, either as co-founder of the Party or as the prospective new great national figure. By the time the *Life* was published in 1943, however, Choibalsang was hailed as "the most beloved and trusted, the best comrade of Sukebatur" (p. 112); and this echo of the manner in which the Russians were then speaking of the link between Lenin and Stalin becomes even more distinct in Tsapkin's book on the Mongolian People's Republic (also cited above), published in 1948, where Choibalsang is referred to as "the friend and comrade-in-arms of Sukebatur, the continuator of his work, the leader of the Mongol people" (p. 38). Similar phrases are, of course, used of Choibalsang by Tsedenbal.

These citations, it must be remembered, are mere random samples. To plot definitively the rising curves in the reputations of Sukebatur and Choibalsang and to diagram accurately the phases through which Choibalsang has been first moved up abreast of Sukebatur and then even ahead of him would require the searching of a much wider literature than has been available to me. Nevertheless what it has been possible to cite here seems to me to justify two tentative conclusions: that the posthumous cult of Sukebatur was from 1923 at least until 1943 perfunctory in comparison with the fervent cult of Sun Yat-sen in China from his death in 1925 until the Communists came to power in 1949—50 [11]; and that Choibalsang, after he had

---

[11] It may be remarked that in China the Kuomintang, after the death of Sun Yat-sen, swung far to the right of the ideas and politics of the last years of his life. It could be argued that the Kuomintang, having become a party of the Right, exploited the Sun Yat-sen cult largely for purposes of lip-service to the ideas and revolutionary phraseology of the Left, which were no longer reflected in the

become not only prominent but preeminent, was given the benefit of a peculiar kind of enhancement of his earlier career, by referring to the positions he held and the things he said, wrote, and did ten, fifteen, or twenty years previously as if he had then not only stood in the front rank of his contemporaries but was then already standing head and shoulders above others in the same rank.

---

actual conduct of the Party. On comparable lines it could be argued that the Mongols, who continued to follow policies much more revolutionary than those of Chiang Kai-shek (although, except for 1929–32, more "evolutionary" and less extreme than those of Russia), had from 1923 to 1943 more of a cult of "the Party" than they did of Sukebatur. It is also interesting that the Kuomintang cult depicted Sun Yat-sen as the single-handed creator of a revolution, while in Mongolia, when after twenty years the first full official biography of Sukebatur was published, the emphasis was on the "united front" origins of his Party.

POLITICAL HEROES: THE PROCESS OF ENHANCEMENT

Historical re-evaluation is a continuous process. Consciously or un-consciously it enters into practically all historical writing. When as-sessing the significance of a problem of this kind in re-evaluation it is important not to jump to the kind of crass conclusion to which the Russians resort when they denigrate "bourgeois" writers as "falsifiers" of history. It would be absurd to say that the careers of Sukebatur and Choibalsang have been fictionized and as fiction made subject to capricious rewriting. The revolutionary pedigrees of both men are indisputably genuine. The problem of evaluating their careers is not one of separating fact from fiction but of trying to delineate the careers in their true proportions, in the context of the times in which they lived. As an aid in attempting an independent evaluation of this kind I have analyzed in the diagram on the facing page the way in which the careers of Sukebatur and Choibalsang have been presented in their official Mongol biographies and the way in which their stature is depicted in comparison with the stature of their contem-poraries.

In this diagram the Revolution of 1911 is taken as a first base line; above it, vertically, are secondary base lines. With 1911 as the point of departure it can be seen that the careers of both Sukebatur and Choi-balsang began between 1911 and 1918, that of Sukebatur as a soldier and that of Choibalsang as a runaway from a monastery who later became a student.

At the year 1918 a secondary base line marks the beginning of the "time of troubles" — Russian Revolution, Chinese invasion, "White" Russian troops, and the intrigues of the Japanese with Semenov and Ungern-Sternberg. The careers of Sukebatur and Choibalsang con-tinue parallel; each of them founded a revolutionary group, and the two later merged.

At the year 1923 a third line marks the death of Sukebatur. From this line upward the graph of Sukebatur's posthumous reputation is continued as a dotted line; but Choibalsang's graph is not continued as a solid line, because he was not immediately recognized as Suke-batur's sole and undisputed successor. He continued to hold impor-tant positions, it is true, but there were a number of claimants to the

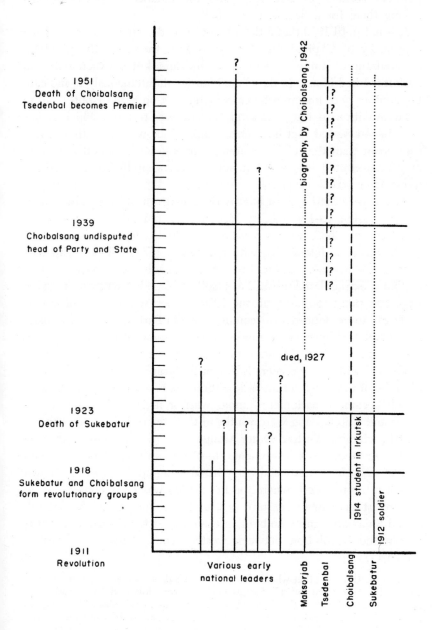

1951
Death of Choibalsang
Tsedenbal becomes Premier

1939
Choibalsang undisputed
head of Party and State

1923
Death of Sukebatur

1918
Sukebatur and Choibalsang
form revolutionary groups

1911
Revolution

Various early
national leaders

died, 1927

biography, by Choibalsang, 1942

Maksorjab

Tsedenbal

Choibalsang

Sukebatur

1914 student in Irkutsk

1912 soldier

political heritage of Sukebatur and the balance of power shifted among them for a decade and a half.

It is not until 1939 that a third line can be drawn, marking the final supremacy of Choibalsang. From this line, therefore, the graph of Choibalsang continues upward as a solid line; but between 1923 and 1939 it is filled in as a broken line, in order simultaneously to indicate the *continuity* of his importance (which is not open to dispute) and to draw attention to the process of "enhancing" through which it has later been asserted that his *relative* importance was at all times more significant than that of his contemporaries — a claim that obviously may be accepted by some but not by others, or by some more un-questioningly than others.

At the year 1951 a fifth line marks the death of Choibalsang and the succession, as Premier, of Tsedenbal. From this year, therefore, the graph of Choibalsang's reputation is carried upward, like that of Sukebatur, as a dotted line, with a tendency for Choibalsang to take precedence over Sukebatur. From this year, also, the graph of Tse-denbal is extrapolated upward as a solid line and downward, to some uncertain point (probably in the 1930's, when we may suppose that he began to be noticed as a "coming man" in Party ranks) as a broken line parallelled by question marks, to indicate that it is not yet known how far the process of "enhancing" his earlier career will be carried.

Parallel with these careers is drawn the graph of Maksurjab, as an example of the career of an early nationalist revolutionary hero. Mak-surjab became a nationally famous warrior in 1911–12 when Suke-batur and Choibalsang were youths in their teens. He played a major part in winning Western Outer Mongolia for the Revolution that set up the Autonomous Government. He played an important part again in 1920–21. He was especially important as a popular hero in his own homeland in the west, where the Revolution was more conservatively nationalist than in the eastern part of the country. Had he not fol-lowed Sukebatur and Choibalsang there might have been a civil war within the Revolution between western conservatives and eastern radicals [1].

---

[1] It is worth noting that when, after Maksurjab's death some time in the middle 1920's, the "excessive leftist" decrees of 1930 were followed by disturbances, including armed risings, the focus of discontent was in the west. These risings are mentioned by Tsedenbal on page 28 of his biography of Choibalsang, but without identification of the geographical area — as is to be expected of an "ideological" writer whose purpose is to discriminate between politically "good" and politically "bad" kinds of people, but not to stigmatize as "bad" the whole population of a geographical area.

Parallel again to the graph of Maksurjab are several graphs which are only schematic but are added as a reminder that from the very beginning in 1911 nationalism and revolution in Mongolia were not completely dominated by a single figure. The importance of some of the early leaders continued not only into the 1920's but into the 1930's and 1940's. Some may still survive, though probably now they are mainly important as "elder statesmen." It is well to bear in mind these continuing though less publicized careers as well as the truncated careers of those who died early, or were purged, or fled into exile.

THE TRACK OF THE ORBIT IN SATELLITE POLITICS

As a complement to the foregoing analysis of the domestic politics of Outer Mongolia it is now necessary to make a corresponding analysis of the peculiarly delicate and quick response of politics in a satellite country to political changes in the protector, or patron, or dominant country, for this response is of the essence of satellite politics and distinguishes it from colonial politics and the puppet politics of, say, a country like Manchukuo under the Japanese. An independent analysis is especially needed because the whole subject is treated by both Mongol and Russian writers in a way that is so stereotyped as to be virtually meaningless.

Ever since the Russian Revolution it has been a fixed convention with both Mongol and Russian writers to refer to Tsarist policy in Mongolia as imperialist, predatory, and exploitative and to present Soviet policy in contrast as an altruistic "big brother" protection of Mongol independence. The truth is that, as I have pointed out earlier, Tsarist Russia saw in 1911 the opportunity to create in Outer Mongolia a buffer state shielding Siberia against possible expansion by both Japan and China. The profits of development and trade were incidental, were not pursued with vigor, and were never vital to the Tsarist state. What was important was not that Outer Mongolia should be developed by Russia, but that it should not be developed by either Japan or China. Tsarist policy therefore treated Outer Mongolia — in spite of the urging of occasional Russian "forward policy" enthusiasts — as an inert buffer zone, not as a zone of forward expansion, much as the British policy of the same period treated Tibet. For the purposes of such an inert buffer it was enough to support the dual system of theocratic authority under the Urga Living Buddha as Bogda Khagan or Holy Emperor and local, territorial feudal power under the hereditary princes.

With the outbreak of the Russian Revolution Outer Mongolia became for the Soviet Russians first a danger zone, because it was being used as a base by "White" Russian counter-revolutionary forces who were supported by Japan; then a zone of hoped-for revolutionary penetration into Asia; then again a buffer zone for defense against Japan in the 1930's; and finally, after the victory of the Chinese Com-

munists, a transition-zone for the development of strategic and economic communication between Soviet Russia and Communist China.

The dates bear out this summary assertion. In 1919—20, when Sukebatur and Choibalsang were organizing their political party and
Partisan detachments, Soviet policy was clearly in the main an emergency policy. Eastern Siberia was organized as a Far Eastern Republic, less Bolshevik in its characteristics than Russia proper, and
the major aim was to defeat Kolchak, Semenov and other counter-
revolutionaries and to bring foreign intervention to an end. In this
period, therefore, the principal activity of Soviet policy was to give
the Mongols military assistance in driving out the remnants of Chinese forces (who were under the command of a general who had
Japanese connections) together with Ungern-Sternberg and the other
"White" Russians. What was useful to the Russians at this juncture
was Mongol unity — something that could not be attained, or could
not be attained quickly enough, through revolution against the existing government, conservative and even reactionary though it might be.

In the 1920's and 1930's the confused cross-currents of Russian
domestic and foreign policies are matched by a similar confusion in
Mongolia [2]. The principal factors were:

1.   Lenin's "retreat" to the New Economic Policy (NEP), permitting
a temporary and partial return to private enterprise from 1920 to 1923.
Some of the NEP measures remained in effect for several years longer.
The NEP restored production but led to the growth of a get-rich-
quick class, the "Nepmen," who were subsequently liquidated by
confiscation and discriminatory taxation.

1a.   This phase was reflected in Mongolia by the rise to power
within the People's Revolutionary Party (which, it should be repeated,
was a coalition of Leftists and of nationalists who had no tinge whatever of Marxism) of such men as Bodo, the first Prime Minister, representing what such Russian writers as Kallinikov refer to as a new,
native Mongol "bourgeoisie." According to Marxist classification such
men, if they were wholly in competition with foreign private capital
and trade were "national bourgeois," to be tolerated within certain
limits; but if they collaborated with foreign "exploiters" they were
"enemies of the people." Bodo was accused of being a friend of the

---

[2] For the chronology of Russian events, I rely here on Sir John Maynard,
Russia in flux, New York, 1948, edited and abridged from two works originally
published in England as *Russia in flux*, 1941, and *The Russian peasant and other
studies*, 1942.

former great Chinese trading firms that had controlled so much of the economic life of Mongolia, and liquidated in 1922 [3].

2.   At the close of the NEP Russia veered toward socialism and a planned economy. In 1924 Stalin announced his formula of "socialism in one country" and in 1929, after much controversy among different factions of the Russian Communists, the First Five Year Plan was launched. In the same years, however, Russian hopes of a spread of revolution, especially in Asia, that would undermine the stability of the capitalist powers and give the Soviet Union time to consolidate, ended in disappointment. The period was one of intense stress and strain, because it involved an attempt to move in two directions at the same time. The internal struggle that ended with the victory of Stalin over Trotsky resulted in what might be called the "conservative" decision to rely primarily on domestic resources, economically; but at the same time the support of revolutions abroad was a "radical" policy. The years from 1924 to 1927, when the struggle with Trotsky was at its bitterest, were also the years when in China the Kuomintang cooperated with the Chinese Communists and with the Comintern, and in these years numbers of Russian and other foreign Communists were active in China as experts of various kinds — attached by no means solely to the Chinese Communists; the most important were those who were working immediately with the Kuomintang.

2a.   This contradictory duality of Russian policy is again reflected by events in Mongolia. These were the years in which the Revolutionary Youth League came near to being an independent second

---

[3] Undoubtedly one of the things the new government feared was the bribing power of these firms, which had immense uncollected debts that the new government was preventing them from collecting — debts of individual Mongols, collective debts of Banners, debts of princes and other nobles for which they were personally responsible, debts of the same nobles which they had managed to pass on to the collective Banner debt, etc. The scale of operations of the larger firms is shown by a well known figure: One firm used to take out of Outer Mongolia annually, as interest only, not as recovery of capital, up to 70,000 horses and 500,000 sheep. The value to the Chinese traders of a system under which they collected livestock as payment of interest, themselves setting the money rates for the valuation of the animals, is illustrated by the story that one Mongol Banner raised 20,000 *taels* (Chinese ounces) of ready silver to pay off its debt; but this was refused by the trader, who preferred to go on collecting interest. See Kallinikov, *National-revolutionary movement*, as previously cited, p. 21. Kallinikov evidently got these figures from Maiskii, *Contemporary Mongolia*, as cited, p. 194. Maiskii adds the detail that the Mongol Banner raised the ready silver from a Russian firm. Maiskii's informants were largely old-time Russian traders who spoke Mongol well and his trade data are probably fairly reliable.

party, and the fact that it was regarded as more Left than the senior People's Revolutionary Party may perhaps indicate that it was in this Mongol group that Russian Trotskyism found its echo. It is in this period that, in Soviet publications, we find the hope expressed that Mongolia might become a model for revolutions elsewhere in Asia [4]. On the other hand, the Leftist trend of the Youth League in these years was offset by the fact that Russian policy in China was supporting, not a Communist revolution but a Nationalist revolution in a united front with Communists. The principal impact on the Mongols must have been the rising fame of the advancing Nationalists, not the Communists; and as mentioned above the only revolutionary warlord who had agents in Outer Mongolia was Feng Yü-hsiang, who was an ally at that time of the Nationalists, not the Communists. Perhaps in part because a too-Communist program in Mongolia would have had a disturbing effect on the United Pront policy that Russia was supporting in China, influential non-Communists survived in the government and the People's Revolutionary Party, in spite of the Youth League, so that Tsedenbal calls 1925—28 a period of "Right deviation" and Friters calls it a period of "feudal-capitalist" revival, as has been mentioned above.

3.   With the split between Chiang Kai-shek and the Chinese Communists, followed by civil war, there came a dramatic turn. Unrest in Asia generally swung away from economic and social radicalism and toward more right-wing forms of nationalism. Russian policy withdrew within its own frontiers, and Stalin pushed swiftly and relentlessly forward to his first Five Year Plan (1929) and to the collectivization of agriculture.

3a.   Once again, the Mongols were not long in following the Russian lead. As far as its Asian frontiers were concerned, Outer Mongolia reverted to something like its old function of inert buffer in the Tsarist period. Internally, the Mongols entered on their 1929—32 course of spectacularly unsuccessful attempted collectivization.

This whole episode was so extraordinary that it calls for special attention. It was manifestly imitative of the Russians, but when it aroused stubborn opposition, sometimes armed opposition, and began to fail, no Russian resources were thrown behind it to force it through. It remains the sole instance of a major Russian-style policy, in a country in satellite dependency on Russia, that was allowed to fail —

[4] See above, p. 3.

regardless of the loss of prestige involved. Nor, after more than twenty years, has the attempt been renewed. The explanation must be interesting; but as there are not enough facts available for a full and confident explanation, all that can be ventured here is a surmise.

Tsedenbal's Mongol account is that the crisis was brought about by Rightists, who with a Machiavellian twist turned themselves into the semblance of Leftist extremists in order to force failures and discredit the régime. This account sounds rather like a facile echo of the charges, in the Russian purge trials of the 1930's, that there was collusion between Rightists and the Trotsky Leftists. As Maynard says of the Russian oppositionists, however, "the logic of events carried them even into alliance with their opposites, who desired the same immediate end for altogether different reasons", [5] and there may have been strange alliances among different kinds of oppositionists in Mongolia.

Even so, however, the Mongol account is inadequate. As for Russian accounts, in no Russian source that I have been able to find is there ever a suggestion that when the Mongols made a "mistake" in attempting to imitate Russian collectivization they may have been acting on a directive from Moscow, or under the urging of Russian advisors. It is simply recorded that the policy was "mistaken." As to this, one surmise might be that the Russians, rather than lose prestige themselves, forced their satellites to take the whole blame. Another interpretation (and the one to which I incline, because it fits well with the general character of satellite politics) is that the Mongols made a headstrong decision of their own, perhaps even against cautionary Russian advice.

There are two arguments in favor of this surmise. One is that Russian agricultural collectivization was only one half of a double program, the other half being the mechanization of agriculture, thus effecting a saving in labor and creating a pool of surplus labor to contribute to industrialization. In Mongolia industrialization was rudimentary, and it was impossible to carry out a dual collectivization-and-industrialization program. The Russians, if this argument is sound, would not have urged such a program in Mongolia unless they had been able to come to its aid with a surplus of machinery; and such a surplus they did not at that time have.

The second argument for believing that the period of extreme

---

[5] Maynard, as cited, p. 324.

leftism in Mongolia was a consequence of spontaneous Mongol emu-
lation of the Russians, rather than a mechanical imitation enjoined
by the Russian themselves, concerns the psychology of satellite politics
in general and, in particular, the political psychology of the Mongols
at this period. The relevant points in the general psychology of satellitism are those that have already been made (see above, pp. 41–42)
— the fact that satellites are not just obedient puppets but eager
disciples and imitators — so eager that if factions develop in the
country in whose orbit they move, they immediately split into imitative factions. Allowance must also be made, however, for the way
in which the general psychology of a political category of state can
be modified by the particular psychology of a people.

To those (unfortunately they are few) who have some first-hand
knowledge of the attitudes of nationalistic Mongols toward such more
powerful peoples as the Russians, Japanese, and Chinese, a certain
kind of suspicion on the part of the Mongols is familiar. When a Russian, Japanese, or Chinese official or advisor or expert has just finished
saying "Such and such is all very well for us Russians (or Japanese
or Chinese) who are more advanced, modern, and sophisticated than
you. At this stage you Mongols should go slowly and pick your steps
carefully. You will get to the more advanced stage in good time, but
for the present you should prepare yourselves for it and not try to get
there immediately" — the instant suspicion of the Mongol is that the
real meaning is "You Mongols got left behind after the days of Chingis Khan and we Russians (or Japanese, or Chinese) are going to see
that you stay left behind. We are going to help you in various ways,
but we are also going to see to it that you stay lagging behind us, so
that we can always keep the advantage." [6]

To this the instinctive answer of the Mongol nationalist is "Very
well, but if we Mongols ever get the chance we'll show you that
Mongols can learn the new ways of doing things as fast as anybody
— that we can not only move as fast as you but catch up with you."
In view of this instinctive reaction, combined with the satellite eager-
ness of the follower who wants to be not merely a follower but abreast

---

[6] For this psychology in several colonial settings see the valuable article by
James McAuley, "Paradoxes of development in the South Pacific," *Pacific Affairs*,
27, 2, New York, June 1954. He quotes the following from a man whose people
had been under successive German, Japanese, and Australian influence: ".... Our
minds, brother, are like a worm under the earth, trying to find a way to the
surface. We go on and on and on, and we are just about to come up when the
whiteman says 'No,' and blocks the way...."

of the leader, it seems to me rational to suppose that most of those who directed the phase of extreme leftism in Mongolia may have been in fact headstrong enthusiasts and not, as Tsedenbal would now have it, exclusively Machiavellian oppositionists; though oppositionists who wanted to discredit both the régime and the Russian association may also have been involved.

4. In 1931 Japan invaded Manchuria. In 1932 it set up there the puppet state of Manchukuo. In 1933 it added to Manchukuo the province of Jehol, including important Inner Mongolian territories. In 1933 also Hitler came to power in Germany. Frontier defense and prevention of a simultaneous attack from west and east now became primary concerns of Russian policy.

4a. The Mongolian aspect of this new situation was the increased importance of Mongolia's function as a buffer. On the one hand, therefore, Choibalsang's rapid rise in this period was probably due in large part to the fact that he was an authentic national military hero. On the other hand the last great political purge, that of the Gendung-Demid group in 1936, probably did uncover not merely an internal political opposition but some oppositionists who had Japanese contacts and believed in the possibility of a combined Outer and Inner Mongolia under Japanese protection and valuable to Japan as a barrier to hold Russia and China apart [7].

Certainly there were Inner Mongolian leaders who, up to about 1935 (by which time the combined Japanese occupation and penetration of Inner Mongolia left them no more initiative), believed that there was enough discontent in Outer Mongolia so that if Japan would arm them to invade Outer Mongolia, carrying with them extra supplies to arm the people, it would be possible to take over the country; but, it was always added, such an invasion must be by Inner Mongolian troops only — if it were accompanied by Japanese troops patriotism would prevail and the people would fight against the invasion. These Inner Mongolian leaders may have been over-sanguine, but they were probably not completely misinformed about discontent in Outer Mongolia. Indeed it may be because he knew of the discontent and the need to allay it that Choibalsang in 1934 sent the conciliatory telegram cited by Tsedenbal (see above, p. 73) admitting that there had been great difficulties and some mistakes but exhorting all to unity in face of the Japanese danger.

---

[7] See the pamphlet by the Outer Mongolian deserter, Captain Bimba, cited above.

However that may be, it is not to be doubted that after the battles against the Japanese on the Manchurian frontier between 1936 and 1939, in which Russian troops intervened on the Mongol side and Russians and Mongols inflicted very heavy losses on the Japanese [8], the psychology of wanting to be on the winning side favored both the ruling party in Mongolia and the Russian association.

Since the end of the war and the victory of the Communists in China, a quite new chapter has opened in the political history of the Mongols. Even the satellite position of Outer Mongolia has changed in a fundamental way. Instead of holding an important flank position, the Mongols are now situated in a geographical zone through which it is of very great importance for the Russians and the Chinese to develop their strategic and economic communications with each other. Of what is being written in this new chapter we know next to nothing. Two major facts do stand out, however: there is no sign of anything that looks like a preparatory move for the unification of Outer and Inner Mongolia; and the policy of China toward the Mongols of Inner Mongolia appears to resemble not the policy of the Russians toward Outer Mongolia, but the policy of the early Soviet years toward minorities within the Russian frontiers.

If the topics that have here been discussed lead up to anything, as an introduction to a political document that was originally designed not to influence foreign opinion but to affect the thinking of the Mongols themselves they lead, I think, to the conclusion that Mongol politics are not an exotic study. There is much here, I suggest, that can be applied to improve our understanding of how other peoples are likely to act who have newly entered or are just entering the world of modern politics. Many of these peoples, but by no means all of them, are in Asia. At first sight, when reading in the Mongol and Russian sources about "monarchists," "feudalists," "reactionaries," "new bourgeois" and so forth the terminology sometimes seems fantastically doctrinaire and unreal, when the events take place within a society primarily of herdsmen, with no industrial proletariat, no native private capital invested in industry, and almost none in trade. In terms of the

---

[8] As far as I have been able to ascertain, the Japanese casualties in the battle of Nomunkhan, 1939, admitted to be 17,000, are the largest ever admitted by the Japanese in a single action — including the Russo-Japanese War and the battles of the second World War. The admission must have been forced on the High Command by the necessity for letting the public know, indirectly, that it was impossible to continue a "forward policy" against the Mongolian-Siberian frontier.

potentials involved, on the other hand — the setting of a trend in one direction and not in another — it can be seen that the issues of the last few decades of Mongol politics have been real issues and the controversies real controversies.

Mongol claimants to leadership have been followed or resisted by no means only because Mongols felt that they were "working for the Russians," or "tied up with Chinese interests," or "agents of the Japanese," but because at the same time, in real and valid terms, they represented conflicts between different groups and different interests that really existed in Mongolia. If a man and his party went in one direction their following would grow; if in another, it would dwindle. It is well not to forget that such things happen among small and weak peoples as well as great and powerful ones.

PART TWO

THE LIFE OF SUKEBATUR

INTRODUCTION

[*p. 5 of text*] Sukebatur [1] was one of the leaders beloved of the hearts of the Mongol people. The fact that the Mongol people were able to escape from a harsh oppression under foreign and domestic oppressors that had lasted several hundred years, and to enter on the road, new in history, of freedom and the peaceful and happy status of independence is linked for ever with the name of our famous leader Sukebatur.

Sukebatur was a son of the impoverished Mongol common people who had suffered harsh foreign and domestic oppression, and was a man who personally experienced and tasted every suffering that the common people tasted.

Twenty-two years ago the Mongol masses were subjected to the fire and sword of the Ko Mings [2], the servants of brutal foreign imperialism, and the butcher Baron [Ungern-Sternberg] and father and son, mother and child, man and wife were separated, as the bandits of the Ko Mings and the Baron, like wolves attacking masterless sheep, plundered the herds and flocks of the Mongol people, and camps and livestock hid among mountains and peaks. The broad and beautiful land of Mongolia suffered all the bitterness and suffering of fire and flood.

In these momentous times when the fate of our motherland and the masses of our people was poised on the brink of extinction, the true son of the Mongol people, Sukebatur, uniting with other like-minded comrades such as Choibalsang, began the great work of extricating his people and motherland from the mire of their despotic enemies and raising them to be free and forever happy.

Comrade Sukebatur did not stop when he had merely delivered the Mongol people from the hands of the brutal foreign imperialists. He also set himself the noble aim of delivering them from the oppres-

---

[1] Sukebatur means Axe Hero. This is a personal name, although it sounds as if it might be a pseudonym.

[2] Before it adopted the name of Kuomintang, the Nationalist Party in China was at one time known as Ko Ming Tang or Revolutionary Party. For this reason all "political" Chinese, whether civilians or troops, were called by the Mongols Ko Ming (Goming) From this usage the word passed from Mongol into Russian in the form Gomin.

sion of the feudal powers within their own society and raising and developing them to be free forever and permanently happy. This pure aim was the same noble aim for which the Mongol people had longed and hoped for a good many hundred years past, and the Mongol people, struggling heroically from generation to generation for the sake of their own freedom and right to independence, had more than once defeated and driven back foreign enemies; but they had never succeeded in escaping from the oppression of their internal oppressors.

Thus the Mongol people, though in its own history it had given birth to not a few patriotic noble heroes, in Sukebatur for the first time gave birth to the great hero of the people who completely delivered the Mongol people from the hands of foreign and domestic oppressors, and led the great struggle to establish a permanent state of happiness free from the exploitation of man by man.

The special distinction of Sukebatur among the other famous patriotic heroes who had stood out in Mongol history lay in this fact.

Not only was Comrade Sukebatur a courageous, heroic, patriotic man who did not spare his ardent spirit and warm blood on behalf of his own people and motherland; he was also a far-sighted and far-thinking great statesman.

In all things Comrade Sukebatur, taking upon himself in times of grave difficulty the noble responsibility of saving his own motherland and people from the bitterness and suffering of fire and flood, was able to distinguish clearly between the friends and enemies of his motherland, and thus profoundly appreciated the beneficial consequences of the mighty October Socialist Revolution which had arisen in Russia. He well understood that the fate and destiny of the Mongol common people were inseparably linked with this Great October Revolution, and that apart from Soviet Socialist Russia our people had no other trustworthy friend.

For this same reason Comrade Sukebatur, personally recruiting and uniting talented sons of the Mongol people, began the creation of our Party and People's Revolutionary Government. Concluding a mutual alliance with the Soviet Union, he obtained aid from the Soviet Red Army and driving out and expelling the hated foreign enemy he cleansed and won back our motherland.

[*p. 7 of text*] Comrade Sukebatur was the founder and creator of the Mongol Revolution, and the first creator of the Mongol People's Revolutionary Army.

In that period when Mongolia was in the hands of the foreign oppressors, and the people could hardly endure the bitterness and suffering of fire and flood, Comrade Sukebatur began to recruit and muster
the People's Volunteer Army on the northern frontier of Mongolia.
When he summoned his people with a call to arise in arms against the
foreign enemy, the people who had hidden in the recesses of the
mountains came down from the mountains to meet him, and the
people who had concealed themselves in the woods and forests came
out of the woods to meet their own beloved leader, and with ardent
spirits and warm blood they fought pitilessly against the hated enemy,
and extricating their motherland from the hands of the foreign enemy
they founded a free and lasting government of their own.

Comrade Sukebatur declared that his aim, after he had led the
Mongol people to drive out and expel the foreign enemy, was to
liquidate the rule of the domestic feudal ruling powers which for
several hundred years had been oppressing the Mongol people, and
eventually to strengthen his Mongol People's Revolutionary Government, and he personally took the lead in the work of developing the
economy, education and military forces of his country.

Sukebatur was a man who devoted himself body and soul to the
cause of the peace and happiness of the people and the motherland,
and an exceptionally self-sacrificing, sincere, and loyal hero.

Comrade Sukebatur's meritorious deeds are recorded for ten
thousand years eternally in the history of the Mongol people, and the
masses of the Mongol people will never forget the deserving record
of Sukebatur, their own famous leader.

The Mongol laboring people, out of their boundless love for their
own motherland and freedom, earnestly desire to study and understand the noble history of their country and the lives of its patrotic
heroes, and especially [p. 8 of text] at this time when the fascist bandits confront all decent humanity with fear and terror, it is more
than ever imperatively desirable to study and understand the history
of our own motherland and the place in it of the life of Sukebatur,
the leader who stood in the forefront of the struggle for the freedom
of the Mongol people.

The biography of Sukebatur, brave hero and patriot, creates an
even greater determination in the Mongol people to go on to ever
new victories. The life of Sukebatur is the history of how the Mongol
people won their own motherland and their own freedom in battle
from the hands of external and internal enemies.

Up to now no full biography of Comrade Sukebatur has ever been published. Accordingly, on the occasion of the twentieth anniversary of the death of our great leader Sukebatur, on the authority of a resolution of the Central Committee of the Mongol People's Revolutionary Party, the Scientific Research Committee has prepared for publication the full biography of Sukebatur, edited for the first time by Nachokdorji. Thus we have now in fact, making good a deficiency, completed an important task which was immediate and urgent.

Although this biography of Sukebatur edited and prepared by Nachokdorji is the first that has been undertaken, it is a fully detailed biography that will be able to satisfy the expectation of readers.

Comrade Nachukdorji, in this biography of Sukebatur, has written down everything from the youth of Sukebatur to the end of his life, and especially has dealt clearly with Sukebatur's early revolutionary activity, his founding of the party, his going to the Soviet Union to ask for aid, his organizing of the struggle for the freedom of the Mongol masses, his driving out of the foreign enemy, and his struggle to consolidate the gains of the revolution.

[p. 9 of text]   Especially he has shown us clearly Sukebatur's love for his people and motherland and how he spared nothing for them; also his heroic courage, his gentle tenderness, his untiring industry, his faith in the masses and his way of learning from the masses; and therefore the members of our Party and Revolutionary Youth should familiarize themselves with the contents of the biography of the people's own great leader Sukebatur and learn from his heroic struggle how to strive to give untiring devotion to the cause of our motherland and the freedom of the people.

PROPAGANDA AND ENLIGHTENMENT BUREAU

OF THE CENTRAL COMMITTEE OF THE PARTY.

CHAPTER I

YOUTH AND YOUNG MANHOOD

[*p. 10 of text*]   Our great leader Sukebatur was born on the second February 1893 in the city of Maimai [Ch'eng] (the present Amogolang-batur) in the family of a poor man named Damdin, nicknamed "White Gown." [1] His father and mother were not especially glad when he was born; on the contrary they thought it would be a burden to bring him up. The impoverished husband and wife, having to endure the hardships of hunger and want with their two previously born children, were barely able to live, and therefore the addition of one more mouth made it difficult to bring up the newly born boy. The time in which Sukebatur was born stands out as the darkest and heaviest time in the history of the Mongol people. At this time the Mongol masses were exhausted by more than two hundred years of enslavement under the alien Manchu empire.

In addition to their foreign enslavers, the Manchus, and to being enslaved by their own yellow [clerical] and black [secular] feudal nobles, the common people were plundered by Chinese merchants, and were suffering a fate of gradual decay and weakening. The Manchu enslavers retaliated with unspeakable cruelty against the Mongol people who more than once sprang to arms to struggle for their freedom.

The condition of the masses at that time was insufferably burdensome [2]. In a petition from the jangghis of the sumuns [3] of one of the

---

[1] "White Gown" is a not uncommon name for a poor man whose winter outer garment of sheepskin, worn with the wool inside and the hide outside, is "white" because he cannot afford to have it faced with cloth.

[2] Mongol accounts of this period always refer, and quite justifiably, to economic decline and widespread impoverishment. Even so, however, it must be remembered that this decline was relative. Absolute destitution, starvation, and beggary never became so widespread in Mongolia as in China and other parts of Asia. One of the reasons for an especially intense anti-Chinese Mongol nationalism in Inner Mongolia, along the margin of the advance of Chinese colonization, was the fact that the replacement of the Mongol pastoral economy by Chinese farming brought with it a lower standard of living and not, as is often assumed, a higher standard.

[3] *Sumun:* Subdivision of a banner (ruled by an hereditary prince); *jangghi:* the

banners of Tsetsen Khan Aimak, presented to their feudal lord, it was stated that: "In the sumuns and bakhs [4] subject to you some of the taijis (nobles) and common people subject to tribute, when we say we are going to collect as tribute their only cow or colt, say that they will not part with them alive, but will slaughter them and eat the meat, though it be for only a few days; and so they behave in unseemly ways; and we, being forced to complete our collection of tribute, and so taking from some by stealth and from some by force, have practically exhausted the cattle, and so we exceed the law and strip men of their possessions and women of their ornaments, and have already caused the livelihood of the people to be completely destroyed. These nobles and commoners are caught in a trap of unendurable hunger and want. Father and son separate, each thinking of his own survival, and filial piety is lost. Husband and wife, forced to think [p. 11 of text] only of themselves, abandon their ties. In search of food they scatter in all directions in distress.... the people are emaciated to the point of death."

This kind of situation was not something confined to one banner of Tsetsen Khan Aimak. Without exception, all the banners of the four Aimaks of Khalkha were the same [5]. The petition cited above is proof that shows us clearly the condition to which the Mongol masses had been brought by the oppression and exploitation of their foreign and domestic despots.

Sukebatur's father, Damdin, was one of the poor commoners who, "having reached the point where hunger and want were unendurable, scattered in all directions in search of food."

Damdin was by origin a poor commoner of the banner of Yosutu

---

minor official (appointed, not hereditary) in charge of the administration of a sumun.

[4] Bakh: Subdivision of a sumun; smallest administrative unit.

[5] Until new territorial divisions were introduced in the 1920's in order to break up the old feudal structure, Outer Mongolia consisted of the lands of the Khalkha tribes plus two special territories. The Khalkhas comprised four Aimaks or tribal leagues, known as Gurban Khalkha, or The Four Khalkhas. From east to west these were: Tsetsen (written form, Sechin) Khan Aimak, Tushiyetu Khan Aimak, Sain Noyan Khan Aimak, Jasaktu Khan Aimak. Of these the two eastern Aimaks were referred to colloquially as jun hoyar, The Two Eastern, and the two western Aimaks as barun hoyar, The Two Western. Urga or Da Kurie stood in the territory of Tushiyetu Khan Aimak. In the extreme north of Sain Noyan Aimak was set aside the special territory of the Darkhad Shabi ("independently administered" disciples) whose taxes and feudal services were owed directly to the Urga Living Buddha. West of Jasaktu Khan Aimak was the Kobdo District in which most of the tribes were Western Mongols, not Khalkhas.

Beise, Dorjijab [6], in Tsetsen Khan Aimak (now Jibkhulangtushirakh sumun, in Jibkhulangtushirakh Aimak), who because he could no longer make a living in his home region some time in the 1890's took his wife Khangtu and, placing his two-year old son Dindub in a basket [7], walked barefoot to Bogda-in Kurie [Urga], accompanying a trading caravan.

The poverty-stricken couple got along by holing up temporarily in someone else's dwelling in the old trading city [now called Amogolangbatur] eight kilometers away from Urga [8]. Later, with great difficulty, they got possession of a battered felt tent.

Damdin was tall and rawboned of body, with a broad, pale face, but though his clothes were tattered and he was poor and destitute, he was in any man's eyes a warm personality, it is said. By nature he was stolid and dependable; he was a man of few words but is said to have been a very intelligent man who could even read a little. His only fault was that he was a little fond of drink. As for Sukebatur's mother, Khangtu was praised as a hospitable, sociable, talkative, voluble woman by her own contemporaries.

After they came to the city the difficult life of the impoverished husband and wife was not lightened or improved. Damdin went around every day doing whatever work he might run into to bring back five or ten cents [*p. 12 of text*] or a couple of grey khatags [9]; and often he met with days on which he did not even get a grey khatag. Khangtu worked at such things as stitching the soles of boots and sewing for people to get five or ten cents and to be a help to her husband in the struggle for life. Because there were plenty of poor men ready to do any kind of heavy work in the city, it often happened

---

[6] In this name Beise is one of the ranks of hereditary Mongol princes; Yosutu ("lawful," or "Law-abiding") is his title (as distinguished from his rank), and Dorjijab is the prince's personal name.

[7] The reference is to the kind of wicker basket, carried on the back, used by Mongols when they go out to gather dry animal dung for fuel.

[8] The old city called Urga by the Russians was called Bogda-in Kurie, "the Enclosure of the Holy One," or Da Kurie, "the Great Enclosure," by the Mongols, and is now called Ulan Batur. Eight kilometers distant was Maimai Ch'eng, the "Traders' City" of the Chinese, now called Amogolang Batur (Amogolangbagatur). The reference is to the quarter called Mai-mai-ch'eng ("Trading City") by the Chinese; this name is simplified to "Maima" in Mongol usage.

[9] At that time worn khatags were used as money [Original note]. The *khatag*, or scarf made of thin, waste silk was a traditional courtesy offering. The poorer qualities were of little value, and hence could be used as "small change." The prevailing color was a very pale blue, hence "grey" implies "soiled," "second-hand."

that Damdin and Khangtu did not get any kind of work and could not even buy a sheep's head for three or four cents, and not infrequently had to go to bed hungry [10].

Because his mother Khangtu was sewing things for people or hired for some kind of work and busy during the day, and unable simply to stay at home, little Sukebatur had to grow up with his two elder brothers making him weep and cry.

When Sukebatur was four or five years old the family moved from Maimai Khota [the Chinese trading city about five miles from Urga] to Kurie [Urga] where they set up their tent and settled on a vacant lot on a little hill to the east of the [Russian] Consul's residence.

After they came to Kurie Khangtu became pregnant and soon gave birth to a daughter and, because of the difficulty of bringing her up, gave her to a neighbor named Dawa to be adopted. Dawa was as poor and destitute as Damdin, but because he and his wife were people who longed for a child, they were delighted to adopt the girl. (The girl's name was Dolgar, and she is still living in the family that adopted her.)

Dawa's wife and Khangtu had first become acquainted when gathering argal [dry animal dung used for fuel] and bits of wood, and then Damdin and Dawa had become acquainted, and after that the two families became very friendly and intimate, and when they were out of things or in need they used to help each other.

Dawa's wife, now old, tells from memory that "I first met Khangtu out on the steppe, picking up argal and bits of wood, and beginning from that time our two families were as friendly as could be, and used to help each other. Damdin's place was on the empty lot on the Consul's hill. They had a poor dingy four-section [11] tent. In the tent, on each side, [p. 13 of text] were plank beds and two old chests, and nothing else whatever. Theirs was a really down-and-out camp. Khangtu had a pipe with no mouthpiece [12] that was never out of her

---

[10] Although the head of a sheep has a place of honor in certain feasts, it is ordinarily one of the cheapest kinds of food.

[11] This description refers to the dome-shaped Mongol felt tent. The "walls" of the tent consist of sections of wooden trellis, called *khana*. The circumference of a tent is indicated by the number of these sections. A four-khana tent is the smallest usual size.

[12] The Mongol or old-fashioned Chinese pipe consisted of a thimble-sized brass bowl, a long wooden stem, and a mouthpiece the material of which (jade, coral, porcelain, etc.) indicated the wealth of the owner. Very poor people smoked directly from the wooden stem, using no mouthpiece.

hand. If anyone came in, she would set out a cup of tea with no milk [13], and a sheep's head or shanks, singed in the fire, saying 'eat this now,' 'drink this now' — that's the kind of person she was. Damdin was a man of few words; he would nod his head now and then, and he was a fellow who was a little fond of drink...."

Sukebatur was six or seven years old at this time. He was a lively, clever and rather naughty child, it is said. He made wooden guns, and a bow with blunt arrows to shoot at sparrows, and was fond of playing the "walnut game" [14] with iron or stone marbles. Also together with his older brothers and the neighbors' children, he played at building houses and corrals with stones. Because of playing with children of the same age, belonging to the Russian employees on Consul's hill, he is said to have become able to talk a little Russian.

In the summer Sukebatur went about in trousers and shirt, with bare feet; in winter in a tanned sheepskin gown. He kept these clothes very clean and was a tidy boy. He liked to work, and when he was trying to make something would sit for several hours without moving. When he went around in town with his elder brother, Rangzan, he would take a bag with him, beg shavings from carpenters, and carry it home on his back, and in such ways was of great additional help to his father and mother, it is said.

Sukebatur wanted very much to read, and especially wanted to learn arithmetic [lit. "how to use the abacus"]. His father, recognizing this excellent disposition in his son, wanted to make him an educated and literate man, but at that time such a thing as education was not so easy a matter for a poor man. In the first place, there was no possibility for a poor man to study, and education was the kind of thing that only nobles and their sons took up. In the second place, a poor man could not give priority to study, but had to give priority to work, in order not to starve to death. At this time Sukebatur's mother had given birth to another child, a daughter.

---

[13] Unlike the Chinese, who do not add milk to their tea, the Mongols consider it an admission of great poverty not to be able to offer a guest tea with milk in it.

[14] In this game the walnuts are placed in front of a diagram (roughly resembling a hop-scotch diagram). The marble is thrown at the walnuts with an underhand, bowling motion, and the score is counted according to where the walnuts roll and come to rest. The marble that is thrown or bowled is called polo — undoubtedly the same word that is used of our game of polo. (The Daghor Mongols of Butkha play a game of "polo" on foot. The teams number five men each, and the ball must be driven between goal posts to score, as in mounted polo. In this game the ball is called *polo,* and the mallet is called *boiko* or *boyoko*.)

Sukebatur's father, Damdin, had been without a job for a long time, [*p. 14*] and his mother, Khangtu, having a small baby, was also unable to work, so that life became even more difficult. Sukebatur's two elder brothers, Dindub and Rangdsan, by running hither and thither for work, were able to bring in a few coppers, but that was not even enough to buy a sheep's head. Damdin, in order to lighten the burden of life, after thinking of everything possible, finally sent his most beloved son Sukebatur to take service with a man named Jamyang-donoi, a rich man of a certain banner, who managed the urte [post relay station] 15 at a place called Khui Mandal. Thus the 14-year-old Sukebatur rode the relay 16 between Burgaltai and Kurie [Urga], the capital. Getting cursed and beaten by the despotic officials and functionaries, the proud and exacting police of the Fifteen Families 17, and the brutal Chinese and Russian officials, he saw their despotic cruelty at first hand and from his inmost heart came to look on them as enemies. One day when he was riding relay with an official, the official's horse shied and reared and my lord the official fell off. The stupid official, suffering from pain and shame, turned his anger against the young post-rider. "You picked out this rotten horse for me," he scolded, coming toward him. When he was about to strike him, young Sukebatur said mockingly to the lordly official: "Go talk to the trees growing out of the ground, 18 or to the stallion for acting up;" and he mounted without further ado and galloped off beyond pursuit.

Sukebatur rode the relay for nearly a year, and then gave it up because the pay he got was so extremely small. Sukebatur's desire to get an education was not forgotten during this period, but became stronger than ever. Unceasingly Sukebatur begged his father and

----

15 Maintenance of these relay stations was considered one of the most onerous feudal obligations in Mongolia. The legal principle was that in each tribal territory certain families had to assume this duty in rotation, either providing the necessary horses and men themselves or hiring others to take their place. In later times this was a practice that led to many abuses.

16 The expression used indicates that he rode with travellers using the official post-relay, in order to bring back the horses when they had been used for one stage.

17 The police of Urga, charged with searching for stolen cattle, etc., were referred to as the Fifteen Families — probably because their duties derived from a feudal service originally confined to fifteen families. There were also a number of other detachments of police.

18 The idiomatic expression "the ground having grown full of trees" (here freely translated) implies that the horse had shied at a tree.

mother to let him learn to read; and as for Damdin, who saw that his son was clever and talented, he had long thought that he must send him to study with a teacher.

Now at that time, near their tent there was a man named Jamyang who was a Jaisang [minor official] of the Shabi Yamen [19] [office of the serfs of the Urga Living Buddha] who lived in the camp of Prince Dokdakho, [whose title was] Achitu Wang. Hearing it said that he gathered the children of the neighborhood together and taught them to read, Damdin determined to bring his son to this Jamyang as a pupil. [p. 15] One morning before Jamyang left for the Shabi Yamen, Damdin gave Sukebatur a khatak [ceremonial scarf] to hold, and took him with him to go to Jamyang's tent and begged him to accept him as a pupil.

Jamyang immediately consented, and beginning from that day Sukebatur sat along with the other students and he taught him the alphabet.

At this time Damdin was serving a term of duty [as a conscript] at the Amban's [20] Prison which was east of the bridge over the Salbi [River], and Sukebatur's home was moved to the yard of that prison. The heart-moving misery of the prisoners confined in this jail strongly drew the attention of the fifteen-year-old Sukebatur. These poor creatures had a frame [21] on their necks, handcuffs on their wrists, and shackles on their legs. They were cooped up in dark loneliness in cells into which neither sun nor air entered, suffering hunger, thirst, cold, and heat, the victims of lice, nits, dirt, and filth. With his own eyes, Sukebatur saw them crying and wailing, and when these prison-

---

[19] This was the office that administered all the "disciples" or serfs of the Urga Living Buddha, both those who lived in the special Darkhad Shabi District, referred to above, and those who, while living in various tribal districts, were withdrawn from the system of tribal taxes and feudal services. The taxes and services of Shabi were lighter than those of Mongols under tribal administration, and whenever a family was withdrawn from the tribe and included in the Shabi it added to the burdens of those who remained under the tribal system, thus causing great discontent.

[20] In Manchu the word *amban* means "great." The Ambans were Manchu officials stationed at various places in Outer and Inner Mongolia and Tibet, directly representing the Manchu emperor. They were supposed to have supervisory functions, but as they added nothing essential to the functions of administration, added greatly to the cost of government, and usually enriched themselves, they were much disliked.

[21] The wooden frame referred to as a "cangue" in eighteenth and nineteenth century books about China. It projected beyond the shoulders, thus preventing the victim from lying down.

ers were subjected to severe tortures and he heard the frightful sounds of their screaming and struggling, it seemed as if his heart would break. When Sukebatur asked his father, demanding to know what wrong these poor creatures could have done to be subjected to such bitter sufferings, Damdin told him the reason clearly. These pitiful creatures were all poor commoners like his father, Damdin. Some had not paid up the interest that they owed to the Chinese merchants of the prince to whom they were subject [22]. Some had been unable to keep up their many and heavy taxes and levies, and when these offenses had been discovered and reported, they were convicted and sentenced to suffer this kind of misery. Pitying their unbearable tortures, he inwardly came to curse the abominable nobles and officials.

Sukebatur wondered why his father and mother and other poor people, who were under the rule of these despots called nobles and officials, remained so meek and did not rebel against their wilful oppression.

Also, when he looked at the hardships of his father and mother and other poor people, they worked hard, but barely escaped dying of [p. 16] starvation, while the nobles and lamas and traders not only did no work but had gold to spend and tasty things to eat, and it was evident to him that their freedom to do as they pleased was grossly unfair and unjust. The impoverished subject commoners, with nothing to eat or wear and barely able to survive, were ordered to provide this and that in the form of services and requisitions, and had to pay over and over again their princes' debts to this or that merchant. When they were not being cursed in anger, they were being summoned to their princes' headquarters, shut up in jail, beaten or slapped until their bones were broken and their flesh was raw [23]. All this to the young and intelligent Sukebatur seemed intolerable. In China lived the Manchu Emperor. He had authority over all the

---

[22] An Aimak was subdivided into Banners ruled by hereditary princes. In each banner there was an office known as the *tamoga* or "seal" office through which the authority of the prince was exercised by stamping his seal on documents. When a Mongol had his debt to a Chinese merchant guaranteed by this office, the debt became a collective responsibility of the banner. In addition, Taiji or men of princely family who did not have the rule of a banner had a number of families assigned to them for their maintenance, known as *khamjilag*, literally "helpers" whose status was somewhere between that of retainers and serfs. A taiji could make requisitions from his khamjilag in order to pay his personal debts.

[23] The reference is to two forms of punishment: beating with a flat-ended wooden staff on the buttocks, and slapping the face with the sole of a shoe.

affairs of Mongolia. Below the Emperor from the Bogda Khagan [24] on down, the lamas and priests, nobles and officials were all in the grip of his hand. Whatever he might say, they said "Yes". Formerly the Mongols had hardly been like this. Only after they had become the slaves of the Manchus had they fallen to this condition. As the saying goes, the poor count their troubles by the score. The common people were oppressed by their own nobles and officials, and in addition by the Manchus and the Chinese. In the final period the Manchu and Chinese oppression and enslavement exceeded all bounds. Not only the masses but the nobles and officials also began to think of escaping from the grip of the Manchus. Hearing his father Damdin say that at the very least they must get out of the hands of the Manchus and Chinese, Sukebatur came to believe that the Emperor residing in China was indeed the greatest of all the crowd who were the plague of the masses.

Thus the circumstances of the time were such that they were observed and drastically reacted to by a naturally intelligent and bright youth, causing him to think and wonder about them. Days and nights went by as swift as arrows in flight, and before long two years had passed and Sukebatur was 17 years old.

[p. 17] Although his father Damdin was on official duty at the Amban's Prison, the pay he received was so little that sometimes for a payment of only two or three paper notes [rubles] from men who had been assigned to duty as guards at the Amban's Prison he would take their place to serve as a guard. Sometimes, when he let a prisoner whom he was guarding escape, he himself would have to serve several days in prison. Although Dindub [whose nickname was] "Roundhead" and Rangdsan [Sukebatur's two elder brothers] were able to work and add a little income, the family remained as poor and destitute as ever.

Sukebatur, during this period, was making great progress in learning Mongol writing and arithmetic with Jamyang Jaisang. During the day he helped his father and mother by gathering dry dung and shavings [for fuel], and carried water or ice [25], or ran errands and did

---

[24] The use of the term "Bogda Khagan" for the Urga Living Buddha, before the fall of the Manchu dynasty, is an anachronism. The commonest Mongol term for him at that time was "Aru Bogda," "The Holy One of the North." In Manchu times, it was the Manchu emperor who was referred to by the Mongols as "Bogda Khagan"; hence the passage of this term into Russian, in the form "Bogdykhan."

[25] In Mongolia it is common in winter to carry snow or ice to the camp instead of water.

odd jobs for others. He never had time to go over the morning's lessons, and in the evening, peering by the flickering light of a lamp filled with inferior oil, he would mumble his lessons; but his mother would say "The light costs money — stop, and go to sleep." Yet these conditions could not in the least deter Sukebatur in his high resolve to acquire an education.

Damdin wanted to do anything he could to help his son acquire an education, and when he had been drinking he would say: "Father and son have the same fate; we two are literate people." At this time, what was going on in the world was much easier for Sukebatur to understand than it had been two years before. In this respect his thinking had become much stronger and was changing. For instance, up to this time when Sukebatur could not understand something, he would merely wonder about it helplessly. Now he knew that what he wanted was to help the masses and to struggle against their enemies. One event of the winter of 1910 especially strengthened this conviction of his. The lamas of Kurie (Urga) had bought some wooden benches from a carpenter's shop, and this had led to a quarrel. Because a mob had rioted at the shop, the Manchu Administrative Resident [26] in Kurie, named Sangdowa, went to restore order, but he was stoned all over his face and eyes and fled, and the matter became one of life and death. Young Sukebatur realized that if the masses could unite everybody's strength in this way and put up a resistance, they could not only frighten their oppressors, but might even crush them. This period was a time when the movement of the masses against the Manchus had risen and spread throughout all Mongol territory, and the Mongol feudal class, which had lost its power and influence, decided that by going over to the side of the [p. 18] masses and making use of their strength it could become independent of the Manchus and Chinese and have everything its own way.

In 1911 the Chinese Revolution broke out [27]. The fact that the

---

[26] The Mongol term used here means "resident great official," and represents the Chinese term Pan-shih [Administrative, or Executive] Ta Ch'en [Minister]. On the next page, the Manchu term Amban is used.

[27] In both China and Mongolia the revolution against the Manchus broke out in 1911. The Chinese, following old custom, take 1912 as the first complete year of the new regime under the Republic. The Mongols, however, take 1911, the year in which the Revolution broke out, as the first year of their independence. Hence the Mongol republic is made to appear to be one year senior to the Chinese republic.

mighty masses of the Chinese people rose against their enslavers and pushed the Manchu Emperor off his throne and overthrew him, raised the movement for national libertation in Mongolia to a new level, bringing it closer to realization and fulfillment. The Mongol lamas and nobles, with Khangdadorji [28] and the Da Lama Tsering-chimed [29] in the lead, under the pretense of "prayers for the longevity" of the Bogda [Urga Living Buddha], held several meetings at Kurie after which they came to a group decision to separate from the Man-chus and to send their own delegates on a mission to Tsarist Russia to ask for aid.

Tsarist Russia had had a long-established policy of controlling Mongolia, and the request of the lamas and nobles coincided neatly with an opportunity to execute this policy, so the request was prompt-ly and willingly approved.

The Amban Sangdowa, learning of all these moves somewhat later, was very much alarmed, but though he tried to stop the efforts of the Mongols, it was in vain. Detachments of Russian troops were re-peatedly entering. The nobles and lamas who had gone to Russia to ask for aid secretly came to Kurie, the capital, and set up a Prime Ministry which was to become a temporary government, and by such means persistently went ahead with the business of establishing in-dependence of the Manchus.

On the 18th of November, 1911, the Prime Ministry, in the name of the Bogda, delivered to the Manchu Resident and civil and military officials a peremptory demand to withdraw. The note read ".... The Mongols have decided to establish a Mongol state with full powers, and to elevate the Jebtsundamba Hutukhtu to be its Emperor, to de-fend all their territory and themselves. Sangdowa and the civil and military officials must leave our frontiers within three days. If they resist, military force will be used to return them to their own country." The Amban Sangdowa, though disposed to refuse, knew that he did not have sufficient force, and bowed his head and submitted to the movement of the Mongol masses. Under the protection of the troops

---

[28] Khangdadorji was a prince of Tushiyetu Aimak, with the rank of Ch'in Wang.

[29] The rank or title of Da (the Chinese word for "great") Lama is applied to any lama who holds an important administrative position. Tseringchimed, who was personally known to the Dilowa Hutukhtu, was by origin a Shabi. He died about the year 1914 at the age of about 50. The Dilowa Hutukhtu considers him to have been a man of great ability, though personally corrupt and of bad repu-tation.

of the Russian Consul he was expelled [*p. 19*] and left for Peking, with the people of Kurie scattering sand and dust after him to speed him on his way with ridicule as a farewell. A month or more later, on the 13th of December the Jebtsundamba Hutukhtu was elevated to be sovereign of Mongolia and seated on the Khagan's throne with great and impressive ceremony.

"....in front of the great gate of the Main Yellow Palace..... countless numbers of people assembled, farther than the eye could reach. In the great gathering were nobles and officials with plumes and buttons [on their hats], ceremonial jackets and court robes. Hutukhtus and Hubilgans [Living Buddhas] and lamas waited in rows... before long the cannon sounded three times and immediately the Bogda, together with the White Tara [30] seated under a golden yellow standard in a handsome four-wheeled Russian carriage. Eight bodyguards conducted the carriage by damnur." [31] Preceding and following were such high lamas as the *donirs, soibons,* and *barabolokchis* [32] in ranks, and two or three nobles girt with swords in red scabbards led the way. A company of bodyguards marched in ranks with their weapons in ceremonial uniform. The Bogda, accompanied by the White Tara, entered their palace by the center gate [33].

"At the outer door of the palace, within and without the red chevaux-de-frise there were brick screen walls with green tiles, on which was inscribed in golden letters 'May all the world mutually rejoice in happiness,' [34] and behind them gathered the multitude of

---

[30] Respectful term used, at that time, for the nominally celibate Living Buddha's consort or concubine. The Taras (of several colors) are female lamaistic deities. The term Tara is Sanskrit. According to the Dilowa Hutukhtu, it was quite common under the older order for the consorts of great princes to be granted such *chol* or honorific titles. The full *chol* of the Living Buddha's consort was Erhe Chagan Tara, Powerful White Tara.

[31] A cart or carriage is drawn by *damnur* as follows: instead of having two shafts, the vehicle has a single tongue, at the end of which there is a cross-bar; instead of having harnessed horses, this bar is carried on the saddle-bows of mounted men. For this occasion the account of a German-eye-witness reads: "The Holy Emperor rode in a heavily gilded Russian mirror-glass coach, drawn by six white horses by *damnur*...." Note that this account gives six instead of eight *damnur* horses and riders; it also describes the Bogda's consort as riding in a separate coach. H. Consten, *Weideplätze der Mongolen,* Berlin, 1919–20, Vol. II, p. 47.

[32] All of these are the titles of high lama functionaries.

[33] To enter by the center gate was an imperial privilege.

[34] The Mongol text has here been conjecturally translated on the assumption that it renders the Chinese auspicious phrase *p'u t'ien t'ung ch'ing.*

ordinary lamas and laymen, who swarmed about just like a newly opened ants' nest. Out of the royal palace came Ponchoktsering, who had formerly served as a Mongol minister, bearing in his hands a very important document. In a loud voice he read 'A decree dispensing grace has been proclaimed.' His words could not be heard clearly, but were something like: 'The Bogda has been elevated to be the Sun-bright, Immortal [35] Holy Emperor, and the White Tara to be Mother of the Nation; the reign-style is to be called Elevated by All; the Great Kurie has been made the central capital of the nation, and a new Mongol nation has been created....'

"Only when night fell did the ceremonies end and the crowds disperse." Thus wrote, in detail, a man who saw with his own eyes the events of that day. (From Volume III of *Words of An Old Secretary*). [*p. 20*] The joyful news that Outer Mongolia had determined its own independence of the Manchus and China and had established a Mongol nation and state spread like a light across the country, from all the borders of the Khalkha land [the news] flew to all brethren of the Mongol nation who had been crushed and subjected to Chinese and Manchu oppression, awakening their nationalism and exciting their determination to arise and struggle.

On this day the hated Manchu rule fell. From then on the fact that the Mongol nation had no concern with them possessed the hearts of all classes of society in Khalkha with pride and joy. On this day Sukebatur could see that the faces of all men were bright and cheerful, their voices loud, and they were filled with pride; and to young Sukebatur it seemed wonderful to hear the boast of the masses that "The Manchu oppression is liquidated and the Mongol people has declared its independence."

---

[35] Lit: "ten thousand years of age."

CHAPTER II

SUKEBATUR THE SOLDIER

[*p. 21*]   In the second year of Elevated by All (1912), and in his 19th year, Sukebatur was conscripted into the Mongol national army. He spent his military service at a place called Khojirbulung ["Soda Patch"].

Before the revolution, the sons of the poor were conscripted for military service. The children of nobles and the rich were not accustomed to enter the army. Sometimes they gave bribes to evade military service and sometimes they hired poor young men of the common people as substitutes and drove them to serve in their places.

After becoming independent of the Manchus and China, the feudal classes created a state that was especially for themselves. Although nominally there was a standing army, they did not consider it important or give the slightest thought to strengthening it. They considered it more important to strengthen their own power and well-being than to strengthen the national army.

Mongol military leaders like Khatan Batur Maksurjab and Manglai Batur Damdinsurung [1] advocated a policy of modernizing the Mongol army to make it like the troops of all civilized countries and proposed this repeatedly to the responsible officials in power, but they paid no attention.

The Mongol army was divided into two sections, one for Kurie and one for the rural districts. The Kurie troops nominally received 9 taels a month per man but often they were not paid and in arrears for months, and most of their pay went into the pockets of the higher officers. The poor souls who had left house and home and all their belongings to serve in the national army as conscripts, experienced the sufferings of hunger and cold and were forced to resort to all kinds of expedients to keep themselves alive, wandering about streets

---

[1] He was a Solon (of a tribe related to the Manchus, not the Mongols), from Barga in northwestern Manchuria on the frontier of Mongolia. His title of honor, Manglai Batur, signifies Forehead or Forefront Hero. According to the Dilowa Hutukhtu, he died in prison under the regime of Hsü Shu-tseng, in 1920.

and courtyards, doing all kinds of hard work that barely kept them
alive, such as sawing firewood and sweeping up dung.

[*p. 22*] Conditions were just as hard for troops serving in the
country districts. Although nominally all their expenses were supposed to come from the aimak and hoshio to which they belonged,
they never even got the lean goat meat which was supposed to be
part of their pay.

The military preparation and training of that period were extremely
inferior. Only the detachment at Khojirbulung specially received combat and drill training from Russian instructors. The Tsarist Russian
instructors were tough and brutal. They oppressed and ill-treated the
Mongol troops, continuously cursing and beating them.

When the 19-year old Sukebatur joined the troops at Khojirbulung,
he was at first a cook and orderly, doing servile work. Before long,
however, his unusual military talent became apparent, and he was
admitted into the ranks of the regular troops. Among the troops at
Khojirbulung at the time there was no one who could keep up with
Sukebatur in military training, it is said, and the Russian instructors,
observing this young Mongol who was so conscientious and clever,
admired him greatly. At the end of a year, having learned his military
skill exceptionally well, Sukebatur was awarded a hat button [2] of the
fifth grade, and was commissioned as a platoon commander. Just at
that time Sukebatur became acquainted with Yangjima [3], the daughter of a poor commoner, in this town [of Khojirbulung], and they were
joined together for life. Comrade Yangjima had known Sukebatur
from the time he was an orderly at Khojirbulung, and although her
prosperous family and relations did all they could to separate and
estrange Yangjima because she had married the son of a poor man,
she paid no attention and went her own way with Sukebatur.

After Yangjima came to Sukebatur (who was then stationed with
the troops at Khojirbulung), and lived with him, they made their
living by her milking the cows of the Russian instructors and such
things as doing sewing for people.

Comrade Yangjima, having tasted with Sukebatur the sufferings of
poverty and hardship, [*p. 23*] became inseparable from him under the

---

[2] This was a survival of the custom under the Manchu dynasty of distinguishing
rank by the material and color of the button on the top of the hat.

[3] This name is from the Chinese *yang*, "shape, form, kind," diminutive *yang-
tze*, "kind, example, sample," which in Mongol has come to have the enhanced
meaning of "beautiful, elegant."

surveillance of reactionary officials, lamas, and foreign imperialists, and all during the hard years of the reactionary régime she kept up her Party work. In the 3rd year [1913] Sukebatur graduated from the machine gun training course and was promoted to be a non-commissioned officer in command of a machine gun detachment. Although he had become an officer he did not become cold and distant toward his soldier comrades. On the contrary, he was very intimate and close to the soldiers under him, and knowing better than anyone else their hardships and sufferings, he did everything he could to be of help to them.

Sukebatur openly opposed the despotic brutality of the Mongol officers and Russian instructors at Khojirbulung, and intervened to protect the soldiers under him, and the troops accordingly respected him and were devoted to him.

For this reason the Mongol officers and Russian instructors of the troops at Khojirbulung secretly detested Sukebatur.

Because the condition of the troops was so bad, their loyalty was undermined and from time to time there were mutinies, and Sukebatur was the leader of this resistance on the part of the troops. According to Comrade Migmar (who at that time was second in command of the machine gun detachment at Khojirbulung): "One day they gave us even worse meat than they usually did. The soldiers were very angry and said 'We won't eat such meat; give us some decent meat;' so they gave us no meat that day. 'What'll happen to-morrow?' the men wondered; but again they gave us none. They must have thought that they could starve us out. Our hunger and anger exceeded all bounds. The next day about noon two cartloads of meat reached Khojirbulung. We all went to have a look at the meat in the carts, and this bad meat was the same old stuff and there was even a stink coming out of it. I don't know how to describe the anger of the troops. They grabbed the deaf lama who had brought the meat, and beat him within an inch of his life. That day Sukebatur was the officer of the day. From some kerosene stored in a hole in the ground at that place he took out a can of kerosene and gave it to us. 'Burn up this lot of meat!' he ordered us. A thousand or more of us soldiers pulled that meat off the carts, threw it on the ground, spilled kerosene on it, and set it on fire.... Then a Mongol officer, Galsang, with the rank [p. 24] of Meiren, came and saw these goings on and was very angry. 'You are the ringleader in this,' he said, and summoned Sukebatur and was about to have him beaten when we, numbering nearly a thousand, said as one man, 'We will never let you beat Sukebatur.' Up against the united determination of all the clamoring soldiers, Galsang Meiren was frightened and lost his head. He bowed his head, stretched out his hands, and pleaded, saying: 'Soldiers, soldiers, please stop!' We troops paid no attention to that. Falling into ranks we declared 'We're going to hear which it is — whether we stay here with food or without food,' and started right off to march to the Ministry of Defense [in Urga]. Then Galsang Meiren, putting on his [official] hat with its plume and button, ran after us pleading desperately "From now on I'll see that you're given everything you need.' So we returned to our barracks. That evening we brought over fat meat from the storage cellar of the Russian troops, and had a fine meal."

Sukebatur, besides striving to protect the rights and interests of the troops, was active in promoting their training and proficiency, to which he devoted much effort and attention. For this reason the troops at Khojirbulung often addressed Sukebatur simply as "Teacher." [4]

Sukebatur, in the many years that he served in the army, frequently saw action on behalf of Mongolia, and unhesitantly exposed himself, earning great distinction.

In 1918, in the army commanded by the famous Khatan Batur Maksurjab, he received the command of the machine gun detachment, and when the Kharchin Duke Babojab [5] rebelled against Mongolia, Sukebatur behaved with conspicuous bravery in a battle on the Khalkha River, for which he was awarded the button of the fourth class by the Autonomous Mongol Government. In certain reactionary quarters an effort was made, out of jealousy, to deprive him of this honor. On this subject Maksurjab, Khatan Batur of the People, has written as follows: " . . . . in the rising on the eastern frontier, Comrade Sukebatur went as commander of the machine-gun detachment with the troops who had been sent from the capital to fight on the defensive against the superior numbers of Chahar [6] troops of the reactionary

---

[4] This form of address implies both more respect and more affection than addressing him by his military rank.

[5] This Inner Mongolian right-wing nationalist leader was not in fact a Kharchin but a Monggoljin Tumet, of a tribe closely associated with the Kharchins. See Owen Lattimore, *The Mongols of Manchuria*, New York, 1934, pages 125, 223.

[6] In Outer Mongolia, the term "Chahar" is frequently used not only of the Chahar Mongols but of any Mongols from Inner Mongolia. This usage undoubtedly arises from a mistaken folk etymology which confuses the name Chahar with the word *jakha*, "frontier." As a result of this confusion, the tribal name Chahar is frequently pronouced Jakhar. It is possible that the true explanation of the tribal name Chahar is to be sought in a term brought back by the Mongols

bandit leader Babojab, who, after completely laying waste and devastating many Banners of Khalkha Mongolia and Barga, had taken and occupied the city of Hailar. [p. 25] Proceeding to the frontier, he led and guided the troops under his command in repeated battles against the hostile bandits. He showed great devotion in personally taking part in all sentry, scouting and outpost duties. In particular, in the pursuit of more than a thousand Chahar troops led by the bandit commander Darjia, from Jangjun Obo Monastery in Barga territory southward to Khangdagaito, Comrade Sukebatur led a detachment in a detour, and by machine gun fire captured the bandit leader, the so-called Duke Sambuu and all his men, and brought back their arms and equipment. Then, when he was on the way back after pursuing and exterminating some bandits who had fled, the subordinate commander Bayar (Maksurjab's subordinate) who had gone out with a small detachment of his own, asserted his authority and seized [from Sukhebatur] all the material that he had captured from the bandits. He stamped his foot and reprimanded them, saying: 'These were men who were trying to surrender to you, and you simply terrorized them.' Comrade Sukebatur, being a man of discipline, though thus abused by the power and authority of an officer of those autocratic times, simply let the affair go by without saying anything, since he had carried out his original mission [the dispersal of the raiders]. (In the end) the high command learned what had happened, and the time came when the merit and devotion of men like Sukebatur who had done the hard fighting and captured the bandit leaders was recognized, praised, and encouraged...."

When Comrade Sukebatur left on this campaign his father-in-law had offered him a bowl of milk, saying, to speed him on his way with blessing:

Go and crush the enemy
Go and come back with the title of Darkhan; [7]

---

from their conquests in the Oxus region where there existed in pre-Mongol times a term *shakir* or *chakir,* meaning literally "servants," but used of "the personal guard of the rulers" (see W. Barthold, *Turkistan Down to the Mongol invasion,* London, 1928, p. 180). In Sinkiang there survived until recently a class of serfs known as *chakar* (Owen Lattimore and others, *Sinkiang and the Inner Asian Frontiers of China and Russia,* Boston, 1950, p. 164). The Chahar tribe may originally have been regarded as the "household" followers or troops of the last Mongol emperors ruling in China.

[7] An ancient Mongol title of honor, originally conferring immunity from taxes and feudal services.

Go and defeat the foe

Go and come back with glory and fame

And in fact Sukebatur did return from the battle of Khalkha River with the honorary title of Darkhan.

Thus Sukebatur, repeatedly going on active service for Mongolia, showed by his actions how devoted he was to motherland and people, by heroically fighting like this without thought for his life and person, like a true patriot. Not only was Comrade Sukebatur a hero himself, but he was one who could inspire heroism in others. [*p. 25*] At the battle of the Khalkha River a soldier named Setergei Tashi who was under Sukebatur's command was lacking in courage and afraid of combat, and just crouched down hiding himself behind a rock. Sukebatur saw this and said harsly: "Are you going to fight Babojab? Or are you going to die at my hand? Is this the way for a man and a soldier to behave? Let's go where the bullets are falling!" Because of this, Tashi from then on gave up his being afraid and hiding and became a very fine combat soldier, and Sukebatur used to praise him highly. Tashi repeatedly used to say, "Sukebatur made a brave man of me." Thus Sukebatur inspired with heroism not just one Tashi, but many and many a Tashi.

Sukebatur served in the army nine years in all, until the bandit Chinese imperialists revoked the autonomous regime of Mongolia and tried to disband the Mongol national forces. To see how the veteran soldiers who served under his command speak movingly of the days when Sukebatur was at Khojirbulung is to realize clearly that Sukebatur was indeed their beloved comrade and good teacher.

CHAPTER III

SUKEBATUR'S FIRST REVOLUTIONARY WORK

[*p. 27*]   The fact that in 1911 Khalkha Mongolia declared its independence from the Manchus and China [1] and by self-determination became an independent country must be regarded as a progressive step in the history of the Mongol nation; but it brought little benefit to the common people. Though on the one hand the oppression of the Manchus and Chinese was ended, yet oppression by the native feudal classes continued as before, and in addition exploitation by the Tsarist government of Russia was increased. The yellow (clerical) and black (secular) feudal classes not only took no measures whatever to improve the conditions of the masses, but followed a course that lost once more to foreign enslavers the gains of 1911. Tsarist Russia and China, after a long struggle over the plundering of Outer Mongolia, later came to an agreement to divide Mongolia and enslave the nation, and in November, 1913, they held a secret conference and in this treaty [2] agreed that Mongolia was a territory belonging to China, and that although Outer Mongolia had authority in its own internal affairs, it was to remain without any power whatever in questions connected with foreign affairs.

---

[1] The formula that independence was declared from the Manchus and from China echoes an important underlying "thesis" as it may be called of Mongol nationalism: namely that China had been conquered by the Manchus, while the Mongols had come under Manchu suzerainty, partly by conquest (in the case of Inner Mongolia), but mainly by treaties and alliances. Thus Mongolia was to be regarded as part of the Manchu empire, but not as a possession of China. When the Manchu empire fell, China and Mongolia, according to this argument, were each free to go its own way. The same argument applies to Tibetan nationalism.

[2] The reference is to the fact that on November 3, 1912, the Tsarist Government had signed an agreement with Mongolia, guaranteeing Mongol autonomy and protection against Chinese colonization, together with a protocol defining Russian rights of trade and investment. When the Russians had secured this agreement, they turned to negotiation with China and finally, on November 5, 1913, signed an agreement under which Russia recognized China's suzerainty over Outer Mongolia while China recognized Outer Mongolian autonomy, and promised not to send troops to Outer Mongolia and to abstain from colonization. See Gerard M. Friters, *Outer Mongolia and its International Position,* Baltimore and London, 1949, especially pages 71, 75.

The Russo-Chinese-Mongol tripartite treaty of 1915 was really an official confirmation of the 1913 Sino-Russian treaty, and had no other significance. Thus Outer Mongolia was unable to become a country with full [sovereign] powers and was restricted to merely autonomous powers. The condition of the masses became even worse than before.

Day by day the masses came increasingly to understand clearly the way in which they had been cheated by the clerical and secular feudal classes, and resistance to the unprincipled oppression by the domestic reactionaries began to develop strongly.

[p. 28 of text]   On 7 November 1917 the great news of the triumph of the Great October Socialist Revolution in Russia sounded like thunder over the plains of the Mongol homeland. The clerical and secular feudal classes suspected the October Revolution like the plague. They strove with all their might to prevent its influence from spreading into this country. They were on their guard lest the masses follow the example of the Russian masses and organize a rising to struggle against them.

Once Tsarist Russia had been overthrown by the October Revolution, the fact that its powerful influence on Mongolia had been terminated greatly encouraged its competitors. At this time China, striving to acquire full control of Outer Mongolia, began to execute with full force its policy of seizing control for itself, and in addition Asia's young imperialist nation Japan, which desired not less than China to rule Outer Mongolia, also began to strive madly for the rule of Mongolia. The clerical and secular feudal classes of Mongolia, fearing the great socialist revolution that had risen in Russia and the spreading struggle of the masses in their own country, hoped to conserve and retain their power and strength by leaning on some foreign country.

Beginning with the 8th year of autonomy (1918) the Chinese capitalists, taking advantage of this, secretly plotted with the feudal classes who held the power in Mongolia, through their own representative in Mongolia, as intermediary; and besides this the Japanese imperialists, making use of certain Inner Mongolian clerical and secular feudal elements, and of "White" Russians, tried for a while to get control of all the Mongol peoples by setting up a so-called "Pan-Mongol Government" at Dahuria Station [1]. Failing in this, they shifted to a new policy.

---

[3] On the Trans-Siberian railway, near the point where the Chinese Eastern Railway (now the Chinese-Changchun Railway) branches off to enter Chinese territory.

The Premier of Autonomous Mongolia, Badmadorji, and the Chinese envoy Ch'en Yi spent days and nights in continuous discussion, but though they were approaching an accord, and the decision had already been made on whether Mongolia was to submit to China or not, there remained some uncertainties on points of give and take.

[*p. 29 of text*] In return for Outer Mongolia's willingness to give up its own government, and to subordinate itself to China, Ch'en Yi drew up the draft of a treaty of sixty-four articles, promising to redouble the powers and privileges of the Bogda Khagan, the lamas and the aristocracy and gave it to Badmadorji, and Badmadorji in due course gave it to the Bogda, asking for his "advice."

The Bogda was fundamentally disposed to approve this treaty, and when the other important clerical and secular feudal personages understood that their own power and privileges would not decline, approval was granted without any great difficulties. Thus a strong link was created between the vacillating Mongol lamas and aristocracy and the Chinese imperialists. They quickly began to prepare the dirty work of overthrowing autonomy. "Bad news has wings," [4] and this vile treachery of the high lamas soon became known, and resulted in arousing the whole people to fear and anger. The masses, when they saw that the autonomous government, which in the eight years of its establishment had not made its benefits very apparent, was about to be terminated, were by no means in favor of relinquishing this limited power that they had enjoyed. The menace of the foreign imperialists reflected on every side of them, was growing in the consciousness of the people. Among the masses an urgent wonder, alarm, resentment, and fear broke out and spread beyond all bounds. Rumors buzzed and spread both in Kurie and the countryside, such as "They are inviting the Bogda to go to Peking," .... "a big army is on its way from the south." That such things could happen in his own country strongly drew the attention of Sukebatur, then serving as an officer stationed at Khojirbulung. When he was 17 years old Sukebatur had seen with his own eyes the great ceremonies of the establishment of an independent country, and the rejoicing of one and all when Mon-

---

[4] The proverb here translated by an equivalent proverb is, word for word, "bad news has a wooden *ulaa.*" The word *ulaa* refers to the post-relay corveé transportation system that provided relay mounts for official travellers and messengers. Thus the translation is "bad news rides a wooden steed." The "wooden steed" is, by allusion, the wooden staff carried by pilgrims, beggars, and other travellers on foot, to ward off the savage dogs that guard Mongol camps. Thus the reference is to such people as carriers of news and rumors.

golia escaped from subjection to the Manchus and Chinese and established itself as an independent country, and like everybody else he had joined in the carefree rejoicing. Yet the masses had not obtained their freedom. Their conditions of life had not improved in the slightest. That oppression and exploitation continued just the same as ever. Sukebatur, like the masses of the people, had seen with his own eyes and knew by personal experience, and, like the masses, he had come to see and to resent, that what was now being decided was an unjust arrangement. Nor was that all. He had long determined to liquidate and put an end to all this. Though he was already opposed to the way in which the clerical and secular feudal interests were covertly holding secret conversations with the Chinese envoy, [p. 30] when Sukebatur learned that their discussions were leading up to the liquidation of the autonomy which was essential to the people and to selling the whole of Mongolia into the power of China, his hostility to the Mongol clerical and secular feudal groups and to the foreign imperialists grew all the stronger.

Sukebatur did not stop at mere hostility. Having made a firm resolve to struggle against them, he set to work. He carried on propaganda among the troops to awaken them to the events of the time. Besides going around and summoning them to be ready to rise and struggle on behalf of the nation at the critical moment, he sought out and contacted friends who would join in and help with this work.

At this moment Badmadorji, the Premier, under pressure from Ch'en Yi, the Chinese envoy, summoned a meeting of the Upper and Lower Chambers, announced the question of the termination of autonomy and submission to China, and told them that they must discuss it. The aristocrats and lamas of the Upper Chamber, knowing that their own power and privileges would be left intact, never hesitated; but the Lower Chamber, because it included patriotic-minded petty civil and military officials, was throughly hesitant about whether to submit to China or whether the right thing was to offer resistance to China by force of arms; and it was so throughly undecided that Badmadorji, unable to do anything, adjourned both Chambers.

After that session Sukebatur well knew that there were men available whose view was that the nation should be defended, and determined that first and foremost he must make friends with them and gradually attract them to himself.

Before long Sukebatur, through Jamjang Jaisang, his former teacher, and others came to know the groups and elements who were deter-

mined to maintain the autonomous government intact, and by his influence he attracted and attached them to himself. Although Sukebatur well knew that their policy was merely to set up the Bogda as
Khagan again just as before, and to establish the autonomous government again just as before, he had determined to make use of their
power. The saving of our country from the danger of foreign imperialist conquest was the most urgent of all problems, and it had
become identical with the problem of uniting, in opposition to the
Chinese, not only the common people who were determined at all costs
not to endure Chinese oppression, [p. 31 of text] but whose who were
similarly minded among the lamas, aristocracy, and officials. Sukebatur
was firmly convinced that unless the foreign reactionaries were defeated and liquidated, it would be impossible to liquidate the domestic
reactionaries; and if both were not liquidated, it would be impossible
to lead the masses to freedom and happiness. First of all, he decided
to set as the first goal the struggle against the foreign reactionaries
who were by far the most formidable. If he could successfully strike
a blow against the foreign enemy, it would be easy to overthrow the
internal reactionaries and obtain freedom and independence for the
masses.

Although Sukebatur did not trust the strength of these "fellow-
travellers" of his in his revolutionary work, he did trust the strength
of the broad masses. Sukebatur was extremely close to the masses, and
worked on the principle of organizing and uniting those among them
who were foremost in intelligence and in loyalty and determination.

Day by day, as the prestige of the government deteriorated, the
murmuring and complaints of the masses steadily increased.

In the ninth year (1919) of the Mongol [Government], at the beginning of autumn, the Chinese general Hsü Shu-cheng, accompanied by
a large number of troops, entered Kurie the capital. As soon as he
got to Kurie he found fault with the envoy, Ch'en Yi, removed him
from office, and repudiated the sixty-four articles he had drafted.
Next, in secret consultation with Badmadorji, he approved and confirmed the policy of liquidating the Autonomous Government. Then,
by parading his troops, he impressed and frightened the officials who
controlled the Autonomous Government and put strong pressure on
them to submit immediately to China. Premier Badmadorji made a
strong report to the Bogda that there should not be a day's delay in
liquidating the Autonomous Government and submitting to China,
and obtained his approval of submitting to China. The Upper and

Lower Chambers, for the second time, were ordered to assemble. As soon as Badmadorji opened his mouth the Princes, Dukes, and lamas of the Upper Chamber gave their approval of submission to China, but the minor civil and military officials of the Lower Chamber showed a much stiffer resistance than before, advocating that on no account should there be submission to China, but on the contrary a forthright resistance.

[p. 32] Under the leadership of Sukebatur some of the men who sat in the Lower Chamber energetically organized the work of enlightening the other members of the Lower Chamber, with the result that they brought about a surge of resistance to the idea of surrendering to China. In spite of this strong resistance among members of the Lower Chamber, however, not only did all the aristocrats and lamas of the Upper Chamber ignore them, but Premier Badmadorji, declaring that "the minority cannot prevail over the majority and the weak cannot suppress the strong," censured and reproved the Lower Chamber, hustled it into adjournment, and immediately delivered to Hsü Shucheng the surrender document with the seals of the Five Ministries affixed [5].

On the second day of the middle month of winter (December) [6], at Kurie the capital, there was carried out the ceremony of liquidating the Autonomous Government and submitting to China. "On this day, there was not a man who carried his head high. All hung their heads. In shame and sorrow, inside and outside of Kurie, down to women and children and old men and women who made the circuit of Prayer (around the temple), all wept and prayed, and the tears falling profusely from their eyes, lamented and sighed." (Choibalsang, *Outline History of the Mongol Nationalist Revolution*, Vol. I, p. 75.)

Nine years before, Sukebatur had celebrated the escape of the masses from the hand of the Manchus and Chinese. Thinking of the way everyone had been happy then, and seeing the shame the people suffered now on falling into the power of China, his heart ached. "No matter what had happened, one task must be carried out", he decided. "The one task to which he referred was to increase the number of Party comrades, strengthen the Party, and step by step to intensify

---

[5] The Five Ministries were: Justice, War, Finance, Interior, and Foreign Affairs.

[6] The reference here is to the old lunar calendar, according to which the new year began usually in February. The year was divided into seasons of spring, summer, autumn, and winter, with a "beginning," "middle," and "end" month of each season.

the work of winning freedom and independence for the people."
(Choibalsang.)

After a few days the seals and documents of the Five Ministries
were seized, their files were impounded, and armed Ko Ming [Chi-
nese] troops were stationed at the gates of every ministry. The subordinate officials under all the Ministries were dismissed from service
and in addition to sending them all home an order was issued to
disband all the Mongol troops in Kurie and the rural districts.

In these heavy days Sukebatur did his share of work with decision
and devotion. He would not surrender Mongol arms into the hands
of the Chinese, and found ways to keep and hoard them. For this
purpose he created a feeling as hot as flame among the Mongol
officers at Khojirbulung, arousing their energy and drawing them
into his own activity. [p. 33 of text] Because of this the army officers
at Khojirbulung, led by Sukebatur, joined in signing their names to a
petition not to consent on any account to surrender Mongol arms to
the Chinese, and presented it to the headquarters of the troops under
their command. At first this move seemed likely to succeed, but later
it failed. Sukebatur purposely met with the soldiers who were being
dismissed and sent to their homes, telling them that the time would
soon come to rise and struggle on behalf of their own people against
the foreigners who had enslaved them, and warning them that at any
time they must be ready. Once the Mongol national army had been
demobilized, Sukebatur was also dismissed from service and came
to Kurie. He stayed at his wife's father's home. Because he had no
official employment it was very hard to make a living, but it is said
that his wife's father did a great deal to help and support him.

As this time there was a great outbreak of resentment among the
people blaming the clerical and lay feudal interests headed by Badmadorji for selling out the national interest, and both open and secret
opposition to them increased. The masses openly showed their dislike
of the imperialistic Chinese aggressors by such things as cutting down
and tearing up and throwing away Chinese flags and banners, and
singing songs that showed the spirit of resistance, such as:

> My lords the nobles in the striped maroon aprons [7]
> Did you look askance when you sold Urga?
> My lords in embroidered gowns,
> Did you look askance when you sold us out?

---

[7] The reference is to a special apron worn when riding to protect the skirts of
ceremonial gowns, and taken off after dismounting.

> For bags and bags of silver
> My lords you sold the Living Buddha himself.
> To fatten your accounts with silver
> My lords you sold the world.

[*p. 34 of text*] These became the favorite songs of men and women, old and young, in Kurie the capital.

General Hsü Shu-cheng, after liquidating the Autonomous Government, set up a Provisional Office for the Northwest Frontier and an Office of the Commission for the Improvement of Outer Mongolia [8]. Besides closely attaching to himself by [gifts of] goods and silver the lamas and nobles who had sold out the national interests, and turning them into sycophantic servants, he secretly organized and mobilized all the Chinese farmers and artisans in Mongolia and added them to his troops, and stationed them where they could control all the vital approaches and passes into Mongolia. He also established again in Kurie, the capital, the usurious Chinese banks, and allowed brothels to open up everywhere and do business. Day by day and more and more the Chinese troops and the civilian artisans and merchants got more haughty and brutal. They cursed and beat any Mongol who showed himself, raped women, and plundered property and money.

In this period Sukebatur prepared himself to devote all his attention and strength to the cause of the people, and by setting to work earnestly to find and recruit men whose views and determination were similar to his he found about twenty men and with them founded a secret group.

The members of Sukebatur's group had a common point of departure, but beyond that their aims were not identical. Thus members of Sukebatur's group like Dangjan [Danzan] [9], Dindub [10], Doksom [11],

---

[8] These are Mongol renderings of his Chinese titles.

[9] According to the Dilowa Hutukhtu, he came from Geling Gung Banner of Sain Noyan Aimak, and was also known as Dangjan Horal. He was of lowly origin, but an extremely able man.

[10] According to the Dilowa Hutukhtu, who knew him personally, he was also known as Undur Dindub — Tall Dindub. The Dilowa Hutukhtu believes that he was by origin a Shabi or serf of the Living Buddha. He was not an especially able man, but a great personal favorite of the Living Buddha.

[11] According to the Dilowa Hutukhtu, he came from Jun Dalai Wang Banner of Tsetsen Khan Aimak. He had held the high rank of Tushimel in the War Ministry. He was well educated. He was one of the delegation of seven who went to Russia with Sukebatur and Choibalsang to negotiate revolutionary support.

and Galsang [12] were former officials, and their main aim was to drive
the Ko Ming troops of the Chinese out of the Mongol homeland and
to revive the Autonomous Government.

One group, headed by Sukebatur, genuinely originated among the
popular faction, and were the children of bitterness and suffering,
and they were not satisfied to stop at driving out the Ko Ming Chinese, but were determined to cast all the clerical and secular feudal
class off the backs of the masses. Because of this there were not in-
frequent disagreements and conflicts among the members of the
group about their work and activities. The Bogda, his reputation dis-
graced by the way his power had been taken from him by the Chinese,
was using every possible means and policy to recover his power, and
was in touch with some of the members of Sukebatur's secret group.

[p. 35 of text]   In Sukebatur's group men like Doksom, Dangjan,
Dindub, and Jamyang [13], before joining with Sukebatur, had presented a secret letter to the Russian envoy in Kurie, asking for help
and protection, and the envoy, Orlov, though himself not knowing
what to do (some people say he was in contact with the Chinese),
was afraid of compromising himself, and said that it was necessary to
have the Bogda's seal attached to the petition, and on this excuse sent
these emissaries back. These official gentlemen, believing what the
envoy Orlov said, went to the Bogda's palace and begged him to have
his personal seal affixed to the petition for help from the Tsarist
government, but the Bogda sent them back, saying "the time has not
yet come."

Some of the feudal interests headed by the Bogda, although they
were in contact with Sukebatur's secret group, did not entirely trust
him and were seeking other support and backing. Some of them were
in favor of relying on America, others wanted to rely on Japan and
the "White" Russians.

Sukebatur however had no great confidence in the help of the
Bogda and the secular and clerical feudal interests. On the contrary,
he put his faith in the support and backing of the people. Because,
in the struggle against the Chinese enslavers, it was important to
know what was going on among them, Sukebatur was working as a
typesetter in the printing establishment set up by the Ko Ming (which

---

[12] This name is unknown to the Dilowa Hutukhtu.

[13] According to the Dilowa Hutukhtu he was a man of learning and good
reputation, who was later head of the Historical Cabinet.

had formerly been the printing office belonging to the Ministry of Foreign Affairs).

In this printing establishment there were three hand-machines and six employees. Their main business was printing and pasting up proclamations. Because Sukebatur did not concentrate on his work, and because he sometimes quarrelled with and opposed the Mongol supervisor and Chinese officials, Ko Ming quarters came to look on Sukebatur with suspicion.

[*p. 36 of text*] The suspicion in Ko Ming quarters was greatly increased by the fact that Party comrades now and then came to see Sukebatur. Knowing that the spies of the Ko Ming surrounded him on all sides, and closely followed every step and move he made, Sukebatur determined to leave the printing office. Several times he asked for leave of absence, on the excuse of trouble and difficulties at home. The Ko Ming officials became all the more hostile to him, and would on no account consent to give him leave, but finally they granted permission. Sukebatur had worked at the Chinese printing office nearly a year.

Then came 1920, the Mongol 10th year. Sukebatur's secret group was continuing its own revolutionary work. The work they were doing was broadened and intensified a great deal, but some members of this group turned against the policy of the majority and went over to the Ko Ming side, putting on two faces and acting as spies and informers, and the nobles and lamas who had become the hands and feet of the Ko Ming were trying by every possible device to track down, expose, and liquidate Sukebatur's secret group.

Thus it had become essential to make the work of this group much more tightly secret. The slightest mistake would make everything known to the Ko Ming and the secret spies it had planted.

Sukebatur assembled the members of his own group and declared: "We have heard the news of the revolution that has broken out in the country of Russia to the north of us. It is necessary to see whether they can help us Mongols in our present crisis or not, to find out whether there is a way to get there and get back".

Sukebatur had frequently heard that the Russian workers and peasants had not only arisen with arms in their hands and overthrown their own despotic Emperor and won their own freedom, but really had a policy of offering help to peoples who, like themselves, had revolted and were struggling for freedom, and this excited his curiosity. In Sukebatur's group it was agreed that in order to escape from the hands of the Chinese, the help of some foreign country was absolutely necessary to Mongolia; but that being so, on what country should they rely? About this there was great dispute within the group, and on this subject they had split into two factions. The first was the faction which was in favor of relying on some capitalistic country. [*p. 37 of text*] The second was the faction which was in favor of relying on the Soviet Government of the Russian workers and peasants. The first faction was the minority within the group, and included the official elements. The second faction, headed by Sukebatur, was the majority within the group and consisted of men who were genuinely on the side of the common people.

Sukebatur bluntly opposed those who said that they should rely on foreign capitalist countries, saying that "If Mongolia should rely on foreign capitalistic countries, we shall never be free from the fear of becoming the slaves of others. This would be to escape from the jaws of the wolf only to fall into the jaws of the tiger, as the saying goes. On the other hand, as for the Russian workers and peasants, they are struggling not merely in enmity against their own despotic reactionaries, but against the despotic reactionaries of the whole world, and have a generous policy of helping the weak and inferior peoples who are seeking to obtain their own freedom, and therefore they will certainly give our people genuine help. It is they who are our friends. The reason is that among poor people all are brothers", he would say. Sukebatur accordingly used to say that "The internal strength for the founding and prospering of our Mongol nation is the masses, and in foreign affairs our prop and stay is the Soviet nation". (Choibalsang.)

Because Sukebatur held firmly to this view and the majority of the members of his group adhered to it firmly and unwaveringly, this view before long prevailed decisively over other, unsuccessful views. After this meeting for consultation Sukebatur's idea was approved and it was decided to send a man specially to investigate and survey the situation in Russia, to the north. Thereupon Sukebatur decided to go north in person and began his preparations. This was in the spring of 1920. At this time Sukebatur's father Damdin had fallen very ill, and was nearing death.

When he was about to leave, Sukebatur sat near his sick father. Taking his father's head in his hands he explained: "For the sake of the people I have to go far away on important business, and so I must leave you here, my old father, because I cannot help it".

Hearing this Damdin admonished him: "There is no need to distress yourself about me, who am an old man and fallen upon sickness. My son, you have had the privilege of being born a human being [14]. [*p. 38 of text*]   Things being as they are, truly it is well that you have straightforwardly made up your mind not to spare life or body in the service of the people. I shall not be able to recover from this sickness, but come what may, if you are able to lead the people out of their sufferings then when I am dead the prayer of your old father's soul will be fulfilled".

When Sukebatur heard his father's noble words he set off for the north with a confident heart. Because this was a time when the Ko Ming spies were then swarming everywhere, he resorted to all kinds of devices to shield himself from their eyes and ears, and with great difficulties and privations barely succeeded in reaching the town of Kiakhta, but though he made every possible effort, he was unable to penetrate any further because the sharp watch being kept by the Ko Ming was too strict, and so he returned.

At this juncture his father had already died. Sukebatur, although he had not yet been able to penetrate into Russian territory, came back with a very clear understanding that the Russian workers and peasants had broken out in revolution in order to escape from oppression and exploitation, and that all the foreign capitalist countries, in order to crush the revolution of the Russian masses, had made a furious attack on them, but were being beaten and driven away.

---

[14] A reference to the doctrine of reincarnation.

CHAPTER IV

THE BEGINNING OF THE BUILDING OF THE PARTY

Following Sukebatur's return, after going north and failing to get through, he worked intensively to increase the membership of his own group and to broaden out its work and make it more active. He had known for quite a long time that there was a secret group on Consular Hill, headed by Choibalsang. Although he had wanted to unite with it, he moved slowly and with caution and secrecy, for fear of the Ko Ming spy system; and though Choibalsang's group on Consular Hill had long known that there was a secret group in Kurie headed by "Gwaming Batur" [1] Sukebatur, they also moved cautiously in everything concerned with it. The policy of the group on Consular Hill was the same as the policy of Sukebatur's group, and it had begun to operate at about the same time. Moreover this group had made the acquaintance of the Russian revolutionary worker comrades Kucherenko and Gembarzhevskii, who were in the capital, Kurie, and were working with their help and advice.

This Kucherenko was a mechanic in the Russian printing office which was then in Kurie. The other, Gembarzhevskii, was the leader of the Russian Bolsheviks who were working in Kurie.

Sukebatur, learning before long that Choibalsang's group was just like his own in its views and policy, became anxious to unite with it.

As for Choibalsang's group, they had decided to join with Sukebatur's group "because it was important to work with united minds and strength", and were waiting for a suitable occasion.

Soon the leaders of the two groups, Sukebatur and Choibalsang, met for the first time. They discussed with cordial agreement the

---

[1] Gwaming is from the Chinese *kua mien,* a kind of spaghetti. Thus "Gwaming Batur" means "Spaghetti Hero". It is said that Sukebatur earned this nickname, which is both derisory and affectionate, in a fight on the Inner Mongolian frontier when his detachment captured some men who were cooking spaghetti; while the others looked for booty and trophies, Sukebatur devoted himself to the spaghetti.

trend of the times. Comrade Choibalsang, recalling that period, has written: "At that time, when I first personally met Comrade Suke-batur, [p. 40 of text] and questioned him in discussion of the serious situation then prevailing, Comrade Sukebatur said significantly 'Mongolia, come what may, must not fall into the hands of the Chinese, and the people must live in freedom for ever. If every brave man's mind is firm and resolute, there is nothing we cannot do'.

"When Comrade Sukebatur said this to me in our first conversation, speaking coolly from the very first, as if there were no cause for caution or suspicion, it must have been because he trusted me.... this first meeting of ours and these direct and manly words spoken by Comrade Sukebatur are to this day clear in my mind".

"....Later when (I) introduced Sukebatur for the first time to the Communist comrades Gembarzhevskii and Kucherenko to make their acquaintance, (he) said joyfully 'We did not know where to go, but now with the great help of you comrades it has become certain that we shall now accomplish our task'" (Choibalsang.)

Without delay the two revolutionary groups began to work together at the beginning of the Mongol 10th year (1920) under the leadership of Sukebatur. When the two groups had begun to work together, their work gradually broadened out. In the work of this revolutionary group the Russian revolutionary Bolsheviks Gembar-zhevskii and Kucherenko were of great assistance. In particular, these two for the first time penetrated among the young Mongol revolutionaries with Marxism-Leninism, and transmitted to them the achievements and experience of the Socialist Great October Revolution that had arisen in Russia, and the revolutionary struggle of the Russian proletariat. Sukebatur deeply appreciated and understood from the experience of the Great October Socialist Revolution that without creating a revolutionary people's party to lead the rising struggle of the masses it would be impossible to defeat the external and internal enemy. For this reason Sukebatur and Choibalsang together worked energetically to broaden and strengthen their revolutionary group which was to become the beginning of the Mongol People's Revolutionary Party, and eventually to organize the Party.

[p. 41 of text] Thanks to the energy with which Sukebatur strove to strengthen the work of his own revolutionary group, the work of his group began to show results and to acquire the quality of general unity. The members of the revolutionary group worked among the people, doing such things as secretly acquainting them with the contemporary situation and pasting up revolutionary posters advocating struggle aginst the predatory Chinese imperialists in parts of Kurie, the capital, where people gathered or passed by. In addition to leading and directing these kinds of work, Sukebatur used to take part in the work himself.

"In the spring of 1920, at a joint meeting of some of the members of our two groups Sukebatur said, in expressing his ideas:

'It is necessary to post up propaganda posters to denounce and attack the imperialist bandit Hsü Shu-cheng and the lamas and nobles [who are on his side] and stirring and rousing the masses to oppose them'. With one voice we all approved [him]. In making and pasting up the propaganda posters Comrade Sukebatur personally took the lead and carried through the work, completing the pasting up without a single case of a man being caught or discovered. Not only that, but he even succeeded in posting up [one of these posters] at the gate of Military Headquarters, without the sentry's even noticing it. After putting out this propaganda, the ideas and behaviour of the masses, and the way they talked, changed a great deal — [these propaganda posters] helped our work a great deal". (Choibalsang.)

Sukebatur also discovered a way to kill Hsü Shu-cheng. One day a friend of his came to report that he had found out, by spying, that in a few days Hsü Shu-cheng would go to Kiakhta by motor car. He assigned two men out of his own group who were good shots and arranged to have them hold him up on the road and shoot him. However, on the day Hsü Shu-cheng was to start, some gunpowder buried at the old Manchu barracks of Hsüan Hua caught fire and exploded with a tremendous noise that echoed to heaven and earth. Black smoke hung all over Kurie, and Hsü Shu-cheng, saying this was a "bad omen", abandoned his journey to Kiakhta. Thus thanks to the powder explosion at Hsüan Hua barracks Hsü Shu-cheng was able to escape from the hands of Mongol revolutionaries.

[p. 42 of text]   About this time Sukebatur began to attract to his side some influential and powerful high lamas and nobles who had become dissatisfied and disillusioned under the Chinese imperialist aggressors, and drew up a policy that would benefit his own cause. This was important and correct. Because the behaviour and arrogance of the Chinese had become insupportable not only for the common people but for important lamas and nobles, these men had begun not only to resent and dislike the Chinese but to think of breaking away from them. Moreover the Bogda Gegen was the leader of these men who were angry because they were deprived of their power.

Sukebatur knew that it would be better to attract and make use of this faction, even temporarily, in the struggle against the Chinese enslavers, than to let them slip into the hands of other "factions", there to be made use of. Sukebatur's group operated very ably, with the result that some of the influential important nobles and lamas in this country (like the Jalhansa Hutukhtu [2] and Ponchokdorji [3], the Da Lama of Doingkur [4]) came to approve of the work of Sukebatur's revolutionary group (in order to profit by it) and frankly ceased to regard them as enemies. This undoubtedly added many potentials to the work of Sukebatur's revolutionary group.

Chinese oppression became more gross with every day that passed. The ordeal and suffering of the people "cried aloud to heaven". Although Hsü Shu-cheng resigned his appointment at this point and returned to China [5], the Chinese military commanders and people like the Chahar Duke Sambuu, who remained, became even more arbitrary and excessive in their behavior. The feudal group was thrown into confusion. Some of them urged sending representatives to the new government in Peking and putting into effect again the treaty of 64 articles recently drawn up by Ch'en Yi, and others sent their own representatives to Japan to beg for help and support, but nothing came of all this and so some of the secular and clerical feudal group headed by the Bogda were at their wits' end and in a panic.

Sukebatur and his comrade Choibalsang understood all these developments clearly, and ably conducted and directed the work of their own group in accordance with the trend of the times.

---

[2] The Jalhansa Hutukhtu was a cousin of the Dilowa Hutukhtu and was the highest ecclesiastical personage and the most outstanding statesman of Western Outer Mongolia. There are striking photographs of him in Consten (already cited), Plate 35, next to page 153, and Plate 46, next to page 184 (together with the Dilowa Hutukhtu). In earlier accounts, even Russian revolutionary writers refer to him as a liberal and progressive man. He died before the purges that separated liberals from leftists. He was in fact a wise reformer, a conservative who advocated conserving the old order in Mongolia by reforming both ecclesiastical and civil abuses. The name is also written Jalhangsa.

[3] According to the Dilowa Hutukhtu he was by origin a Shabi, an able man, a strong nationalist, and a great favorite of the Urga Living Buddha.

[4] Doingkur, the name of a Buddhist deity, was also the name of one of the administrative divisions of the Urga lamas under the Bogda.

[5] Hsü Shu-cheng was one of the leaders of the Anfu Clique in China which relied on Japan, and had come to Mongolia as an agent of the Japanese imperialists. This clique dominated China for short time, and when it collapsed the government organized by this clique was changed, and this was the reason why Hsü Shu-cheng was recalled. (Note in original text.)

At several meetings of the secret group Sukebatur reported that it had become important to take up urgently the question of establishing relations with "the Red Russians up north", and asking help and protection from them.

In the spring of 1920 Comrade Sorokovikov, the special delegate of the Far Eastern branch of the Comintern, came to Mongolia to acquaint himself with the circumstances of the Mongol Revolution, and met Sukebatur and his associates, and this event was an event that had most beneficial consequences for the work of Sukebatur's group. "From today the way has been opened to the fulfillment of our great task" was the way in which Comrade Sukebatur expressed his high evaluation of the benefits of this meeting.

Sukebatur planned, after this meeting with the Comintern delegata, to complete quickly a number of important tasks. These questions, too urgent to be delayed, were: to unite the two groups as a matter of high policy and lay the foundations of a party, to draft and confirm a code for the guidance of members, and to appoint delegates to go to Russia.

Although the two secret groups of Sukebatur and Choibalsang were on terms of mutual understanding in aims and ideology and had been working together, they had not yet been able to effect a complete amalgamation, with the result that there was not a single and centralized leadership, a single discipline, or a single plan of work. Thus it was extremely important and urgent to unite the two groups and create a heroic, devoted People's Revolutionary Party which would then lead the already spreading struggle of the masses.

Moreover in view of the lack of a party program, there had been cases in which members of the group had gone astray on points of theory, which made it important to provide party members with a program as a plan of action.

[p. 44 of text]   Under the leadership of Sukebatur, a joint meeting was called immediately of all the members of the two secret groups of Kurie and Consular Hill. This meeting confirmed the complete unification of the two groups and an "oath of loyalty" for members of the party, and decided that the party should have a seal and badges.

In view of this, this meeting was the historical meeting which laid the foundations of our Mongol People's Revolutionary Party and confirmed the party program. At this meeting another important question was discussed and decided, and this was the business of selecting some comrades as delegates, headed by Choibalsang, to go to the Soviet Government of Russia to ask for help. After this meeting Comrade Choibalsang and others took over the responsibility for completing the work of preparation for a prompt departure for Soviet Russia to ask for aid, and set off in haste.

After he had sent Comrade Choibalsang off to the north Sukebatur took charge of several important matters. He directed the activity of party members among the masses, the preparation of arms, the carrying out of such things as constant surveillance of the Chinese and the lamas and princes connected with them and, simultaneously, he directed all the work of improving the methods and technique of the party group and making it secret, and also the work of getting the Bogda's seal affixed to the document asking for help from Russia.

Although Sukebatur well knew that with or without the Bogda's seal Soviet Russia would give the help to the Mongol masses that was asked for, he considered it important to get the Bogda's seal affixed to the document requesting help. In the first place, in his own group there were certain official elements connected with the Bogda who wanted to get the clerical and secular feudal interests headed by the Bogda to take part in this matter of appealing for help, and their number was growing. Hoping to make their own reputations important later, when the undertaking had succeeded, they insisted that it was absolutely necessary to have the Bogda's seal affixed, and some of the Party members were in some ways taken in by their arguments, so that in the group itself this idea won out. In the second place, in the question of whether the Bogda's seal was or was not to be affixed to the document asking for help, the fact of the matter was that getting the Bogda and other influential feudal interests to take part in this affair involved no particular danger to the revolution; and moreover, it would make it possible to remove, [p. 45 of text] even though only temporarily, the hostile attitude toward the revolution of its internal enemies, and with no direct opposition from the domestic reactionaries to certain important activities of our own Party, and the possibility of going ahead against the opposition only of the Chinese and the minority faction which was collaborating with them could in some ways be considered as concretely a help to the work of the revolution at that time.

Sukebatur viewed it as important, for these fundamental reasons, to get the Bogda's seal affixed to the document asking for help from Soviet Russia. He gave a special directive to the members of his own group, and they did everything they could, but did not succeed, and the matter was deferred. The reason was that the Bogda and the lamas and nobles did not want, come what may, to ask for help from Soviet Russia. In the first place, there was no group which supported and upheld them — in other words no oppressive group — in Soviet Russia. In the second place, they were afraid that the Mongol masses, following the example of the Russian masses, might overthrow and liquidate them, and so were on their guard. The failure to complete this move, however, did not greatly worry Sukebatur. On the other hand, what did disturb his hopes was the fact that there was no report or news whatever from his representive Comrade Choibalsang, who had gone north. If Comrade Choibalsang had been unable to get through the frontier and had been discovered and captured by the Chinese, everything would leak out and there would be a serious state of affairs. Though Sukebatur sent out members of his group in all directions, and tried in every way to find out, there was no news whatever to be learned, and he was worried by the feeling that he must have been captured. In the meantime Choibalsang had sent two code telegrams, one after the other, to Sukebatur. The second wire read: "Business is good. The friends who were to follow have not come. Why are they delaying. I suggest that it is important that they should bring the Bogda's present with them".

[*p. 46 of text*]   ("Business is good" meant that the planned undertaking could be carried through, and "the Bogda's present" meant "bring the document with the Bogda's seal".)

From the day he received this wire Sukebatur worked energetically to speed up the business of getting the Bogda's seal affixed to the document asking for help, and to prepare for selecting additional delegates and sending them to Soviet Russia.

CHAPTER V

THE JOURNEY NORTH

The water of the Tola River runs laughing in the summer sun. From a fireplace on the ground outside a little tent, the side-felts of which have been rolled up [to make it cooler], blue smoke is rising in puffs. In the pot, fat mutton is stewing. By the fire a young layman occasionally stirs the meat in the pot or adds dry branches, leaves, and twigs to the fire. His handsome young face is beaded with sweat in the heat of the sun.

He keeps a close watch all around, as if he were on the alert for something.... Inside, the little tent is crowded with men. They are drinking fermented mare's milk and talking together about something. Though from their behavior you would think they were idle men with nothing to do but drink good fermented mare's milk, eat fat meat, and disport themselves in the clear water of the river, they seem to be conferring about something secret. At the back of the tent sits a tall, pale young layman, wearing only cloth trousers and shirt. In a low voice he is saying something. The others, whether old or young, laymen or lamas, are listening with great attention to his words.

The young layman who was boiling the meat in the cauldron outside took the meat out. Suddenly his expression changed. He ran into the tent. "The Ko Mings are coming", he cried, and went out again. Soon ten or more mounted Ko Mings arrived at a gallop, and dismounted outside the tent. The Ko Ming who seemed to be the leader took two soldiers with him, went straight into the tent, and after he had jabbered some words a Ko Ming soldier asked in bad Mongol, "What are you all doing, so many of you?"

Hearing this, the pale young layman smiled, showing his even white teeth. "We are here for a summer rest, and to amuse ourselves and cool off in the water," he said, and added, "Honored friend, eat some meat and drink some mare's milk, and enjoy yourself with us", and he took a gourd that was brimful of fermented mare's milk in front of him, [p. 48 of text] and offered it. The Ko Ming commander took a little taste, smiled faintly, and went out, without saying a word.

The young layman who was sitting by the kettle of meat smiled contemptuously as he watched the Ko Mings ride off pell-mell.

The men inside the tent stopped drinking mare's milk and began listening attentively again to the words of the pale-complexioned young man.

This pale young layman was Sukebatur, and he had specially set up a tent by the river in order to be concealed from the eyes and ears of everybody. The appearance of pasturing horses and cattle and bathing in the water was in order to hold a meeting of a party group. At this meeting Comrade Sukebatur brought up the proposal that it was necessary to choose additional delegates to send to Soviet Russia, and that it had become important to get the Bogda's seal quickly affixed to the request for aid.

Thereupon the members of the meeting of the party group selected five men, headed by Sukebatur, as delegates to go to Soviet Russia, and assigned to their member Jamyang the responsibility for quickly getting the Bogda's seal affixed.

From that day Sukebatur began to prepare to go northward. In the interval the Jaisang Jamyang barely succeeded, by running to and fro and trying everything, and by great effort, in carrying out successfully his assignment of getting the Bogda's seal affixed to the document asking for aid.

The clerical and secular feudal interests headed by the Bogda did not really want to ask for help from Soviet Russia, but to seek help from America or Japan. But because the feudal interests were not convinced of help from America and Japan, they reached the conclusion to adopt a parallel policy of seeking aid from Soviet Russia. On this point Jamyang said to his comrades of the party group:

"Simultaneously with affixing the seal for us, the seal was attached to two documents asking for foreign help; one was a document seeking aid from America, and this he gave to Jalhangsa Hutukhtu. The other was a document asking for aid from Japan, and this he gave to Sitar Chechen. They considered the business of stamping the seal on both these requests for aid very important, but hesitated when it came to stamping the seal on our document. Only after making us wait a good long time did they stamp the seal and give it to us. They seemed not to be willing to consider [our document] very necessary".

Once they had the document stamped with the Bogda's seal ready, and being under suspicion on the part of the Chinese, it became important for Sukebatur and his companions to start.

Accordingly on the 15th of July of the 10th year (1920) Sukebatur and the others left Kurie one after the other, heading for the north. Not only did they keep apart from each other and travel by roundabout ways, but as a deception they said to anyone they met that they were travelling on trading business. Because the few dollars collected and given to them by party members for their needs along the road were far from sufficient, Sukebatur sold his own tent to someone to get money to take along for use on the journey.

Comrade Yangjima and her child were left behind in the gatehouse of a residence. Sukebatur and the others travelled for six overnight stops till they halted at the tent of an old acquaintance named Ponchok, who lived in the district south of the Jiruge [Yeru] river. There they stayed two nights to rest themselves and their horses. This Ponchok (a fine herdsman of the people of Gentei Aimak) had formerly first come to know Sukebatur at Khojirbulung. They got on together very well, and he had heard indirectly from others of the revolutionary work in which he [Sukebatur] was engaged. He [Ponchok] had very much wanted to go to see him [Sukebatur] but he had been unable to do so on account of the great distance, so when the man he had wanted to see turned up, he was very glad.

During the two days and nights he spent at Ponchok's tent Sukebatur did not tell him a single thing about his mission; but Ponchok, with cheerful faith, saying he would do his best for the cause, gave his firm oath and was helpful to Sukebatur and the others in getting across the frontier. From there Sukebatur and his companions, travelling with Ponchok, stopped at a Buryat camp known to Ponchok which was at a place called Buritutu, near to the east of Old Kiakhta, and here they had a great many discussions and consultations on how to get across the frontier. They decided to split into two parties, and to pass as ordinary merchants.

[p. 50 of text] When Sukebatur, taking Ponchok with him, got to the Mongol border, the Ko Ming troops immediately halted and rounded up the two of them and severely examined them as to the business on which they were crossing the frontier. "My name is Temur, and with this man I am crossing the frontier in order to buy a four-wheeled cart from the Russian [town of] Degetu Sibegen [= Upper Gate Verkhneudinsk]," said Sukebatur imperturbably. Some of the Ko Mings stripped them both of all their clothes and searched them. Others jabbed at Sukebatur's naked body with their bayonets, giving him a third degree questioning on why he was really crossing the frontier.

Sukebatur, standing naked in the midst of the Ko Mings, insisted that he was just going to buy a four-wheeled cart. Ponchok, watching, thought, "Now is the time we are going to die. The Ko Mings are going to see the document around Sukebatur's neck", he thought to himself in prayerful fear, because Sukebatur had wrapped the document with the Bogda's seal in a khadag (scarf) and hung it around his neck like an amulet. The Ko Mings, after behaving extremely cruelly and arrogantly for a while, finally let them through, and Sukebatur and Ponchok hurriedly went on to the Russian town of Troitskosavsk, where they stayed at the Commandant's headquarters. Ponchok then went back and brought across the frontier the two men who had been left on the other side.

When Ponchok went back, Sukebatur assigned to him the mission of moving nearer to Kiakhta, entering the service of the Ko Ming if he could, maintaining liaison between the delegates who had gone to Russia and the party comrades left behind in Mongolia, and gathering intelligence on the affairs of the Ko Ming. Ponchok carried out this assignment very well.

After that Sukebatur, with the other delegates, met the Consul in that town, and in due course went to Ude Town [= Udinsk]. They were escorted by the Comintern delegate, Comrade Sorokovikov. Having met old comrades and triumphantly talked over what had happened, they got on a steamer and continued their journey together.

Soon they got to Verkhneudinsk, and got off at the place where the steamer stopped, where two men had come to meet Sukebatur and the others. One of these was Comrade Choibalsang, and not having met for a long time the two friends were overjoyed at this meeting.

[p. 51 of text]   From there they all went to Verkhneudinsk town, where they stayed at an inn and "planned how to accomplish their final aims, sometimes rejoicing and laughing and sometimes anxiously wondering". (Choibalsang.)

A few days after they had got to Verkhneudinsk, Sukebatur and his companions met secretly and talked with authorities of the Far Eastern Republic, and then, to go to Ergeu [= Irkutsk], Sukebatur and his companions travelled in a special train provided for them and reached Irkutsk.

After a few days Sukebatur and his companions met in this city (at noon on the 19th of August) with Comrade Kupun, the head of the department dealing with Far Eastern affairs.

The Mongol party delegates clearly stated the business on which they had come, and gave to Kupun the document with the Bogda's seal asking for aid. On this point Comrade Choibalsang has written: "In the autumn of 1920, when our delegates went to Irkutsk and met with the delegate of the Far Eastern bureau of the Comintern, Comrade Kupun [1], and talked with him, Kupun said: 'You delegates have brought a document with the Bogda's seal.

'It is something that will be in the record for you in the future. But in this matter it is important that you delegates should submit a document which makes clear your own desires and carries the seal of your own party.' In this there was no small disagreement among us.

"Some of us said that while we were in Kurie we had suggested drafting a document with the Party's seal, but had decided that it was not yet time; now it was important to draft such a sealed document. Some said that since we already had the document with the Bogda's seal, there was no need for a document with the Party's seal. There was a dispute between these two diverging views. For a good half day the two groups would not speak to each other, or even walk on the street together.... Sukebatur would not approve what Dangjan and Doksom said, that there was no need for a document other than the document with the Bogda's seal, but said that, on the contrary, since it had become imperatively important to have a document with the Party's seal, it would be all right to make a draft and give it [to the Russians]". [*p. 52 of text*] (Choibalsang's article, "Sukebatur was truly our beloved leader".)

The contents of this declaration, written through the direct urging of Sukebatur, proposed in a remarkable way a policy for the Mongol People's Revolutionary Party for the immediate present and the future. [It read:]

"....We men of the People's Party, having received great help from Russia in the name of the People's Party, and having formally concluded friendship with the elected [Russian] officials, after having made use of their military strength to obtain autonomy will elevate the Hutukhtu (Bogda) to be a sovereign with limited power. Relying on their [the Russians'] power, we shall use the method of destroying most of the hereditary aristocracy. When we have entirely escaped from the hands of others, simultaneously with obtaining the power

---

[1] This name is given according to the Mongol transcription, which may not agree with the Russian orthography. I have not come across the original in any Russian text.

in our own country, we shall follow with all our strength the road of giving to one and all a culture which will include foreign civilization and especially the rights of the people. When we have made a little improvement, the moment we see that [the people] begin to understand within one or two years, we shall renew the revolution, and if we liquidate the few who hold power we can complete our task with little internal destruction and without foreign criticism, and the way of mutual aid and eternal friendship of the Russian and Mongol People's Parties will be at hand...."

After this document [had been completed] Comrade Sukebatur discussed it with his comrade delegates, in order to decide on dividing up the work they were to do, and accordingly some delegates went to Omsk, the capital of the province of Siberia, on the mission to get aid, while other delegates were sent back to Kurie, the capital, to lead the party work.

It was decided that Sukebatur himself, together with Choibalsang, should stay at Irkutsk, in order to add to their military knowledge and training and to undertake the general leadership of the work.

Without delay, according to this decision some of the delegates set off to Omsk while others started on their return to Kurie.

Sukebatur and Choibalsang both remained in Irkutsk and entered the officers' school of the Red Army and began to study. Sukebatur, being a soldier to begin with, soon learned everything that was taught. [p. 53 of text] "In the end he was even teaching a class of Russian troops in drill and command". (Choibalsang.)

Sukebatur and Choibalsang studied hard together as special students at the military school, and worked industriously together at studying the orders of command. Because Sukebatur knew little Russian, Comrade Choibalsang helped him as much as he could by explaining everything that was taught, and the two helped each other a great deal in their studies. After 10 days or so Sukebatur became very ill with a cough and fever and had to stay in bed, and Choibalsang nursed him. Because of this a special instructor of the scout section of the Fifth Army came to their quarters to teach them the course. Before long, Sukebatur recovered. In the meantime a telegram reached Sukebatur and Choibalsang from the delegates who had gone to Omsk, saying that they had been sent on to Moscow and were discussing their main business. In addition, repeated telegrams of alarm came from the party comrades in Kurie, saying that the situation in Kurie was getting much worse, that the majority of the Party members had been arrested, and that it had become much more dangerous to carry on their work.

Sukebatur and Choibalsang, "When they heard all this, were both disturbed at heart, and wondered what to do. Helplessly, they talked over every day the situation in Kurie and the affairs of their comrades who had gone to Moscow as they waited and hoped for whatever news might come from either direction", but almost a month went by with no news whatever from either direction.

The young Mongol revolutionaries fully recognized that the troops of the White butcher, like the reactionary Ko Ming Chinese, were the implacable enemies of the Mongols, and considered it very important to struggle against them. [p. 54 of text] Therefore on the second of November 1920 in a statement and petition to the Comintern Far Eastern section and the authorities of the Soviet Fifth Army, Sukebatur and Choibalsang said: "Fighting has begun in Mongolia between the White troops and the Chinese. In view of this we delegates, after considering the matter, are convinced that apart from the fact that this is the final disaster for our country, Mongolia, and adversely affecting the Soviet government, we Mongols absolutely cannot think of using the homeless, fleeing and dispersed troops of the reactionary Semenov to achieve the great purpose of our country [i.e. independence]. As we Mongols have already come to ask for aid and protection from the Soviet government.... we urgently beg that you immediately send troops to Mongol territory to clear out the reactionary troops of Semenov and to deliver us from the hands of the Chinese.

".... If your Red Army should enter Mongol territory, we Mongols will mobilize troops and will certainly render mutual help. In this connection we submit this note, asking to know whether you can or cannot promptly send to the frontier supplies for our use, especially supplies in the form of weapons".

Then, after a few days, about the 10th of November, there came a telegram from the delegates who had gone to Moscow; "The main object of our hopes has been completely accomplished. Everything goes well. We are returning immediately".

Sukebatur and Choibalsang were overjoyed. After a few days the delegates who had gone to Moscow reached Irkutsk.

The great Soviet nation and its leaders, Lenin and Stalin, and all the Soviet toiling masses determined to extend warm support to the struggle for freedom of the Mongol masses. The Mongol delegates having already completed the mission on which they had left, it was now necessary for them to return immediately to their homeland to direct and organize the struggle of the people.

[*p. 55 in text*] In this connection, it was first and foremost necessary to organize the People's Revolutionary Party as the director, organizer, and guide of the people. The revolutionary struggle that was bursting into flame and spreading everywhere naturally required the immediate organization of a People's Revolutionary Party.

It had become necessary for Sukebatur to return to the Mongol homeland to begin and direct this great task, but it was not yet possible to penetrate directly into Mongol territory and set to work. The reason was not only that the plundering Chinese conquerors were making every effort to find and catch him and Comrade Choibalsang, but that the majority of the responsible members of the Party had already been caught by the Chinese and put in prison.

The remaining members of the Party, not to mention being followed by Chinese spies and unable to carry on party work, had no way even to get to their own homes, and were wandering hither and thither in concealment.

Since it had already become impossible to penetrate into Mongol territory, it was necessary to work on the far side of the frontier.

Therefore Sukebatur determined to move to the Verkhneudinsk section of Kiakhta, because it would be closer and more convenient for revolutionary work in the Mongol homeland. Accordingly Sukebatur and Choibalsang left Irkutsk on the 19th of November and on the 22nd reached Verkhneudinsk.

CHAPTER VI

THE DIRECTION AND ORGANIZATION OF THE ARMED RISING OF THE WORKERS AND PEOPLE AGAINST THE EXTERNAL AND INTERNAL ENSLAVERS

Beginning from the day he reached Verkhneudinsk, Sukebatur busied himself with the work of preparing the calling of the first plenary Assembly of the Mongol People's Revolutionary Party. The problem was, in calling the first plenary Assembly of the Party, that it was important to direct and organize it on the basis of realities, and to determine the leading propositions that were to be laid before it. He began to make connections with whatever Party members were in Mongolia, and to direct them by letters, and he directed the work of secretly disseminating in Mongolia the propaganda leaflets calling for a struggle against the foreign conquerors which he had printed after setting up in Irkutsk a Party printing office.

He also energetically carried on the work of recruiting partisan troops. Under the orders of Sukebatur, Comrade Choibalsang secretly entered Mongol territory and, travelling through the Banners of Somiya Beise and Prince Khadan Batur, carried out the important work of recruiting partisan troops, and Sukebatur himself, crossing the frontier, energetically directed the work of recruiting partisan troops at the East Outpost [1] of Kiakhta and other places.

So the year 1921 began. A new danger confronted our country and people during February 1921, and this was the turn of events when the White bandits headed by Baron Ungern in their second battle dispersed and drove off the Chinese and took possession of Kurie.

Baron Ungern was a tool of the Japanese imperialists, and a trusted friend of the White bandit Ataman Semenov; and as soon as Semenov

---

[1] The East Outpost and West Outpost were Mongol frontier stations where taxes were collected on cattle being driven into Siberia. — D.

had been beaten back by the Red Army, he had nowhere to turn
and entered Mongolia with the support of the Japanese imperialists.

[*p. 57 of text*]   The Japanese imperialists, who had several times
endeavored to carry out their intention to make themselves the
masters of Mongolia and, not having succeeded, were now at the end
of their resources, determined to make use of the mad Baron Ungern
for this purpose, and by aiding and supporting him were trying to
get into Mongolia. But Baron Ungern, when he had got Mongolia
out of the hands of the Chinese, arrogantly promoted himself as a
man of glory and soon seized all power in Mongolia. The clerical
and secular feudal group, who had at first praised Baron Ungern as
a man to whom they were grateful and who was useful to them, and
who had even honored him as the reincarnation of the Fifth Bogda [2],
gradually recognized that he was becoming a dangerous factor and
were trembling with fear of him.

Baron Ungern, beginning from the day he came to Kurie, conducted
himself in an unspeakably savage and ferocious way, robbing, raping
and hanging the people. The people, falling from the hands of the
Ko Mings into the hands of Baron Ungern, considered that it was like
"escaping from the maw of the tiger and falling into the jaws of the
wolf."

Though Baron Ungern was in control of Kurie, this was far from
being the same thing as dispersing the Chinese troops and driving
them entirely out of Mongolia. Here and there in Mongol territory,
and especially in the north, quite a few thousand Chinese troops
remained as before. In addition the Chinese, knocked about by the
Whites, worked off on the Mongol people the terror they felt, oppressing and tormenting them like madmen. The oppression of the foreign
enslavers was rousing the anger and resentment of the masses, and
bringing them to the point of rising to struggle.

The work of organizing the People's Revolutionary Party to guide
and lead this expanding struggle of the masses and to bring it to
victory had become all the more forcefully imperative. In the meantime the fundamental work of preparation for getting under way the
meeting of the first general assembly of the Party had been carried
out, so it was agreed that the time had come to summon the meeting
of the general assembly immediately.

---

[2] The Urga Buddha was the Eighth incarnation; the Fifth was regarded as the
greatest of the line. — D.

Accordingly on the first of March 1921, in Verkhneudinsk [3] under the direct leadership of Sukebatur, the first general assembly of the Mongol People's Revolutionary Party was held. At the same time that it clearly set out and affirmed the objectives to be accomplished by the People's Revolutionary Party, this assembly, besides confirming the Party program (the ten aims) it was hoped to attain, and the practical organization of the party [p. 58 of text], and choosing the Central Committee, passed resolutions for organizing a temporary People's Revolutionary Government and a People's Revolutionary Army. This assembly also proclaimed to the Mongol people the organization of the People's Revolutionary Party. "Recognizing the signs that the time has come for us, the whole Mongol people, to achieve our own independence and freedom, we should act with united strength in the struggle to achieve our own independence and freedom" was the wording of this summons. Thus the Mongol People's Revolutionary Party was organized just at the time when the people's struggle against the foreign enslavers was expanding and spreading. The great leader who first carried out the primary and fundamental organizing of the party which led it was Comrade Sukebatur.

Soon after, on the 13th of March, 1921, by resolution of the Central Committee of the Mongol People's Revolutionary Party, an assembly was held of delegates of the Partisan Army and all Banners and Shabi [districts], and a Mongol People's Temporary Revolutionary Government was organized.

This assembly gave a clear directive to be carried out by the authority of the People's Temporary Government: "The fundamental objectives of the masses of the people, acting with arms in their hands, are (1) to free their own land from the cruel rule of the Chinese and to cleanse it of others who have invaded it with the support of a foreign country;

"(2) to set up a government capable of truly protecting the interests and well-being of the masses and capable of promoting the development of culture in our own country. Accordingly the responsibility entrusted to the Temporary Government is to deliver the territory under our sovereignty from the power and rule of the Chinese, to clear out all armed robbers such as the troops of the Russian White

---

[3] The Mongol name as given in the text is Degetu Sibegen, "upper gate." The word *ude*, door, is an alternative for *sibege*, gate; hence the Russian place-name Verkhneudinsk, "upper place-called-ude" is partly a translation and partly a Russianizing of the Mongol name.

faction and the Chinese [4] bandits, to establish relations between the Mongol people and countries which treat us with friendliness and equality, and to summon a General Assembly of delegates of the Mongol people to create a permanent government and to decide on a constitution."

Out of the partisans who had previously been recruited and mobilized Sukebatur organized a People's Revolutionary Army, and thereupon urged before the People's Revolutionary Party and the Temporary Government that an armed rising be organized, and suggested that they first and foremost attack and capture Kiakhta.

[p. 59 of text]   The justifications were: (1) Kiakhta and the vicinity were the main strength of the Chinese army; and (2) if Kiakhta were seized, it would facilitate the spreading and promoting of the revolutionary work in Mongolia.

The People's Revolutionary Party, besides passing a resolution, in accordance with the suggestion of its own leader, to unify the partisan detachments and create a People's Revolutionary Army, appointed Comrade Sukebatur and Comrade Choibalsang respectively Commander in Chief of all troops and [political] Commissar.

At this time the Partisans, thanks to the intensive work of Sukebatur, had reached a number of more than 400. They were quartered at a place called Altan, in the pastures of the Orkhon and Selengge. "Although the troops who had been recruited did not have enough in the way of camping equipment, bedding, or food and provisions, they got felt and cloth tents by begging for them from others, and sometimes the local people gave them felt or cloth tents, to help them. [The troops], because their thoughts were for the well-being of the people, thought not the slightest of their own suffering and hardships, such as hunger and cold, and for bedding they used the hides and skins of cattle and horses which had died or which they had killed and eaten, and wood or stones for pillows. Like children of the same father and mother, they slept in each other's bosoms, and those who had a portion of provisions, shared it to eat with those who had no provisions. Also, sometimes those who had acquaintances among the people of the locality went out and got things to eat from others, and

---

[4] Howadza, a contemptuous term for Chinese. Probably derived from the Chinese expression k'ua-tze, "one who speaks in a rustic manner." It is frequently applied by Chinese to men from Shantung province, and sometimes used by Mongols to distinguish men from the eastern part of north China from the Shansi men who are the largest group among the Chinese traders in Mongolia.

sometimes newly arriving men brought with them such things as lard and pork, mutton and beef, and curds and butter, and divided them up with their comrades to eat. The Commander in Chief Sukebatur, when he came out from Verkhneudinsk to make the rounds of these troops, brought with him such things as curds, mahor [5] tobacco, cigarette paper, and matches, and distributed them.... the way Comrade Sukebatur supported and helped them could be compared to the way a wild bird nurses its eggs that are just hatching." (Choibalsang, *Short History of the National Revolution of the Mongol People*, Vol. II, p. 36.)

Sukebatur worked earnestly to redouble and solidify the strength of the People's Revolutionary Partisan Army. He organized the Partisan Army as a whole into four battalions, and appointed battalion commanders. Out of the People's Revolutionary Army emerged such admirable and fine commanders as Comrades Bomchangtu, Khasbatur, Ponchok, Sodnamtashi, and Nangjat.

Because Sukebatur personally gave the Partisan Army its combat training, while Comrade Choibalsang was in charge of Party and national work, the troops' preparation for combat and their understanding of nationalism increased and improved in a short time.

The exceptionally great [qualities of] leadership of Sukebatur and his remarkable skill and cleverness gradually convinced the fighters of [their ability to] crush the enemy and he became a legend and a model to them.

At the place called Shamar-un Shara Tohoi [6] more than a hundred Ko Mings came to get a load of grass [hay]. Taking three troopers, he charged at the middle of them, and by this heroic display overawed and terrified them, scattering them like a bolt of lightning. With the butt of his rifle he struck and killed a Ko Ming who came out of an ice-hollow. Openmouthed, all the troopers praised and talked about this incident. With complete belief in Sukebatur's skill and cleverness, they strained and longed to be heroes like him.

The Partisan troops, from the day they were first organized, began to capture arms here and there from Ko Ming detachments and individuals that they killed, and the military prestige they thus acquired stirred and encouraged the hearts and spirits of the people in the region, so that they won their warm support in the struggle.

---

[5] The Russian *mahorka*.

[6] "The Yellow Elbow of the Shamar." The Shamar is a stretch of pasture below the junction of the Orkhon and Selengge. — D.

Moreover the local people who volunteered to join the Partisan Army increased daily. On this subject Comrade Choibalsang has written: "All the Mongols, who had had their fill of suffering, rejoiced as soon as they had this rallying point and support. Singly and together, with nothing but a horse to ride [7] or straggling along on foot [8], one after another you could watch them gathering, old and young, lamas and laymen, the lame and the halt and the blind [9], Tibetans, Buryats, Chahars [10] — men of all kinds. Day and night alike, in detachments and bands they swarmed in. Sometimes those who were well off brought extra mounts and arms and freely gave them to help men on foot who had no horses to ride and no weapons, and helped to build up our strength." Once everything had been done to make ready and prepare for an armed rising, it was important to attack and capture Kiakhta immediately.

Comrade Sukebatur had been busy pushing on the preparations for organizing the armed rising. The Party Central Committee and the Temporary Government approved and confirmed his plans and preparations for attacking and taking possession of Kiakhta. Moreover in the whole army, because Comrade Choibalsang as [political] Commissar had firmly directed the work of acquainting all the troops with the significance of the armed rising and explaining it to them, "The heart of every soldier was stirred, and it was apparent that their morale and their conviction that the enemy must be harried and absolutely crushed was as high as heaven."

All the preparatory work for attacking and taking possession of Kiakhta had been completed down to the last detail.

Before assaulting the town of Kiakhta, Sukebatur sent an ultimatum to the commandant of the Chinese garrison in the town. The document read: "You must call in the arms of the troops under your command and surrender them to us, together with the Mongol city of Kiakhta. If you do not reply, or refuse to accept this ultimatum, then our Mongol army will have no alternative but immediate attack; and

---

[7] *I.e.* with a horse to ride, but with no arms.

[8] Lit. "Walking and naked" — a common way of speaking of a man with no horse to ride.

[9] In Mongol, *eremdeg-jeremdeg*, a "jingle" expression, in which jeremdeg supplies the jingle while eremdeg means "blind in one eye." The translation is therefore a free rendering of the jingle.

[10] In Outer Mongolia, the term "Chahar" is frequently used loosely for any Mongols from Inner Mongolia, and does not necessarily mean "a member of one of the Chahar Banners, in Chahar Province."

in that event you must accept the responsibility for any damage or untoward occurrences. [Signed] General Sukebatur, Commander in Chief of the Mongol People's Patriotic Army."

As no answer came from the Chinese troops, there was no hope that they would surrender.

On the 18th of March Sukebatur assigned to the entire army the duty of taking the town of Kiakhta by assault. The People's Revolutionary Partisan Army, under the command of their own leader and General, Sukebatur, set out for the assault and capture of the town of Kiakhta, with the 10,000 Chinese troops dug in and nested there, on the night of the 18th.

Marshal Choibalsang has magnificently and beautifully written of how the People's Patriotic Partisan Army assaulted and took the town of Kiakhta: "On that day, as the [late] sun slanted, the weather conditions finally became cloudy and overcast. The troops brought in their mounts, prepared tea and food, polished and cleaned their guns and weapons, and received their ammunition. The noise of going to and fro made an uninterrupted tumult. As soon as night fell, suddenly damp, wet snow began to fall. The troops, making their preparations and getting ready, waited until about 10 o'clock, when they went up the Valley of the Wall, which leads from Altan to Kiakhta, crossed the Pass of the Chestnut Horse, and along the ridge of Straggling Spruces, in the Valley of the Jinong [11]. The snow in the air kept falling more and more heavily. It was getting bitterly cold.... As the sky began to lighten, the snowfall became less. Just at the yellow light of dawn, suddenly the ranks moved, trotting steadily forward. All along the horizon it was getting clear and bright. The clouds rose, the blue sky appeared. When the first glow of the sun had just struck the tops of the distant mountains, the order to go into action came from the commanding general Sukebatur. He divided and assigned the detachments of troops according to the previously prepared plan. As the main force of the army reached the place called Shirege Burhan (Enthroned Buddha), on the West Ridge of Kiakhta, they split into deployment southward and northward and then the machine guns were set up and preparation was made for battle. The first detachment of the main force, according to assignment, began by opening fire on the Ko Ming outposts. The Chinese troops, abandoning their

---

[11] A former title, derived from the Chinese *chün wang*. See Pelliot and Hambis, *Histoire des campagnes de Gengis Khan*, Leiden, 1951, Vol. I, p. 363.

outposts, galloped off in the direction of Kiakhta. As the People's Patriotic Army kept up its fire, a lot of troops and civilians, overcome with terror, mounted men and people on foot milling around, fled out of Kiakhta in the direction of Altan Bulag. Here and there in the town of Kiakhta shells were exploding. The officers of the Chinese troops, abandoning their men, fled in haste in motor cars across the Russian frontier.

". . . . the counter-fire of the Chinese troops from Kiakhta was truly like hail, and although the People's Patriotic Army battled like this against the nearly 10,000 hated Ko Ming troops nested in Kiakhta, yet the great numbers of the Ko Ming troops enabled the Chinese cavalry gradually to begin to reform its ranks.

". . . . fighting back and forth, the Patriotic Army of the People's Party came down the ridge and advanced to the Bagasutu Gol [12] between this ridge and Kiakhta.

"The northern column of the People's Party's troops advanced from northwest of the town of Kiakhta. [p. 63 of text] The center body headed directly for the town of Kiakhta. The southern column attacked the outskirts of the town of Kiakhta. Some of the Chinese troops broke out at a gallop from all the gates of the town of Kiakhta, and as the fight went on, at eleven in the morning the Patriotic Army of the People's Party was on the point of taking possession of Kiakhta. As they were gradually closing in on the town, suddenly a crowd of Chinese cavalry deployed and charged from the southern end of the western ridge. The Chinese troops who had fled to Altan Bulag were coming back to make a fight for the town. . . .

"When they set out, the Patriotic Army of the People's Party had been given 200 cartridges per man. Now, after fighting so long, these were exhausted, and the 15 [cartridges] distributed to each man in the interval when ammunition was being brought up were also already exhausted.

"The troops of the People's Party barely numbered 400. About fifty men had been dispatched to fight the Chinese troops at Ulan Burgasun [Red Willows], and the remaining 300-odd were scattered, having been divided up by tens and twenties here and there, or into several detachments outside and inside the town, and their strength was thinned out. The strength of the Chinese troops was concentrated, their numbers great, and each man had several hundred cartridges,

---

[12] Lit. "Dung river"; i.e. the stream carrying off the sewage of Kiakhta.

and thus the People's Party's Army was unable to capture Kiakhta completely that time, and had to withdraw and retire. After they had thus withdrawn and retired.... ammunition and supplies were brought up from the rear in horse-drawn wagons, their arms and supplies were replenished, and they formed and kept up their fire. Moreover two cannon which had been left in the rear were dragged up and placed in position, one on the Ridge of Straggling Spruces, with the main force, and one in the ravine to the northwest. A telephone wire was laid between the two, to receive reports by voice, and when they had fired a few times the Ko Ming troops which had returned to the town of Kiakhta and emplaced themselves, fled in panic to the southeast; [and when from their rear] cannon and small arms had fired on them repeatedly, the Ko Ming troops gradually disintegrated and the whole lot of them fled, passing by way of Hiling Nur [13] and entering the Toji spruce forest; after which, at twelve o'clock of the same night, the People's Patriotic Army captured and occupied the town of Kiakhta."

[*p. 64 of text*] As soon as they had taken and occupied Kiakhta, Sukebatur issued a special proclamation, pacifying and reassuring the common people and ordinary peaceful civilians [14].

On the next day the Central Committee of the Mongol People's Revolutionary Party and the People's Temporary Government moved from Verkhneudinsk to the town of Kiakhta, and went on with their duties. On the same day the Central Committee of the Party and the People's Temporary Government jointly held an important meeting, and besides urgently discussing external and internal policy they organized the People's Temporary Government for regular business, organizing Departments of Defense, the Treasury, and Foreign Affairs.

Thereupon the People's Revolutionary Temporary Government announced and proclaimed the fact that the power of government had passed into the hands of the people.

"Our Mongol country must separate itself from the cruel rule of the Chinese Government! Let us gather together throughout our land,

---

[13] Hiling Nur is a corruption of Hili-in Nur, "Frontier Lake"; Toji means "Wilderness." — D.

[14] Apparently the meaning of the word *irgen* here is "civilians," although the same word is used frequently (but less frequently in Outer than in Inner Mongolia) to mean "Chinese" — a usage that began in Manchu times, when Manchus and Mongols were considered to be "military" followers of the Emperor, while Chinese were his conquered "civilian" subjects.

drive out and clean up all plundering and robbing bandits, all the treacherous evil pack of thieves with arms in their hands who go about telling all kinds of lies, and bring peace and rest to our Mongol homeland!

"We have organized a government which will temporarily hold executive authority, in conformity with the spirit of the times, until delegates can be summoned to assemble from all the people of our Mongol nation; we shall hold a National Assembly and, after public consideration and discussion, we shall duly organize a government of this country that will, after careful examination, determine a lawful constitution to respect and preserve the power and authority of the people [15]. Henceforward, because throughout our Mongol land the power and authority of the Chinese are no more, the supreme power and authority of our Mongol government have passed entirely into the hands of the Mongols themselves.

"The mass of our Mongol people, one and all, emphasize the triple unification of opinion, aims, and action. The momentous time has come to organize a new People's government in place of the former hated imperialist government."

[*p. 65 of text*]   Although the revolution flourished thus at Kiakhta, the Chinese troops had been driven off, and a People's Revolutionary Government had been set up, yet this did not mean that the struggle was over. Throughout the country there were remnants of the Chinese troops, and there were still nests of White bandit troops. Thus the Party and the Revolutionary Temporary Government were confronted by the duty to liberate our country completely from the White bandit troops.

The news that the revolution had broken out in the town of Kiakhta spread like wildfire through the land. The first victory of the People's revolution awakened and aroused the determination and enthusiasm of the oppressed and troubled broad masses of the people, and brought them into the revolutionary struggle. The people's revolutionary struggle moved like a wave throughout the land.

When the clerical and lay feudal interests headed by the Bogda heard the news that the people's revolution had triumphed in the north, they were startled and astonished. Although they had secretly disliked Baron Ungern's autocratic ruthlessness and had been trying

---

[15] In the original the words *arad amitan* are used, a double expression of the kind so characteristic of the Mongol language, meaning literally "people spirit-having." The sense is, idiomatically, "people as human beings," or "souls."

to get out of his clutches, yet such a thing as the outbreak of a people's revolution promptly caused them to change their minds. To them a people's revolution was beyond all comparison more to be feared than Baron Ungern's autocratic domination. They were thrown into panic by the idea that they might be extinguished and crushed by the rising and spreading people's revolution. The people's revolution also startled and panicked the bandit Baron Ungern no little. Baron Ungern-Sternberg called revolution "worse than infectious plague or the cholera," and clearly stated the principle of their struggle and his own: "I am at war with the revolutionaries who are the enemies of the human race." He claimed that the creation of a world-wide imperial rule with unlimited powers was the only good way to struggle against revolution, and since the revolutionary doctrine had become strong and flourishing among the masses of Europe, in the West, his opinion was that it was necessary to revive and propagate an imperial order in the East, in order eventually to wipe out and liquidate revolution. Above all, he hoped to liquidate the Soviet government, because it was the example for the proletarian masses of the whole world who thought of escaping from imperial rule and capitalist oppression. [*p. 66 of text*] From the day that revolution broke out in Russia the bloody Baron Ungern had struggled as an enemy of the Soviet Government, and the lightning blows he had suffered from the heroic Red Army had made all the stronger his determination to persecute and struggle against the Soviet Government.

No sooner had he dispersed and driven out the Chinese troops and won a foothold in Mongolia than he rallied the forces opposed to revolution under his own banner and earnestly undertook preparations for the task of raiding and harrassing the Soviet government.

With regard to Mongolia, Baron Ungern hoped to make Mongolia a base in fighting against the Soviet nation, and his intention was to make the Mongol people once more the slaves of the Manchus and Chinese. In August 1921 when he was caught by Mongol and Soviet troops, he openly admitted under interrogation that he had held these principles.

It was now obvious that the Mongol working masses, led by Sukebatur and Choibalsang and the People's Revolutionary Party, had risen to struggle against both the foreign and internal enslavers, and that these, in turn, were in panic and confusion. But as the clerical and secular feudal group and the Tsarist-minded reactionary Baron

Ungern were exactly similar to each other both in their fear and dread of the revolution and in their hate and detestation of it, they soon found their voices and tongues and mobilized all their strength to choke and exterminate the people's revolution that had arisen in the north. All kinds of irredeemable elements which had crept into the party, speculating for profit, had already turned over to the side of the enemies who opposed the revolution and united with them. Some of them were men who had turned against the Chinese because they had not been given rank and honor. Some were men who had hoped not to have to share the enjoyment of the ruling power of the state with foreign conquerors. Their ultimate aim was the hope of reviving the defunct autonomous regime. They had never had any thought of giving up the sovereign power into the hands of the people. The present policy of the revolutionary party was that, since they had come to a decisive parting of the ways with the hopes of these fellow travellers, they must be looked on as enemies of the revolution.

All the reactionary forces of Mongolia, having thus united, began the struggle against the people's revolution.

[*p. 67 of text*]   Baron Ungern, in order to extinguish and liquidate the Mongol people's revolution, and eventually to invade the Soviet nation, began to assemble his own dark forces. Defeated by the Red Army he had escaped with his life and had gathered together the bands and remnants of White bandits who had taken refuge in Mongolia, and had even recruited into his forces some detachments of Chinese troops which, after being dispersed by the People's Partisan Army, had fled southward in defeat. He levied the horses and cattle of the people for mounts and provisions for his army, and not stopping at that he conscripted the people themselves into his troops. For mounts for his troops and for transport use alone Baron Ungern levied from the common people more than five thousand geldings and some four thousand gelding camels. In May, 1921, Baron Ungern's cavalry had reached the number of 11,000.

The Bogda Gegen's government, with the intention of aiding Baron Ungern, had issued an official order to the people of the Banners of Tusiyetu Khan Aimak, where the influence of the revolution was strongly flourishing, that the People's Party and Government were not to be believed in. The order read: "The subversive movement is the red movement which is the enemy of the people of the whole world. It is opposed to God, princes, and true virtue, and deadly to the great purpose of creating a Mongol state. Therefore it is not allowed to believe in and follow the words of the Red Party faction. In Tusiyetu Aimak there are many stupid or wrong thinking elements who follow the Red Party faction which, deceiving the ignorant people, has, without the permission of the Bogda Khagan, put out a proclamation declaring that it will organize a subversive party. It should be understood by one and all that if a Red Party should appear it would be poisonous and destructive to religion and the Mongol state. To liquidate this subversive party promptly, Sukebatur and the others whose names appear in the party's manifesto shall personally come forward to submit to the Bogda Khagan. If they do not conform, they are to be liquidated immediately by force."

Moreover the clerical and secular feudal interests and Baron Ungern, taking advantage of the fellow travellers within the party, resorted to the basest agitation to persuade them to overthrow the leaders of the party. From so-called "party comrades in Kurie" two letters came to Sukebatur and Choibalsang, revealing that these fellow-travellers had definitely turned against the revolution and gone over completely to the side of the enemy. [*p. 68 of text*] In the words of one of the letters: "As to our original agreement, the essence of the agreement was to obtain help from any likely quarter, to set up the Bogda as Khagan, to organize an autonomous government, and not to allow the loss of our old institutions. Now, judging from what we see and hear of the growing activities of certain comrades, they are uttering words that are totally different from our original agreement, and that do not accord with the great reputation of the People's Party." It went on: "This means that we must be careful of the possibility that this might become a calamity that might completely wipe out the Mongol religion. At present Baron Ungern is organizing the autonomous government that we had hoped for and has aided in elevating the Bogda to be Khagan, and in obtaining a respite for the life of the poverty-stricken Mongols; there is no assurance, however, when someone among the many Powers may secretly aid Baron Ungern by the use of force, so you [Sukebatur and his faction] should abandon your ambitions at once; if you come back, you can have prestige and reputation and obtain protection. The allocation of the various requisitions is being equalized; people have been appointed to official duties at an equal ratio between aimaks and shabi [16], and

---

[16] As noted above (p. 104, n. 19), the favoring of the shabi, or direct subjects of the Living Buddha in the demand for services and taxes, had aroused resentment among the aimak ("League") and hoshio ("Banner") authorities. What is here described is an attempted equalizing in this respect.

consequently the minds of the people at large have been conciliated and unified, and thus all functions of the government have been strengthened, and if there is no war or disturbance, and we go on living in peace and quiet, that will be the end of it. There is no need to strive after anything else."

Sukebatur and Comrade Choibalsang together immediately wrote and sent off a letter in reply to these so-called "party comrades," and in this letter, in addition to characterizing the clerical and secular feudal interests and the fellow travellers bluntly as "elements driving the Mongol people like cattle along a course of terrorizing the people, amassing wealth, arming Ungern, and cutting short the national existence of Mongolia," they said that "to organize a People's Party, to exert ourselves without sparing life or body on behalf of the Mongol people, supplementing harsh or gentle expedients with the use of the strength of sharp weapons is our only policy." After this letter in reply, the "Party comrades in Kurie" ceased their letter-writing. The enemy, having tried to calm down the revolutionary movement and halt it, and not having succeeded, began to oppose it as if they had gone completely mad. Adopting a policy of defaming and vilifying the reputation and dignity of the Mongol People's Revolutionary Party, they spread all kinds of poisonous propaganda among the people. The Bogda distributed all over Mongolia a proclamation declaring "the present Mongol People's Party has now become like the intimate friend of the brutal Ko Ming, [*p. 69 of text*] and those who give aid of mind or strength to the People's Party are in fact helpers of the enemies of Mongolia; therefore under the law of the land they are on no account entitled to mercy."

The enemy stirred up the minds and hearts of the people, and in order to estrange them from the revolutionary struggle, they spread this kind of baseless and slanderous propaganda like a deluge, and simultaneously they determined to suppress the people's revolution immediately by force. Accordingly Baron Ungern, with the intention of drowning the Mongol People's Revolution in blood and eventually cutting off the Far Eastern Republic from its dependence on Soviet Russia and capturing it, divided up his army to form four divisions, and advanced northward in haste by four routes. This took place during May 1921.

The opponents of the revolution, headed by the Bogda, in alliance with the bandit Baron tried, in their opposition to the People's Revolution, to defame and defile its reputation and dignity, but did not succeed. The masses of the people resented and did not believe the prejudiced ideas of these enemies; on the contrary, they began to believe in and follow the People's Revolutionary Party. The internal oppression by the feudal interests and the insane behavior of Baron Ungern aroused the masses and impelled them to take part in the decisive struggle.

In the meantime the Mongol People's Revolutionary Party, under the leadership of Sukebatur, was able to rally its forces for the support of the revolutionary struggle of the masses and for the struggle against the enemies opposed to the revolution.

On the 28th of June 1921 there was a joint meeting of the Central Committee of the Party and the People's Temporary Government. The important decision was made to strike a lightning blow at the offensive of the White bandits, and then go on to capture Kurie, the capital. Comrade Sukebatur, simultaneously with preparing the general plan for taking Kurie, the capital, prepared a plan for intercepting the routes by which detachments of Ungern's army were advancing from the south, and for annihilating them by a sudden onslaught. At this time, by way of aid to the struggle of the Mongol people for independence, the Soviet Workers' and Peasants' Red Army had already arrived.

According to the plan devised by Sukebatur, the advance guard of Ungern's main force, the troops of the Chahar Duke Bayar [17], would be met and engaged by the People's Revolutionary Partisan troops under the command of General Sukebatur. The White bandits moving to the attack along the line Kuder Karaul [18], Modun Kul [19], Jelter Karaul [20], constituting the main strength in the detachments under Kasagrandi and Rezukin, would be engaged and exterminated by the joint strength of the independent detachment constituting the

---

[17] This Inner Mongolian leader, one of a number of Inner Mongolian Right-Wing nationalists who were active in Outer Mongolia at that time, was not in fact a Chahar; but in Outer Mongolia the term "Chahar" is frequently applied to anyone from Inner Mongolia. It is the belief of the Dilowa Hutukhtu that Bayar was probably from the Gorlos Banner of Jerim League, in Western Manchuria.

[18] Karaul (written form, Karagul) is an outpost, watchpost, or frontier post. Kuder is the name for the musk deer.

[19] This place name means "Wooden Leg."

[20] In this place name, the Mongol orthography makes it impossible to decide which of several alternatives is correct: Jaltar, Jaldar, Yaltar, Yaldar, Jelter, Jelder, Yelter, or Yelder. It is the recollection of the Dilowa Hutukhtu that there was a place named Jelter, a word of unknown meaning.

western column under the second in command, Choibalsang, and the detachment of the Workers and Peasants' Red Army under the command of Comrade Stenkin. Moreover before this, in order to liquidate the nests of White bandits in the Altai, Kobdo, Kubsugol [21], and Urianghai [22], under Kazantsev and Kaigorodov, Comrade Khasbatur and others had been assigned special troops and despatched on this mission [23].

By the end of May the advance guard of Baron Ungern's main force, the troops under the Chahar Duke Bayar, had encountered and wiped out the troops stationed at Ibchig [24] to protect the Mongol People's Temporary Government, and then, advancing through the Spruce Wilderness, headed straight for Altanbulag, to take it by assault.

The Mongol People's Volunteers commanded by Sukebatur, joining forces with the Workers' and Peasants' Red Army, not only repulsed the troops of the Chahar Duke Bayar and captured Duke Bayar, but pursued and harassed the fleeing troops as far as the Yeru Gol [25].

After a few days, on the fifth of June 1921, Baron Ungern with more than 3,500 men moved to attack Altanbulag and Troitskosavsk, and the Mongol People's Revolutionary Army, together with the heroic Soviet Red Army, met and engaged them. At the end of a fierce battle lasting two days and a night without cessation, Baron Ungern's army was repulsed. Baron Ungern himself was severely wounded, and the Mongol troops who had been taken by force into his army came over to the side of the People's Revolutionary Army in groups and detachments. For these reasons Baron Ungern, with the few troops he had left, forded the Yeru Gol and fled for their lives to join the troops of General Rezukin. At first, when Baron Ungern attacked Altanbulag, the main force of the Soviet Red Army had not yet quite been able to reach the town of Troitskosavsk, [p. 71 of text] and were still on their way, and so Sukebatur with barely 700 fighters had to put

---

[21] The lake marked "Kossogol" on most maps, following the Russian mispronunciation of the Mongol name.

[22] The area also known as Tangnu-Urianghai, Tannu-Tuva, and Tuvinian People's Republic. Finally annexed by the Soviet Union in 1944.

[23] For details of these various "White" detachments, see I. I. Serebrennikov, Velikii otkhod (The great exodus), Harbin, 1936.

[24] A place name probably meaning "a defile, a narrow ravine."

[25] In the text, the name of this river appears as "Jiruge," but the reference appears to be to a stream flowing into the Orkhon and appearing on maps in the forms Iru, Iro, Iroa, etc.

up a fight against Baron Ungern's several thousand men. Although
the strength of the People's Volunteer Army was small, they fought
fearlessly against the overwhelming strength of the enemy, and many
were the warriors who laid down their lives like heroes in this severe
and unequal battle. At the time of this battle Sukebatur said to a close
friend of his: "I have never yet done anything to be ashamed of before the people, and now that it looks as though we may lose Altanbulag to the enemy, I shall fight to my last breath to defend it."

The determination and inspiration of the great leader succeeded in
instilling in his soldiers the conviction that they would triumph over
their enemy. In truth, the People's Volunteer Army fought with a
lion-like courage. By the time the relieving army arrived, they had not
only succeeded in defending the town of Altanbulag, the cradle of
the revolution, without losing it, but had been able to repel most of
the forces of the formidable enemy. At this moment the troops of the
independent detachment forming the Western column, under the command of the deputy commander, Choibalsang, joining forces with the
heroic Soviet Red Army, had not only like a thunderbolt virtually
eliminated the other remnants of the White bandits, but had captured
the mad Baron Ungern. Having succeeded in destroying the White
butchers, it immediately became important to take possession of the
capital, Kurie. Accordingly on the 28th of June the great leader Sukebatur, taking command of the whole army in company with the
Workers' and Peasants' Red Army, set out to take Kurie, the capital.
The People's Volunteer Army moved along the road leading from
Altanbulag to the capital, Kurie, fighting and exterminating White
remnant troops. In the neighborhood of the Yeru Gol they destroyed
the detachment under Colonel Imchinov which Baron Ungern had
left as a defense, and gradually moving forward on the offensive,
they also made ashes and dust of the fragment of White bandits at
the place called Manghadai [26] on the Kharaa Gol [27], and continued
their offensive without halting in the direction of Kurie, the capital. In

---

[26] This name apparently means "place of dunes"; in that case the normal pronunciation should be *manghatai,* but the Dilowa Hutukhtu confirms that the
usual pronunciation is *manghadai.* The Mongol spelling is the same for either
form.

[27] As this name is printed on maps (*khara*) it suggests the meaning "black"
river, which is misleading. The text shows that the written form of the name is
kharaha or *kharaga,* pronounced *kharaa,* with the meaning "sight" (as in gun-
sight). This form of the name is confirmed by the Dilowa Hutukhtu, but the
reason for the name is unknown.

this advance, "If iron mountains had barred the way, they were strong enough to hack and cut their way through," as Comrade Choibalsang has written.

When they heard the news of the People's Revolutionary Army gradually approaching Kurie, the capital, the commanders of the White troops who were at Kurie fled in panic. [*p. 72 of text*] The Autonomous Government headed by Manjusri Hutukhtu [28], made a panicky attempt to halt the advance of the People's Revolutionary Army. The Bogda for the second time issued an edict saying "lay down your arms and return," and sent out a special emissary bearing it, but the People's Volunteer Army kept on without halting toward Kurie, the capital, and as they continually drew nearer the clerical and secular feudal interests decided to go out to meet them ceremoniously.

The leading detachment of the People's Volunteer Army, advancing together with the special detachment of the Soviet Red Army, moved forward and at 4 o'clock on July 6, 1921 penetrated into Kurie, the capital, and seized the communications, telephone exchange, and similar important places.

After two days, on the 8th, the Mongol People's Revolutionary Party Central Committee, the People's Temporary Government, and the whole People's Volunteer Army reached Kurie, the capital.

From the old Gangda [29] Bridge to Consular Hill the people of Kurie, the capital, supporting the old and lifting up the infants [30], came out to give a warm welcome to their own great leader Sukebatur and the Mongol and Soviet heroes.

---

[28] The "head of the government" in this context is a reference to the office of the Premier, not to the "Urga Living Buddha," who as Bogda Khan was head of the state. Actually, the Manjusri Hutukhtu was deputy Premier. The titular Premier at this time was the Jalhansa Hutukhtu (a cousin of the Dilowa Hutukhtu), one of the most able and enlightened ecclesiastical statesmen in Mongolia; but at this moment of crisis he was away in western Outer Mongolia. The Manjusri Hutukhtu was the head of a monastery not far from Kurie, high up in the Bogda Ula range. He was considered a benign churchman, but an inept administrator. He was, together with the Dilowa Hutukhtu, one of the accused in the great state trial of 1930, and was at that time released under suspended sentence; but while the Dilowa Hutukhtu escaped, and went into exile, the Manjusri Hutukhtu was later arrested again, sentenced, and executed. These matters are dealt with in the Dilowa Hutukhtu's *Autobiography* (not yet published).

[29] Name of one of the temples in Kurie. — D.

[30] A flowery way of saying "young and old"; the picture is one of helping old people, no longer able to walk, and carrying babes in arms. This literary expression is a translation of the Chinese *fu lao, hsieh yu*.

On this day among the masses of Kurie, the capital, it was as if the dark mist lifted and the bright sun shone through; but among the oppressing elements it became dark as night.

The great leader Sukebatur, at the head of the whole army, where the red standard fluttered in the wind, sat erect on his handsome charger, greeting as he rode the rejoicing masses that had come out to meet him. Behind him, browned by the sun and wind, the Mongol and Soviet heroes, sitting askew [31] on their chargers, making their weapons glitter in the sun, rode singing their song of victory:
[p. 73 of text]

> Bright-lettered banner of ours
> Bear it high over our heads
> Beyond numbering were the Ko Mings
> Beaten by us to the dust [32]
> Ei-hu! Ei-hu!
> Patriot soldiers of the People's Party, Hu! Hu!

As they sang, the tune was caught up by the youth of Kurie, the capital. At the old War Department the authorities of the Autonomous Government obsequiously met the authorities of the Government of the People's Party and Sukebatur. They still had in mind the idea of getting them to make a compromise, but this they were not able to do.

Comrade Sukebatur, on behalf of the Central Committee of the People's Party and the Temporary Government, made a brusque speech to these assembled lamas and nobles: "On behalf of the masses of the people, who have hoped to escape from the mire of the imperialists and reactionaries, foreign and domestic, we have already created a People's Temporary Government, in order to promote the people's freedom and independence which they have won by an effort unsparing of sacrifice of life and person, and have determined to reform the government of the country in every respect. Having reached this point, we ought to decide things with a strong hand in

---

[31] To sit askew in the saddle is an indication of relaxed discipline and a "devil-may-care" attitude. The Mongol saddle is very short between bow and cantle, and when riding relaxed it is easy to sit with one thigh wedged in the saddle instead of sitting squarely. Young men consider it "dashing" to ride like this — and also with the hat askew on the head.

[32] For the sake of preserving the alliteration, in the Mongol manner, I have translated freely. The literal rendering of this line would be "[we] have made to become powderdust indeed."

a true revolutionary way; but since all you lamas and nobles have not opposed us this time, we will be gentle with you, and recognizing the national situation, we will elevate the Bogda to be a sovereign with limited powers, in order to create a united government of popular sovereignty, and you must in an orderly way hand over the seals of office and business of all offices of the old government."

Why did Sukebatur say that the Bogda would be retained as sovereign, on the basis of limited powers? Why did he not immediately declare the overthrow of Bogda from his imperial throne and the organization of a people's revolutionary republic? It was entirely correct for Sukebatur to speak in this way. The reason was that our revolution in its own peculiar conditions was not a proletarian revolution, but was a bourgeois democratic revolution [33]. The Mongol revolution, however, must in no way be likened to previous bourgeois revolutions. "The bourgeois revolution is limited by being merely the exchange of one group of exploiters for another group of exploiters in power over the government," (as Stalin has said). Thus our revolution, by eliminating foreign and domestic oppression, and in laying down a policy of giving the sovereign power to the people, was absolutely different from previously known capitalist revolutions.

[*p. 74 of text*]   Comrade Tsedenbal has called the Mongol revolution "a new kind of capitalist democratic revolution."

In a word our revolution, because it is a bourgeois democratic revolution in a colonial country, in its first phase took the line of turning the spearhead of its struggle directly against foreign imperialism, and because the fundamental struggle had a national significance the domestic feudal interests took part in it. When the national democratic revolution in the successful struggle against the foreign imperialist agressors had consolidated itself, then only was

---

[33] This part of the text illustrates the changing Mongol vocabulary in a significant way. In most of the narrative purely Mongol expressions are used. *Arad tumen,* "people myriad," may stand in a general, imprecise way for "people," "common people," or "the masses." *Ejerheg,* "lordly," may stand for "imperialist." *Kharhis,* "cruel(ty)," "brutal(ity)," may stand for "reactionary." In this part of the text, however, where a precise "ideological" terminology is required, Russian neologisms appear, such as *burjuilig,* "bourgeois;" *proletari,* "proletariat;" *kulani,* "colony;" *peudal,* "feudal;" *reserv,* "reserve" (military); *imperialism,* "imperialism," etc. Another form of neologism is the use of Mongol words or roots in a new sense, creating new expressions. Examples are *hurunggeten aradchilaksan,* lit. "wealth-havers made to be like people," with the meaning "democratized capitalism," or "democratic capitalism;" and *horcha ujugur,* "sharp point," in the sense of "spearhead."

it necessary, in passing over into its second phase, to direct the spear-head of the struggle against our domestic enemies. Thus the first phase of our revolution was not yet completely carried out; or to put it in another way, the danger from foreign enemies was not yet entirely wiped out. On the other hand, the revolution had not yet been able to triumph throughout the country, and moreover the influence of the clerical and lay feudal interests headed by the Bogda had not yet been entirely weakened. At such a time it would not have been right to suggest that our revolution should go into its second phase and struggle directly against the clerical and secular feudal interests. "If, in thus opposing the aggressors, the reserve strength of the revolution had been cut off, the main revolution would have been weakened, and its expansion would have run into danger." (Tsedenbal, "The Road of Struggle and Victory.") It was already a case of "Without consolidation of the positions that have been won in battle, without allocation of one's own strength, without preparations for the supplying and unification of the front, without mobilization of the rear, it is impossible to attack the class enemy successfully." (Stalin, "Problems of Leninism: a reply to comrades and fellow workers.") Sukebatur therefore considered it important to put off the immediate organization of a republic, and in recognition of local circumstances to raise the Bogda to be a sovereign with limited authority, creating at the same time a government under the people's power.

When the danger from the foreign enemy had been liquidated, the revolution had triumphed completely throughout the country, and the masses had universally come to understand, believe in, and rally around the benefits of the Party and Government, then, he considered, it would be necessary to turn the edge of the struggle against the internal enemy, and to decide on the organization in our country of a truly revolutionary republican government. [p. 75 of text].

The authorities of the Autonomous Government, when they heard Sukebatur's words, though they had passionately hoped to be able to resist, [34] understood that they were already powerless. Sukebatur's brusqueness was not his brusqueness alone. It was also the brusqueness of the one million Mongol people. Therefore the weak rulers of the failing autocratic government, in face of the people who had revealed their determination, bowed their heads and gave in. After

---

[34] Lit. "Action-of-resisting (acc.) ten-thousandly had hoped although-having-been."

two days, on the 9th of July, 1921, the Mongol People's Revolutionary Party Central Committee and the Temporary Government jointly held a meeting, which following the suggestion of Sukebatur made the historic decision to limit the power of the Bogda and, acknowledging him as sovereign, as before, to initiate a limited constitutional government under the power of the people. On the 9th of July the authorities of the old government presented a memorial to the Bogda Khaghan, saying, "We recommend that the official business of the Autonomous Government be transferred to the jurisdiction of the People's Party and the Temporary Government." The Bogda, except for [the ritual expression] "We have noted it" [35], was unable to utter another word. On the next day, the 10th, they began the work of organizing a People's Revolutionary Government. On this day at three o'clock the official business of the old government was transferred to the authorities of the People's Revolutionary Government and Sukebatur.

And so the People's Revolutionary Government issued a proclamation to all the countries in the world declaring that an independently determined revolutionary Mongol state had been created.

Thus our national democratic revolution, under the leadership of Sukebatur, for the first time in the history of the Mongol nation, shouldered its own responsibility for its own people [36].

The great ceremony of the transfer of the sovereign power to the hands of the people who had been enslaved for many hundred years was carried out on the 11th in Kurie, the capital. To all the people who had assembled in a gathering Comrade Sukebatur, besides making the proclamation that sovereignty had been transferred to the hands of the people, admonished them [as follows]: "From now on, in ever firmer and stronger friendship with the Soviet nation, after promptly liquidating and cleaning out all the foreign imperialist aggressors and especially the detachments of White bandits, the true promotion of the nation that we have independently established for ourselves will be the responsibility of the Mongols themselves."

[*p. 76 of text*]   The words that Sukebatur spoke aroused the flame of rejoicing of all the people.

---

[35] The text uses *medebe*, the Mongol translation of the Chinese *chih-tao*, the formula used by the Manchu emperors to indicate that a document had been personally read. See No. 1783 in H.A. Giles, a *Chinese-English Dictionary*, London, 1892.

[36] I have here translated idiomatically. The original reads "caused to become a body the back-burden of its own in front of its own people myriad."

CHAPTER VII

THE STRUGGLE FOR THE CONSOLIDATION OF THE GAINS
OF THE REVOLUTION

[*p. 77 of text*]   Comrade Sukebatur, beginning from the first day
of the creation of the People's Government, was entrusted with and
worked at the duties of Minister of War and Commander-in-Chief of
the Army. The task of leading the People's Revolutionary Army which
the Party and Government had laid upon Sukebatur was not without
reason and significance. At that time the remnants of the White
bandits were roving hither and thither in Mongolia, continuing to rob
and kill the people, and the foreign imperialist aggressors were a
danger that threatened to encroach on and attack the frontiers of our
country. In these circumstances our People's Revolutionary Army had
scarcely yet been able to become a consolidated force. The People's
Revolutionary Army had been formed out of partisan detachments
recruited as genuine volunteers, and the warriors of the partisan
detachments had not spared life or person in their devoted efforts on
behalf of the revolution, but they lacked the ability, by this kind
of strength [alone], to deliver a hard blow to the enemy. Moreover the
warriors of the People's Revolutionary Army suffered from lack of
food and provisions, clothing and equipment, and housing, and were
poorly and insufficiently supplied with arms and weapons. Above all,
there was no military training. The business of organizing immediately
a powerful army capable of defending at the first call of the people
their power and welfare was an immediate emergency confronting the
People's Revolutionary Government and not to be deferred. For this
reason the Party and Government charged Comrade Sukebatur with
this heavy and important matter. In addition it certainly cannot be
said that Comrade Sukebatur worked only for the strengthening and
development of the People's Revolutionary Army. Comrade Sukebatur was the leader of the People's Revolutionary Party and one of
the authorities of the People's Revolutionary Government, and therefore he also personally guided and directed every single task of the

Party and Government. [*p. 78 of text*] It is proper to say that every policy and measure undertaken by the People's Revolutionary Party and Government was carried out by the initiative and leadership of Sukebatur. How hard and difficult it must have been to lead and execute every function of the newly arisen People's Government at that time!

Our country had been severely damaged and laid waste by the repeated terror of the brutal Chinese troops and the White bandits opposed to the Russian Revolution. The economy of the people had weakened and declined. The number of head of cattle had fallen and decreased. The routes of trade and commerce had been blocked and cut off. Goods and commodities had become scarce. The finances of the country had fallen to the last point of extremity. The treasury was exhausted and depleted. On the other hand the broken remnants of the White bandits who had not yet been completely expelled from our country were plundering and creating confusion and their terrorising of the common people was getting worse and worse, and the foreign imperialist aggressors, having assembled superior forces on our frontiers, were on the point of attacking and invading us. Simultaneously, the enemies opposed to the revolution, with the intention of debasing and insulting the reputation and prestige of the Party and Government, were spreading poisonous reports, and confusing the hearts and minds of the backward people with doubts.

There was another reason for the severe difficulty of leading and guiding this country — the job of breaking up the whole of the old national apparatus and the whole of the old machine which had governed and administered the country. The leading apparatus [1] of the country was not only intact as before. In addition the old elements which for a good many years had been accustomed to make use of the Bogda and the clerical and secular and feudal personages still remained intact in their places as before, and were conducting and managing the business and affairs of our country. They were not the kind of people who had yet learned how to protect the power and interests of the herdsmen and workers; on the contrary they were the elements which had learned how to defend to the last gasp the power and interests of our class enemies. Therefore how could they think of making a genuine and sincere effort on behalf of the masses? In every

---

[1] In the text, here and above, the Russian neologisms "apparat" and "mashina" are used.

possible way they injured and obstructed the great tasks of the people. Therefore it was necessary to break up the old machinery of the nation and in its place to create a new machinery; but this was not such an easy matter. We did not just at that time have a capable force of our own ready to take over the business of government and take the lead immediately. It was absolutely necessary to prepare such a force. [*p. 79 of text*]

Comrade Sukebatur, while our country was in this sort of condition, took the reins and led all its business and affairs. At this time Comrade Sukebatur was carrying out a great task that truly exceeded human strength. Besides working assiduously to create the People's Revolutionary Army, he was doing the additional work of completely wiping out the remnants of the White bandits who were destroying the people. On several occasions Comrade Sukebatur personally took troops and led them into battle to exterminate remnants of these White bandits.

In the dangerous and serious period when brutal foreigners were on the point of encroaching on and molesting our frontiers, Comrade Sukebatur made tremendous efforts to strengthen and defend the important approaches and defenses of the frontier of this country. Late at night he used to make tours to inspect the guards and sentries of this capital city. Over and above this Comrade Sukebatur conducted the bitter struggle against the enemies who were trying to obstruct the development of the revolution against imperialist aggression and feudalism. Above all, he struggled against the Bodos [2], who were endeavoring to restore in this country the regime of a monarchy with unlimited powers, and also against the representatives of the trading firms [3] who hoped to develop this country along the road to capitalism. Although Comrade Sukebatur frankly considered the Bodos and the representatives of the trading firms to be, one as much as the other, the irreconcilable enemies of the revolution, he decided that the reactionary monarchist-minded Bodos were to be struggled against first. The reason for this was that at that time the Bodos were receiv-

---

[2] The name Bodo appears in the Russian sources in this form, but in the text it is spelled Bodoa. The plural, "Bodos" (in the text, Bodoa tan) is used of "the Bodos" as a category. According to the Dilowa Hutukhtu, Bodo was a Shabi by origin, and had served as an interpreter-secretary at the Tsarist consulate. He belonged to the conservative wing of the Nationalist Party, and was a supporter of the Urga Living Buddha.

[3] The term used is *dangjantan,* from the Chinese *tang-chia-ti,* "manager" (of a trading firm).

ing the aid and support of the old reactionary forces within this country, and thus were better based and stronger than the representatives of the trading firms, while on the other hand there was no harmony and reconciliation [4] between the Bodos and the representatives of the trading firms. Therefore he followed a policy of temporary friendliness with the capitalist-minded representatives of the trading firms, and was at pains to make use of their strength in struggling against the Bodos who held monarchist views. As for the others, the capitalist-minded representatives of the trading firms, our Party would inevitably have to struggle against them at some point, sooner or later.

In their meeting of January 1922 the leaders of the Central Committee of the Mongol People's Revolutionary Party, at their sixth session, at the urging of Comrade Sukebatur, summarily discharged Bodo from his position as Premier and expelled him from membership in the Mongol People's Revolutionary Party. Moreover his friends and accomplices, the deputy premier Lama Chakdorjab and the deputy premier and Minister of the Interior Ponchokdorji were all equally removed from office.

Before long Comrade Sukebatur in August 1922 discovered and liquidated the counter-revolutionary group headed by former Premier Bodo.

The monarchist-minded Bodo and his friends Chakdorjab [5], Ponchokdorji, Toktahu [6], and Dindub, resenting their being driven from office, had hoped to lead a counter-revolutionary rising, to overthrow the People's Revolutionary Party and Government, and to organize an autocratic monarchist government relying on foreign imperialist aggressor countries.

Bodo, after being expelled from his official duties, while living as a private citizen in East Kurie, had established contact with more

---

[4] It is interesting to find in a "revolutionary" text that the word used for "reconciliation" is *tungjin*. According to the Dilowa Hutukhtu, a better spelling would be *tungjing*; and according to the same authority this is a "literary" word of Tibetan origin, religious in connotation and little understood in common speech.

[5] According to the Dilowa Hutukhtu, who confirms that he was a friend of Bodo, he was also known as Tsetsik Chakdorjab or Flowery Chakdorjab. He had travelled in India and Tibet, and was a Shabi by origin.

[6] According to the Dilowa Hutukhtu, he was a layman of Sain Noyan Khan's own Banner in Sain Noyan Khan Aimak. He was well educated and strongly anti-Chinese. He had escaped arrest during the period when Urga was occupied by Hsü Shu-tseng.

than 200 Russians, Mongols, and Buriyats, living in the capital, Kurie, White remnants such as the *terigun* Tsewang [7], who had secretly prepared arms and weapons. Storing such things as machine guns and other arms and ammunition in the Bogda's palace, they had prepared to fight against the People's Government and had secretly organized cooperation with such Tibetan oppositionists as Saji Lama [8], who were imprisoned in the jail. During 1922 Bodo and the Bogda had sent their own representatives to arrange with the reactionary Chinese General Chang Tso-lin "whether to govern the Mongol nation as a part of the Chinese Three Eastern Provinces [9]." Moreover they had secretly consulted and decided with the bandit Dambijangtsan [10], who was in the mountains called Ma Tsung Shan, across our south-west frontier, to liquidate the People's Party and Government.

Comrade Sukebatur, after discovering and liquidating Bodo's coun-ter-revolutionary group, considered it important to liquidate the bandit

---

[7] The term *terigun* here is used as an abbreviation for *terigun taiji*, a "taiji of the first class." A taiji is any male member of one of the princely families claiming descent from Chinggis Khan. Such families were divided into different "classes," according to the title held by the head of the family. Tsewang was a brother of the Darchin Ch'in Wang of Tusiyetu Khan Aimak. He was primarily responsible for inviting Ungern-Sternberg to support the Bogda Khan against the Chinese, and was therefore at odds with his elder brother, the prince, who was a leader of the pro-Chinese faction. The family, a branch of that of the Aimak princes of Tusiyetu Khan Aimak, was closely connected with the Urga Living Buddhas through the fact that it had provided the second "incarnation" (in Outer Mon-golia) of this line of dignitaries, and Urga or Ta Kurie was built on what had been originally its "banner" territory. — D.

[8] The Saji Lama was put to death in 1922. The Dilowa Hutukhtu, never having met him, does not know when he had come from Tibet or how long he had been in Ta Kurie, but believes that it may be true that he had connections with Dambijangtsan, as Bodo almost certainly did.

[9] i.e. Manchuria.

[10] Dambijangtsan was the Russian Kalmuk who has already been mentioned, above. He is mentioned in both the *Autobiography* and the *Political Reminiscences* (not yet published) of the Dilowa Hutukhtu. The Ma-tsung Shan, a no-man's land between Inner and Outer Mongolia, was his last stronghold. This name appears in the text as "Ma jing Shang," a corruption of the Chinese Ma-tsung Shan, "Horse-hoof-print Mountains" (see Owen Lattimore, *The Desert Road to Turke-stan*, Boston, 1929, especially pp. 235—242, with photographs of Dambijangtsan's fort). As a matter of fact, the name Ma-tsung does not really mean "Horse-hoof-prints." This is a "folk" etymology current among Chinese caravan men. The name is really a Chinese corruption of the Mongol *mechin* (*bechin*), vernacular *mekch*, "monkey." (See the legend "metsin" on Russian maps.) Legends of "man apes" abound in this region of Central Asia. I have mentioned one of these legends in the *Desert Road to Turkestan*, but the subject is worth further study. These legends are probably a part of the same folklore pattern as the "abominable snowman" much publicised in the recent literature of Himalayan climbing.

Dambijangtsan who was his ally. He carefully prepared the plan for liquidating Dambijangtsan, [*p. 81 of text*] and personally chose the men to carry out this business, and paid great attention to all details. To the commander of the detachment that went to liquidate Dambijangtsan, the Partisan Nangjat, he said: "If you three cadres [11], putting your brains together, are not able to carry out everything simultaneously in accordance with directives, do not look upon my face. If I meet with you, I will meet you with the edge of this sword." So saying, he gave him one Vintovka [12] cartridge, and a sword with a brass belt and a fine black hard-leather scabbard with Russian letters on it, and taking Nangjat by the hand he sped him on his way with these words: "Comrade, you are a Party member, under oath to devote body and soul unsparingly on behalf of the masses of the people. May you complete your mission according to my plan with only this cartridge and sword, and return."

In the autumn of the 12th year [1922], at a meeting of the leaders of the Central Committee of the Party, a Mongol covered with dirt and dust who looked as though he had come from afar entered and gave a letter to Comrade Sukebatur. This letter had been sent by Nangjat and his companions who had gone on the mission to liquidate Dambijangtsan according to the directive of Sukebatur.

Comrade Sukebatur opened the letter, read it, and learning that the mission of Nangjat and his companions had been fulfilled, it is said that he clapped his hands in great rejoicing and said, in Russian, "It's done, it's done," jumping up and down.

Thus Comrade Sukebatur carried on an implacable struggle against counter-revolutionary enemies, and consolidated the gains of the revolution. Moreover Comrade Sukebatur's greatest glory was that he joined the masses of our country to the Soviet masses, hand in hand, and won and gave to us their immeasurable and genuine support and friendship. Comrade Sukebatur understood before anyone else that only the Soviet nation would genuinely assist the struggle of the masses for independence, and also understood before anyone else that the further development of the young revolutionary Mongol nation born in the period of the 1921 revolution would still have to depend heavily on the watchful support of the Soviet nation. Therefore Comrade Sukebatur in the autumn of 1921 himself went to Red

---

[11] "Cadres" appears to be here the appropriate translation of *edeged*, often used to mean "elements", etc.

[12] Name of an old model of Russian rifle, now obsolete.

Moscow, met the great Lenin, and concluded a treaty of friendship with the Soviet nation.

[*p. 82 of text*]   Comrade Sukebatur thus carried out a great and superhuman undertaking; and yet he did not pass by lesser and unimportant matters unheeding. Comrade Sukebatur daily dealt with scores of people either in the Central Committee of the Party or in the government or in the Ministry of War, and found time to lead them either personally or by telephone, or by telegraphic reports. Sometimes people who did not know Sukebatur feared, until they met him, that he might be high and mighty; but Sukebatur, in dealing with people, was completely without grandeur and perfectly commonplace in his manner, so that such people found themselves talking to him right away, without formality, in "words straight from the heart." Comrade Sukebatur, listening very attentively to what they said, was able to grasp and understand what they wanted.

Did Comrade Sukebatur have enemies? one may ask. He had many enemies. The clerical and secular feudal interests, when their power and authority were diminished, strained every effort to eliminate the People's Party and Government at all costs, and to kill Sukebatur at all costs. That is why they killed him by poisoning.

CHAPTER VIII

HIS DEATH BY POISONING AT THE HANDS
OF HIS ENEMIES

[*p. 83 of text*] The enemies of the people had endeavored, beginning from the first day of the Revolution, to kill Comrade Sukebatur by poisoning.

The clerical and secular feudal group headed by the Bogda, defeated by Sukebatur in several attempts to liquidate the Party and the Government, regarded him with a most extreme resentment, and their hope was, in their thoughts by day and their dreams at night, to find some way of doing away with him. They did not stop at mere hope, but kept on trying in their endeavor to accomplish this evil design. Comrade Sukebatur's favorite soldier, who had been his bodyguard, the Partisan Comrade Ponchok has said: "Before the White remnants had been cleaned up the clerical and secular feudal elements headed by the Bogda were extremely agitated and worried. At the time when surreptitious enemies like Bodo and Dangjan were working in the Party and Government leadership, and opposition groups like Saji Lama and Dobchin [1] Hubilgan were stirring in open opposition, they were [all] trying to poison and kill the great leader of the Mongols, Sukebatur, and there was any amount of spying and surveillance going on. We repeatedly encountered suspicious business, like unknown characters peeping into the enclosure in which he lived, peering over [walls], and men on foot and on horseback patrolling around. In this very difficult time Comrade Sukebatur, besides always keeping me beside him wherever he went, was fully armed night and

---

[1] His full name was Dobchin Shiukchin Badma Nimbo Namjil Dubi Doyi. His monastery was in Sanbeise Banner, in the eastern part of Outer Mongolia. He was executed in 1923. He was connected with a group which hoped for Japanese intervention in Outer Mongolia. Of these 18 were arrested, and all or most of them executed. Among them were the Manjusri Lama, the Hajit-un Hubilgan, Serenen Otochi (physician to the Bogda Gegen), Baldun Gung (duke), Tseringpil Bichichi (secretary), Tsewan Norbu, and a man named Dangjan (not the Dangjan named in the text above), who rode out of Outer Mongolia to make contact with the Japanese in Manchuria, and consequently was known as "the man who rode to Japan." — D.

day and extremely alert and cautious." Since [our] contemptible [2]
enemies were unable thus openly to harm [3] the beloved son of the
people, they bided their time waiting for a suitable opportunity.
Finally, at a moment when the great leader was lying exhausted with
an attack of the coughing sickness [4], and his closest assistant Choibalsang had gone to the eastern frontier on special business and his
place was not filled, our enemies were able to take advantage of this
opportunity and succeeded in carrying out their evil design. When
Comrade Sukebatur first had the coughing sickness, he disregarded
his sickness and in the severe cold of a late winter night went out on
a round of the city garrison troops, making his cough much worse.
Sukebatur's comrade in battle, now secretary general of the Central
Committee of the Mongol People's Revolutionary Party, Honored
Comrade Yangjima [5], has said to us, from her recollections: "Sukebatur one night when he went to sleep gave me his watch and told
me, 'Wake me at exactly four o'clock,' and so I called him at four
o'clock, sharp, and he dressed and went out to make his round of his
troops. He came back at six in the morning, and said he was going
out again, but be complained of a headache, lay down, and was
unable to get up. On that day I too suddenly had a fever and went
to bed. We were both unconscious. At that time they separated us
and put me in another tent, and it is said that several physicians of
the Bogda and a doctor from Manchuria [6] took turns in giving him
medicine. After lying sick for seven days, Sukebatur died. When they
examined his body, his stomach had turned completely black, and
was wrapped around with Chinese cloth." Thus the blind Bogda [7]
had given directives to his own cunning doctors to take advantage of
Sukebatur's having fallen sick to dose him with poisoned medicine
and kill him by poisoning [8].

---

[2] The Mongol *uchuhen,* like the Chinese *hsiao,* is used to mean "petty" in the
sense of "contemptible."

[3] The word "to poison" is here (as is quite common) used to mean "to harm,"
"to kill in ways other than by poison."

[4] This vague term was formerly used for tuberculosis, among other things, and
that is probably the meaning here.

[5] i.e. Sukebatur's widow.

[6] A Russian doctor who had lived in Manchuria and was known in Urga as,
word for word, "Manchuria Doctor." — D.

[7] The Bogda Khan, or "Urga Living Buddha," was blind for about the last
20 years of his life, including the whole of the period from 1911 when he ruled
as Khan. — D.

[8] The Dilowa Hutukhtu never met Sukebatur personally, but heard a number

Comrade Sukebatur, even when he had climbed the black pass that leads to death, troubled over affairs of state.

When he lay at the point of death Sukebatur sighed and said, in a low voice: "What is to become of our cause? What is that I hear in the street? I greatly suspect that it may be a riot of the faction of Tseringpil, taking advantage of the New Year...."

At that time enemies like Secretary Tseringpil [9], in collusion with a foreign country [10], were on the point of starting a counter-revolutionary disturbance and disorder, and it was a dangerous period.

Sukebatur, gasping for breath, said:

"Life is golden, but mine is passing;
Let my comrades whose thought is selfless continue my work.
Let them in all things work and strive:
Long live the people's state." [11]

And so saying he died. This was the 22nd of February, 1923 [12].

At that time Comrade Sukebatur was only thirty years old. The black news that Sukebatur had been poisoned by the enemy and had died echoed in a flash over the limitless broad snowy plains of Mongolia, [*p. 85 of text*] casting into immeasurable grief the herding

---

of stories about him. One was that Sukebatur was not unreservedly devoted to the Soviet alliance, and that some of the conservatives hoped that he would eventually declare for a Mongol nationalism independent of Russia. The Bogda Khan was one of those reputed to have held this view, and was therefore not unreservedly hostile to Sukebatur. One of these stories about Sukebatur's death is that his last illness began after he had dined with the Soviet consul, and that he was therefore poisoned by the Russians, who had come to suspect him. The Dilowa Hutukhtu was told by a Mongol doctor (i.e. a practitioner of the traditional Tibetan medicine) that "a Russian doctor" (the Dilowa Hutukhtu does not know whether this was the "Manchuria doctor" of the text) told Sukebatur that the traditional Mongol Tibetan medicine was bad for him; though Sukebatur himself was inclined to put faith in the traditional medicine. The Russian doctor gave him a purging medicine, and it was after this treatment that he died. The political accusation of assassination by poisoning is a tradition in Mongolia — for an example, compare the legend that the father of Chingis Khan was poisoned by his enemies. In more recent times, the same accusation has been common in Russia. In the case of Sukebatur the outside observer may well, on the evidence presented, arrive at the Scottish verdict of "not proven." It seems quite possible that Sukebatur may have died of influenza or pneumonia, or tuberculosis, without being poisoned by either a Russian or a lama doctor.

[9] This was the Tseringpil of the pro-Japanese faction, mentioned above, p. 174, note 1. — D.

[10] *I.e.* Japan. — D.

[11] The translation here is free, in order to preserve an alliterative form parallel to that of the Mongol.

[12] Hence the reference above to the New Year is to the lunar New Year.

people who had been living carefree in their warm tents. Their bitter grief was like that of orphans deprived of their fathers and mothers. At first they would not believe that Sukebatur had died. They could not really believe the word that that noble man who had saved the distracted and suffering Mongol people from the midst of terror had suddenly died; but nevertheless their beloved son had died, poisoned by the enemy. On the 26th of February, 1923, at the capital city, Ulanbatur, they escorted Sukebatur on his final journey. In the unendurable cold of winter, on a melancholy day, three generations of Mongols followed Sukebatur's coffin: his elders and the aged; those of his own generation, who had striven in the cause of the people with Sukebatur; and the children and youth of our country, whose friend and teacher Sukebatur had been. At the head of the procession were such comrades as the leaders of the Central Committee of the Mongol People's Revolutionary Party, members of the government, and the plenipotentiary representative in Mongolia of Soviet Russia. Sukebatur's body, covered with red silk, was put in the coffin and placed on a gun-carriage. The horses drawing the coffin and General Sukebatur's beloved charger were also covered and decorated with red cloth. Before his body went several men carrying in honor the Order of the Star of the Red Banner and the silver sword bestowed on him by the Soviet Government.

In the procession carrying Sukebatur to burial from Kurie to Consular Hill the crowd was continuous. It was in truth a procession such as had not yet been seen in Mongolia at that time. The procession moved on until it reached the place of burial, Altan Ulugei [Golden Cradle], and then Sukebatur's chosen aide Khatan Batur Maksurjab, on behalf of the Party Central Committee and the Government read the funeral oration. In its words: "On behalf of the People's Government of Mongolia, and representing the masses of the people to manifest the most sincere feeling of deepest grief and sorrow that you, Comrade General Sukebatur, have departed this life; you it was, Comrade General Sukebatur, who first and foremost responded passionately when imperialist and reactionary forces were on the verge of liquidating our Mongol autonomy and extinguishing our state. Uniting in determination and spirit with like-minded patriotic comrades, and without the slightest regard for life or person, you strove ahead and, obtaining help from a neighboring country, took the leadership of the People's Army and, with clear purpose and valiant strength, instantly extinguished in battle our imperialist aggressor enemies. For such things as having led the masses of your people out of the bitter suffering of fire and water, having set up a constitutional people's government limited by the power of the people, and won freedom and independence for the people, your admirable reputation and bright fame are renowned throughout the world and, Comrade General Sukebatur, we are profoundly convinced that you have become a prop and support, as firm and strong as a pillar of steel, to the Mongol state forever. But now that you have thus unexpectedly departed this life, there is no end to the sorrowing and grief of the masses of the people from the very depths of their extremity. Yet, though this be so, there is no remedy for the fact that this is a world in which nothing lasts forever; but at least there are no few patriotic comrades who are of like mind with you and, respecting and faithful to your heroic spirit and admirable fame, they will all, Comrade Sukebatur, go forward without departing from the path of your guidance and leadership, and certain it is that they can further strengthen and make firm forever our present state under a people's government, so that, Comrade General Sukebatur, your admirable fame and merit will be inscribed on monuments of stone and witnessed in histories and chronicles that they may be celebrated universally unto ten thousand ages. And so, Comrade General Sukebatur, all the masses of the people, manifesting their profound sorrow and grief in sincerity of heart, escort your honored remains to the grave with full ceremony." All who had assembled at the reading of the document of mourning, standing there for the last time in the presence of their own beloved leader, gazed upon him intently as if to absorb and retain his image in the depths of their minds and hearts. Overhead, countless numbers of black-bordered flags fluttered and flew in the winter wind, and amid the crunching noise of snow and the whinnying and snorting of the cavalry chargers, here and there could be heard sharply and clearly sobbing and crying and deep sighs. After the document of mourning the men who had worked and struggled with Sukebatur made speeches to express their grief.

Thus pale, frozen, and shivering, all the people, men and women, old and young, completed the ritual of parting for the last time from their dear leader, and as they lowered the coffin into the ground the noise of cannon boomed and the music played mournfully and solemnly.

CHAPTER IX

UNDER THE LEADERSHIP OF CHOIBALSANG ON THE ROAD OF SUKEBATUR

[*p. 88 of text*]   Though Sukebatur died, his work and his ideas are as alive as ever, and continue to lead and guide our million people.

Sukebatur achieved a memorial monument for himself such as no craftsman could achieve. That monument consists of Sukebatur's ideas, Sukebatur's work, Sukebatur's teaching, and the whole of his life. Sukebatur's death has also become a great monument of our generation. This death left a deep and ineradicable impression on the hearts of a whole generation, whose consequence has produced a movement encouraging the continuation and realization of the deeds and work of Sukebatur.

Sukebatur created the Mongol People's Revolutionary Party and left it as his gift to us, and this was the noblest legacy of all that he left us. If there were no People's Revolutionary Party, we should not have been able to triumph over foreign and domestic imperialists and reactionaries. If there were no Party, we should not have been able to lead our country out of conditions of extreme backwardness and primitiveness, and to advance to a new development.

The fact that the Party in this interval has produced and trained its own future successor, the Mongol People's League of Revolutionary Youth, has also become a great strength. Our Youth League has become the true helper of the Party by continuing to train the many thousands of the youth of the people in the tradition of Sukebatur, and they are ready to take over our great task.

Our Party, after the end of the life of Sukebatur, though suffering the great loss of its own leader, has from its midst, from among the most reliable members of the Party, chosen and installed as its own leader Sukebatur's most beloved comrade, Choibalsang.

[*p. 89 of text*]   That Comrade Choibalsang was one of the founding organizers of our Party, and the most beloved and trusted, the best comrade of Sukebatur, you and I know. After parting from Sukebatur, under the leadership of Comrade Choibalsang we have gone on struggling with all the enemies of the people, and in these 20 years have fought for and won truly admirable achievements.

In the wide and vast Mongol homeland the horse herds and cattle have grown and multiplied many fold. Our completely new economy and production are being continuously reorganized; roads and communications are being developed and improved with admirable speed; the influence of culture shines into the farthest corners and nooks of our country.

Lower, middle, and higher schools, libraries, and a national theater, cinema, and circus have been organized and are gradually growing and developing and science is flourishing.

In our country a completely new kind of humanity has appeared and is conducting the affairs of the state.

The economic conditions of the people are day by day becoming prosperous and highly developed. It can truly be said that every household is contented and every individual happy, and with no sufferings of oppression, exploitation, bitterness, deprivation, hunger, and cold, our standard of living is genuinely satisfactory. Our most reassuring achievement is the fact that the People's Revolutionary Army which Sukebatur founded and organized has been developed to become a force capable of dealing a devastating blow to the enemy. Our People's Revolutionary Army, in these more than 20 years, has been able to defend this country's self-determination and the people's happy livelihood from hostile encroachment, and everybody knows that not a few times it has dealt hard blows to encroaching enemies.

[p. 90 of text]   All of these achievements our people have secured under the leadership of the Revolutionary Party that Sukebatur created and gave us, and of his comrade, Choibalsang.

We attained all of these achievements by consolidating and developing our friendship with the people of the great Soviet Union, and with the sincere aid of the country in which socialism has triumphed. "These achievements of the Mongol People's Republic are the fruit and outcome of the profound and great fatherly initiatives laid down by the great leader of the working masses of the world, and our most affectionate friend, beloved Comrade Stalin." (Choibalsang.)

Now the Mongol people are struggling to defend the progress of the present and the future from the danger of the enemy persecuting mankind, fascism.

To aid and help, with all our strength, the Soviet people who are conducting a patriotic war with reactionary fascism has become today our noblest duty.

Our Party and Government, under the leadership of Comrade Choibalsang, besides striving and working to adapt, change, and direct the entire economy of the country and its people in accordance with wartime conditions, and to reinforce and strengthen our forces for the firm defense of the nation, are directing the work of aiding, with all our strength, the heroic Red Army of the Soviets.

[*p. 91 of text*] The work of strongly aiding in the task of quickly crushing German fascism, and of safeguarding the swift development of our motherland free of fear, is fully understood by our working people. The responsibility of working in patriotic sincerity is at this time steadily expanding and increasingly urgent.

The Mongol people, on the road of Sukebatur, under the leadership of Choibalsang, and with the great aid of the Soviet nation will without fail fully accomplish the war objectives that it has set before itself!

BIBLIOGRAPHY

BOOKS USED IN WRITING THE BIOGRAPHY OF SUKEBATUR

1. J. Stalin: *Questions of Leninism,* 11th edition, 1939.
2. J. Stalin: "A reply to Comrades and Fellow-workers," in *Questions of Leninism,* pp. 305–321.
3. Kho. Choibalsang: *Concise history of the original organizing of the Mongol People's National Revolution,* 2 vols, 1934.
4. Kho. Choibalsang: Sukebatur was indeed our beloved leader. Lecture on the great leader Sukebatur, by Marshal Choibalsang, to the students of the New Strength Higher School, 3 September, 1942. Printed in the journal *Party Organization,* 1942.
5. Kho. Choibalsang: The remarkable fortune of the Mongol people. Printed in the volume, *Twentieth anniversay of the Mongol People's Republic.*
6. Tsedenbal: *The way of struggle and victory,* 2 vols.
7. Yangjima: *Favorite sayings of Sukebatur.*
8. Maksurjab: Speech on "The commander of the machine-gun detachment." Printed in the newspaper *People's Army,* 1924.
9. The book entitled *Matters connected with the history of the Mongol People's Revolutionary Party* [no date].
10. *Decrees and resolutions of the first national assembly,* 1924.
11. Documents of the revolutionary period of 1921, preserved in the national archives of the Ministry of Culture. Notes on the recollections and stories of partisans, in the Historical Cabinet of the same ministry.
12. Nawangnamjil: Sayings of an old secretary. MS. preserved in the Historical Cabinet.

INDEXES

(Articles are cited in quotation marks, books in italics)

PART I

archery 12

Author, unknown *Monggol-un arat tu-men, erke chiluge, tosagar toktanil-un tukhai temecheksen* 6

banditry 26

Bimba, Capt. *Krasnaya ruka nad vnesh-nei Mongoliei* 74, 78

Binsteed, G. C. "Mongolia" 21

Bodo 83

Boxer Rebellion 18

Buryat Mongolia 30

Caroe, Olaf *Soviet empire* 8

Chiang Kai-shek 27, 28, 45, 77

Chidenbal (*see also under* Tsedenbal) *Nukur Choibalsang-un uiles ba ami-dural* 62, 63, 67

China 3, 9, 10–14, 17, 18, 30, 31, 42, 44, 52, 65, 72, 89, 94

Chinese Communists 29, 65, 66, 72, 84

Chinese Revolution 22, 27, 30, 31, 52

Chinese trading firms 84

Chingis Khan 6

Choibalsang 67, 79 *sqq.*

Choibalsang *Arat-un Khatan Bagatur Maksurjab* 64

Choibalsang *Concise history of the Mongol revolution* (*for different Mongol titles, see p. 64*) 31–33, 37, 54–56, 58

client government 36

collectivisation 73, 75, 85

colonization 16, 17, 19, 20, 21, 22, 23, 26

Comintern 84

Consten, H. *Weideplätze der Mongolen* 61

Dambadorji 26, 72

Dambijantsan 9, 19, 56 *sqq.*

Dedijer, V. *Tito* 65

De Francis, John (translator) *Chinese agent in Mongolia* 70, 72

Demid 74

Dilowa Hutukhtu VII

Dilowa Hutukhtu *Autobiography* 49, 50, 53, 59, 61

Dilowa Hutukhtu *Political memoirs* 50–53, 61

Doksom "Istoricheskie uroki 15 let revolyutsii" 33, 34, 73, 75

duguilang 23, 24, 34

education 29

Far Eastern Republic 83

Feng Yü-hsiang 13, 85

Finland 42, 45

firearms 10

Franke, O. *Geschichte des chinesischen Reiches* 10

Friters, G. M. 3, 33, 59, 70, 72, 73, 85

Gendung 74, 75

Grousset, René *Histoire de la Chine* 11, 12

Goodrich, L. Carrington *A short history of the Chinese people* 10

Gungjo Gegen *Gung-un joo-in gegen-u surgal* 25

Haenisch, Erich "Sino-mongolische Do-kumente vom Ende des 14. Jahrhun-derts" 6

Hummel, Arthur W., ed. *Eminent Chinese of the Ch'ing period* 18

Inner Mongolia 3, 7, 22 *sqq.*, 27 *sqq.*

"irreversible minimum" 44 *sqq.*

Ja Lama *see under* Dambijantsan

Japan, Japanese 13, 25, 29, 37, 39, 82, 88, 89

Jebtsundamba Hutukhtu (Urga Living Buddha) 48 *sqq.*, 58, 64, 82

Jehol 15, 26, 88

Kallinikov, A. *"Aratskoe revolyutsionnoe dvizheniya v doavtonomnoi Mongolii"* 18, 19, 23–26, 58, 69

Kallinikov, A. *"Natsional'no-revolyutsionnoe dvizhenie v Mongolii* 21, 71, 75, 84

Kalmuks   8, 9
Khalkhas   7, 8
Khorchin Mongols   18
Kobdo   60
Kolarz, Walter *The peoples of the Soviet Far East*   4
Kuomintang   27 *sqq.*, 45, 72, 84
Kozlov, P. K.   59

lamas, Lama church   28, 38, 58
landlords   13, 14, 26
Lattimore, Owen "China and the barbarians"   14
Lattimore, Owen *Desert road to Turkestan, The*   57, 61
Lattimore, Owen "Historical setting of Inner Mongolian Nationalism, The" 3
Lattimore, Owen "Inner Asia from inside and out"   6
Lattimore, Owen *Inner Asian frontiers of China*   12
Lattimore, Owen "Introduction" to Friters (q.v.)   33, 45, 68, 70, 71, 73
Lattimore, Owen "Introduction" to L. M. J. Schram, C. I. C. M., *The Monguors of the Kansu-Tibetan frontier*   49
Lattimore, Owen *Mongol journeys*   26
Lattimore, Owen *Mongols of Manchuria, The*   19, 20
"left deviation"   73, 75, 76
Levenson, J. R. "Western powers and Chinese revolutions"   36
Living Buddhas   28, 38

McAuley, J. "Paradoxes of development in the South Pacific"   87
Ma, Ho-t'ien, *Chinese agent in Mongolia* 70, 72
Maiskii. I. *Sovremennaya Mongoliya* 59–61, 84
Maksurjab   64, 71, 76, 80, 81
Manchus 5–10, 12, 15, 16, 18, 19, 26, 30
Manchuria   16, 17, 19, 20
Marxism   83
Mavrodin, V. "O poyavlenii ognestrel' nogo oruzhiya na Rusi"   10
Maynard, Sir John *Russia in flux* 83, 86

Mehra, P. L. *The Younghusband expedition, an interpretation*   35
Ming dynasty   6, 11, 12
monastic foundations   22, 25
Monggol-un arat tumen, etc., *see under* Author unknown   6
Mongol People's Revolutionary Party 70, 72, 75, 83, 95
Mongol People's Temporary Revolutionary Government   70
Mongol Revolutionary Youth League 70–72
Mostaert, Father A. *Dictionnaire ordos* 24

Nachukdorji, Sh. X,
nationalism   6, 13, 17, 22 *sqq.*, 27
Needham, Joseph *Science and civilization in China*   11
New Economic Policy   83
nobles   25, 38

Obruchev, V. A. *V debryakh tsentral'noi Azii*   61
Oirat (Ölöt, Eleuth) *see under* Western Mongols
Ordos   18, 23
Ossendowski, F. *Beasts men and gods* 71
Outer Mongolia   3, 7, 30 *sqq.*

Petech, L. *China and Tibet in the early 18th century*   35, 49
Pozdneev, A. M. *Mongoliya i mongoly* 48–50, 57
Preobrazhensky, A. G. *Etymological dictionary of the Russian language* 10
Price, Ernest B. *The Russo-Japanese treaties of 1907–1916 concerning Manchuria and Mongolia*   20
princes   22, 24, 28, 30, 58

railways   13, 17
Russia   3, 15, 31, 36 *sqq.*, 70, 80
Russian expansion   43 *sqq.*
Russian Revolution   36, 53, 82
Russo-Japanese War   17

satellite state, politics, satellitism 3, 6, 36, 41 *sqq.*, 53, 82 *sqq.*
Senggerinchin   18
Serebrennikov, I. I. *Velikii otkhod* 71
Serruys, Father Henry   6
Shabi administration   52, 58

Shoizhelov, S. "Natsional 'no-osvoboditel' noe dvizhenie Mongolii" 3
Shoizhelov, S. "Zapadnaya Mongoliya" 3
Soviet Union, Soviet Russia 38, 43, 83
Stalin 84
Sukebatur 3, 53, 54, 62 *sqq.*, 67 *sqq.*, 76, 78 *sqq.*
Sun Yat-sen 3, 24, 76, 77

Te Wang (Prince Te) 28 *sqq.*, 38
Tibet 8, 35, 49, 82
Trotsky 84
Tsapkin N. V. *Mongol'skaya narodnaya respublika* 68, 76
Tsedenbal *see also under* Chidenbal 63, 67, 70, 72, 76, 79, 80, 85, 86, 88

Tumet Mongols 25
Turkey 3, 44, 47

Ulanfu 26
Uliastai 18
Ungern-Sternberg 37, 53, 64, 83

Vreeland, H. H., 3rd. *Mongol community and kinship structure* VIII, 58

Warlords 13, 22, 28, 31, 39
Western Mongols 7, 8, 9, 12, 30

Yangjima *Favorite sayings of Sukebatur* 63
Yugoslavia 39, 40
Yün-tze *see under* Ulanfu

PART II

America 125, 137
Autonomous Mongolia (government) 119 *sqq.*, 124, 162, 164, 165

Babojab 114
Badmadorji 119 *sqq.*
Bayar, Duke 158, 159
Bodo 169—171
Bogda Khagan *see under* Jebtsundamba Hutukhtu
Buryats 149

Chahars 114, 149
Chen Yi 119, 121, 132
Chang Tso-lin 171
China, Chinese 106, 117, 118, 120, 122, 123, 131, 145
Chinese merchants, trading firms 98, 105, 169, 170
Chinese Revolution 107
Choibalsang 94, 127, 129 *sqq.*, 139 *sqq.*
Choibalsang, *Outline history of the Mongol nationalist revolution* 122, 148
Comintern 133, 139, 140, 142
Consten, H. *Weideplätze der Mongolen* 109

Dambijangtsan 171, 172
Damdin 98—107, 127
Damdinsurung 111
Dangjan 124, 125, 140
Dawa 101
Dilowa Hutukhtu 108, 109, 111, 124, 125, 132, 158, 161, 171, 175

Dindub 124, 125, 170
Dobchin 174
Doksom 124, 125, 140

education 102, 104, 106, 107

feudal, feudal classes 98, 108, 111, 117, 118, 120, 123, 134, 137, 154, 157, 173, 174

Friters, G. M. *Outer Mongolia and its international position* 117

Galsang 125
Gembarzhevskii 129, 130

Hsü Shu-cheng 121, 122, 124, 131, 132

Jalhansa Hutukhtu 132, 137
Jamyang 104, 106, 125, 137
Japan 118, 125, 132, 137, 144, 145, 176
Jebtsundamba Hutukhtu (Urga Living Buddha, Bogda Khagan) 108—110, 119, 121, 125, 131, 134, 135, 137, 140, 153, 155, 157, 163, 171, 174, 175

Khangdadorji 108
Khangtu 100, 101
Kiakhta 150 *sqq.*
Ko Mings 94, 123, 125, 126, 128, 136, 138, 139, 145, 148, 150 *sqq.*
Kucherenko 129, 130

lamas 109, 131
Lattimore, Owen, and others *Pivot of Asia* 115
Living Buddhas 109

Maksurjab   111, 114
Manchus   106—108, 110
Marxism-Leninism   130
military service   111 *sqq.*
Mongol People's Revolutionary Army
    146, 147, 151, 155, 158, 161, 167, 180
Mongol People's Revolutionary Govern-
    ment   165, 167
Mongol People's Revolutionary Party
    95, 130, 133, 140, 143, 144, 146, 152,
            158, 162, 165, 167, 170, 179
Mongol People's Revolutionary Youth
    League   179
Mongol People's Temporary Revolu-
    tionary Government   146, 149, 152,
                            162, 165
Moscow   142

Nachukdorji, Sh.   91, 97
National Army   111, 112
nobles   131

October Revolution   95, 130

Partisan Army   144, 146, 147
Ponchok   138, 139, 174
Ponchokdorji   132, 170
Ponchoktsering   110
princes   105

Rangdsan   106
Russia (Tsarist) 108, 112, 117, 118, 125

Sangdowa   107—109
Semenov   144
Sino-Russian Treaty of 1913   118
Sitar Chechen   137
Sorokovikov   133, 139
Soviet Red Army   158—161
Soviet Russia, Soviet Union
        95, 127, 134, 137, 142, 154
Stalin   163, 164

Tibetans   149
Tripartite Treaty of 1915   118
Tsedenbal   163, 164
Tseringchimet   108

Ungern Sternberg 94, 144, 145, 153—160
Urga   100, 101
Urga Living Buddha *see under*
    Jebtsundamba Hutukhtu

Verkhneudinsk   143, 144, 148

Yangjima   112, 138, 175